CONTAINER gardening

CONTAINER
gardening

ANTONY ATHA

This is a Parragon Publishing Book
This edition published in 2003

Parragon Publishing
Queen Street House
4 Queen Street
Bath BA1 1HE, UK

Created and produced for Parragon Publishing by
The Bridgewater Book Company Ltd.

Creative Director Stephen Knowlden
Art Director Michael Whitehead
Editorial Director Fiona Biggs
Project Editor Sarah Bragginton
Illustrations Anne Winterbotham
Line artwork Coral Mula
Photography and Picture Research Liz Eddison
Studio Manager Chris Morris
Designer Terry Hurst

ISBN: 0-75258-721-8
Printed in China

*Front cover photograph of Harvey Groffman's garden,
London, photographed by Steve Wooster*

NOTE
For growing and harvesting, calendar information applies
only to the Northern Hemisphere (US zones 5–9).

contents

The container garden

Containers can embellish every garden, large and small. This book covers the whole range of container gardening, from selecting containers and designing their arrangement in the garden, to choosing the many colorful and shapely plants that can be grown in them.

Containers in the garden

Containers are used in different ways in different gardens. In a traditional garden, containers can be filled with special plants. In a small patio garden all the gardening has to be done in containers. Plants have to be bought, planted, fed, and watered through the year. This book shows you how.

the importance of planning

The first thing you have to do when planning a garden is to measure the available space accurately. This is particularly important when planning a small patio garden, because the smaller the space, the more care is needed to insure that every part of the garden is used to the very best advantage.

What is the garden used for?

Once you have measured and assessed the garden, you need to think how it can be used by the family. Space is the key. In a very small garden there may only be room for a table and chairs, somewhere to eat outside in summer. In such a restricted space the gardener may have to be content with just a few containers filled with herbs for the kitchen, or summer annuals and flowering climbers to brighten up the walls.

The larger the garden though, the more possibilities there are and the more problems that might occur. First, think

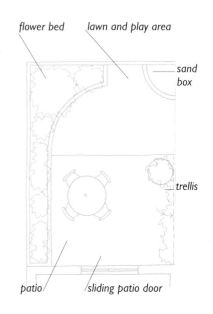

▲ *A small garden at the rear of a town house. The trellis and tree on the right help to break up the space.*

◀ *A well-designed patio with a splendid hosta in a container. The bright orange and yellow flowers of the nasturtiums complement the green foliage.*

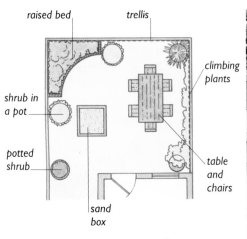

raised bed   trellis

climbing
plants

shrub in
a pot

potted
shrub

table
and
chairs

sand
box

▲ *A smaller version of the design on page 10
for a town house with a side passage. The sand
box can be seen from the kitchen. The containers
provide accent points around the edges.*

▶ *A sophisticated patio where the main feature
is the square pool surrounded by ferns. The balls
of clipped box soften the right angles of the pool.*

about the family. Many boys fancy themselves as young soccer stars but ball games and plants do not mix, and hydrangeas do not make good goal posts. Girls are usually quieter, but all children are likely to want an area to ride their bikes and very young children appreciate a small sand box, which can often be included even in a small patio garden. (If you include one make sure it can be covered against the unwelcome attentions of neighborhood cats.)

The vital questions It is a good idea to draw up a series of questions. Is the garden for eating outside in the summer? Is it an extra room? Does the family sit there? How much competition for the space is there between the gardening and

nongardening members of the family? When you have answered these questions you can answer some of the specific gardening queries. Which direction does the garden face? How much sun does it get, or is it totally shaded? Once these questions have been answered you can decide, for example, whether there is room for a raised bed around a patio area, the type of containers that you need to buy, and the type of plants that you want to grow. Raised beds have many advantages—they are more easily reached by the elderly and disabled, they provide sufficient space for more permanent trees and shrubs, and they give a container garden more substance. If you are planning to build a raised bed, do allow space between it and the walls

of the house, otherwise the damp course will get blocked and become damaged.

Essential rules Whether the space is large or small, certain rules apply. All the elements of a container garden must be easily reachable, and there must be a clear plan to the area. This may seem obvious and unnecessary but it guarantees essential factors, such as space to walk out of the back door. It also makes sure that you can reach all the containers to water them properly, and that you can reach permanent plants to train or prune them as necessary. Don't forget you will need easy access to any outside faucet for watering purposes, and make sure that kitchen windows will not end up covered with foliage that blocks out the light.

containers as focal points

Nothing is more challenging to the garden designer than an ordinary narrow rectangular garden, open to view, revealing everything. This is not what gardening should be. All gardens, even the smallest, need secrets, and the judicial use of containers can help the designer add many little extras.

A small formal garden using containers

Formal gardens are laid out in geometric patterns and have developed from the Elizabethan knot gardens of the late 16th century. Squares, rectangles, and circles are the easiest shapes to use, and they can look very good in a small space. Faced with a fairly narrow rectangle the garden designer could start by narrowing the shape even further. Plant a dark green yew hedge around the garden or, if there is not room, train dark ivy up all the walls. Then, build a brick or flagged path right down the center of the garden leading to a striking container at the end to draw the eye down the path, through the garden. Next, divide the garden more or less into four equal parts by creating a circle in the center. This gives you four equal borders with a quadrant cut out of each in the center. Edge each quadrant with box, *Buxus sempervirens*, to create the outlines. At the corners of each segment place matching containers. Plant these with the gold-leaved, *B. s.* 'Marginata' that can be clipped into balls. Because the balls are in containers they will appear higher than the low-growing box hedge, and give the garden vertical interest. Also, because they are evergreen, they will give the garden shape and form during winter. Planting the four borders depends on their size and your personal preference. Keep the planting as symmetrical as possible, and use plants of differing heights.

◄ *A rustic summerhouse in a formal garden, flanked by standard wisterias and tubs of lilies and auricula primulas. Euphorbias frame the steps up from the herbal knot garden.*

An informal town garden Another approach to the same basic shape involves informal curved lines, using plants and containers to alter the perspective of the garden. Map out the garden on a piece of graph paper and then make a series of curves around the edge. These will be the flower borders. Put lawn in the center of the garden and then position a slightly winding path of stepping stones through the middle leading to a circular area where you can stand a striking container or sundial. Then place small containers where each curve joins the next. Some will not be visible from the house, or they will be partially obscured, and will therefore provide the garden with a series of secret spaces, each one highlighted by a container. Such a garden can be framed by planting one or two trees or large shrubs that initially draw the eye away from the shape of the beds, giving the whole garden an added air of mystery.

Planting a garden should vary with the seasons. Smaller spring bulbs, such as crocuses and chionodoxa, look lovely early in the year. In the early summer, colorful garden perennials, such as aquilegia and corydalis, are very useful and attractive. And, depending on the space available, do not forget smaller roses to provide color throughout the summer, while the containers can be filled with bright summer annuals.

▶ *A monumental antique jar in a formal garden surrounded by neat low hedges of clipped box. Any unusual container or garden statue helps to draw the eye and makes a good focal point.*

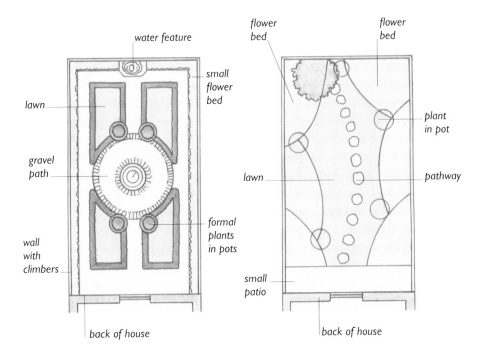

▲ *Formal and informal designs for a long town garden. The planting in the formal garden (left) can be varied with the seasons. The informal design (right) can contain a variety of plants.*

creating rooms and features

One of the best ways to use containers is to divide one area of the garden from another. This applies just as much to large, formal gardens in the country as to small town gardens. They are an easy way to create a barrier, and if you change your mind after a season, they can always be moved.

Using containers in a small town garden

A typical small town garden has a paved area outside the back door that leads to a lawn flanked by flower beds. Two design ideas for this type of garden have been suggested on pages 12–13, but if you have a particularly long and narrow garden that you want to separate into two or three divisions, then why not go even further and divide it cross wise?

To make the first division, range an even number of fairly formal containers along the edge of the patio. They do not have to block the patio from the lawn but they do create the illusion of a division, and if they are planted with colorful annuals in summer, such as petunias and lobelias, they will attract more attention. (They will also attract butterflies and bees during the hot weather.) These plants in turn make a stronger visual statement.

If there is room you could think about making a slightly raised bed at the end of the first division. Build a small retaining wall, say two or three bricks in

height, with a single step in the middle, and position four containers in front of it, two at each end, and two flanking the center step. You can complete this design by positioning a garden seat right at the end of the garden, flanking it with a further two containers to provide a slightly formal focal point.

Containers for paths The same idea lies behind containers placed at regular intervals down a garden path, flanking the walkway rather like soldiers. This idea requires quite a large garden because, ideally, any formal path should be wide enough for two people to walk down it side by side, or for the gardener to push a loaded wheelbarrow down its length.

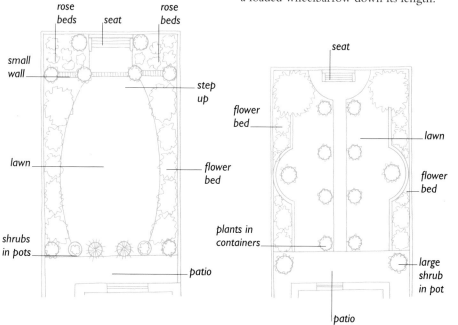

▲ *A most effective design for a larger town garden dividing the space into three "rooms" using containers and varying levels.*

▲ *A formal garden that relies on symmetry for its effect. Matching containers flank the path down the center of the lawn.*

◀ *Rough sketches of
different areas show the
number and type of
container you will need.
Here the gardener plans
to surround a seating area
with scented plants.*

❶ *Lilium* Golden Splendor

❷ *Nicotiana* Domino Mixed

❸ *Phlox* Palona Mixed

❹ *Nicotiana* Domino Mixed

*Planting containers for emphasis and
accent* The beauty of using containers in
this way is the variety that they bring to
planting schemes, and the color accents
that they provide. In the summer, bright
red and white pelargoniums can be
planted together, or in separate
containers. Blue lobelias can also be
included for a red, white, and blue effect.

Another approach is to use the softer
colors of mixed petunias in lilac, pink,
and white. Gray-colored stone, concrete,
or fiberglass containers are an ideal foil
for these paler colors, for the neutral
color of the container will blend in
with the plants. Beware of using colored
containers in such positions though,
because they may produce an
unpleasantly jarring color contrast.

▶ *A particularly striking and unusual display,
showing sunflowers and ceanothus. Late
daffodils will achieve the same color contrast.*

the importance of background

Plants never appear in isolation—colored flowers are softened by green foliage, trees are silhouetted against the sky, and white clematis growing up a trellis will appear differently from one rambling up the wall. Always remember your garden background, and make sure that you use it well.

◄ *Any number of variegated grasses can be used to recreate this startling design. Secure the polystyrene foam with nylon netting.*

Easy backgrounds

Some backgrounds are simple. The easiest is the classic hedge of dark green, evergreen yew, *Taxus*, against which all colors will appear brighter and stronger. White plants in matching containers are particularly effective. Lacking a yew hedge, a similar color effect can be obtained by covering a wall with ivy, *Hedera*. If you are growing ivy as a background to other plants, then choose one of the dark green varieties. If you want the wall itself to appear more interesting there are many forms of ivy available with variegated gold or white-splashed leaves. They look more attractive on their own, but are not so successful as a background, because the variegated leaves tend to detract from the color of the plants.

Brick backgrounds

Many backgrounds in small gardens are the plain brick of the house or the

Contrasting containers are a clever idea against a neutral fence. Here blue meets green.

Terracotta looks best against a brick wall. All plants look well in classically designed pots.

Avoid a color clash with a strong background color with both the plants and containers.

garden wall. In fact most bricks are red or yellowish, although this can also depend on the age of the structure. If you have a brick background then you may be tempted to paint it white, but do not. The predominant color of plants is green, which goes well with the red, orange, and dusky yellow color of most brickwork. Also, plants grow quite quickly and the leaves will soon cover the new paint. Before that stage, the white really makes too bright a background and drains color away from the plants. And white also excludes a wide range of excellent white or pale cream climbers. You cannot grow a white plant effectively against a white wall.

Using smaller containers against informal backgrounds
Most plants grow in front of other plants. The standard design rule of tallest at the back, shortest at the front, is as applicable to plants in containers as in any herbaceous border. Many containers are made from terracotta and

this forms a pleasant background suitable for most plants. If you have new pots they can always be aged by applying a coating of sour milk and yogurt to dull the new clay and help algae form on the surface.

Also, take care to balance the color of the leaves with the color of the pots, and the pots against their background. The only area where there may be some difficulty is on a roof garden. Erecting a trellis around the edge of a roof garden will enable you to enclose the space with green-leaved climbers, but the best and cheapest solution when it comes to containers for roof gardens is to use fiberglass or plastic. These are lighter than clay, stone, or wood and, if wanted, they can be painted in a variety of colors. However a roof garden is probably the one case where it is best to have uniform white containers, and let the planting provide the color.

▶ *Madonna and regal lilies are good scented plants for containers. Unless they are grown in a very sheltered site they require staking.*

containers in doors and arches

Doorways and arches are the most important points in any house or garden. The front door of a house announces the style you are aiming for. Similarly, an archway in a garden makes a statement about what is to come. It follows that any containers used need to emphasize your design.

◄ *A delightful garden with containers of hostas and dicentras and an archway of honeysuckle. Cut this back hard to keep it within bounds.*

Framing formal doorways

A much used, ever popular theme for the formal front door of a Georgian town house is two Versailles tubs, each planted with a standard bay tree, *Laurus nobilis*, clipped into a mophead. It is unnecessary to add anything else, although the trees can be mulched with stones or gray gravel to highlight the planting. Clipped box, *Buxus*, in antique terracotta pots, or spiral-shaped standards are equally good alternatives. If you want to add some color then substitute a standard marguerite daisy, *Argyranthemum*, for its gray leaves and white flowers.

Creating a colorful welcome In less formal surroundings with more room, you can contrive a very different effect, whether your house has a front garden or a paved area for a number of containers. In a cottage garden you can plant a climbing rose, such as the climbing form of 'Iceberg', which you can train over the door: its nodding white flowers are even more delicate when viewed from below. The rose can be surrounded by any number of containers planted with blue and white flowers, such as *Geranium* 'Johnson's Blue', *Lavandula angustifolia* 'Hidcote' with its dark blue flowers, complemented by white petunias or *Penstemon* 'White Bedder'. Planted in weathered terracotta pots against a matching background of brick, plants such as these provide an immediate welcome.

Formal arches

One of the most striking aspects of any garden is an archway in a formal evergreen hedge, flanked by terracotta or stone urns filled with plants of a single color. In such cases it is almost impossible to improve on a pure white scheme, for the dark green complements the white so well, although white and blue is also very effective. Make sure that the containers suit the hedge: if you have a formal yew hedge, for example, then grand terracotta pots always look stylish.

framing a doorway

1 Measure the space around the door and then erect the trellis using battens and Rawlplugs. If you wish you can train wires instead of trellis.

Planting care If you have decided to plant matching bay trees, or any formal evergreens, in pots, then you must insure that the plants are properly pruned to shape, watered, and fed. Annuals can be

2 Choose matching containers for the climbing plants and stand them on blocks to keep the containers off the ground to allow free drainage.

changed every year and cost relatively little, but a trained standard tree is a hefty capital investment that, with care, can provide enjoyment for many years. Alternative suggestions include conifers

3 *Clematis* 'Jackmanii Superba' and *Rosa* 'Zéphirine Drouhin', the thornless rose, are good choices for a front door. They provide color in the summer.

or even an olive tree, *Olea europaea*, which is planted in formal tubs. The latter often needs protection in the winter, and should be placed under glass during cold weather to protect it from frost.

KEEPING DOORWAY DESIGNS IN PROPORTION

One thing not to forget, when you frame the front door of a house, is the height of the door itself. Keep the container in proportion with the doorway, tall enough to make a statement, but not so tall that it is out of proportion. Try out the container, and then add the height of an imaginary plant to see what sort of effect you have achieved. Also be certain that the style of the container matches the house. Weathered terracotta pots suit old brick cottages but formal town houses look best flanked by Versailles tubs or classical urns and planters.

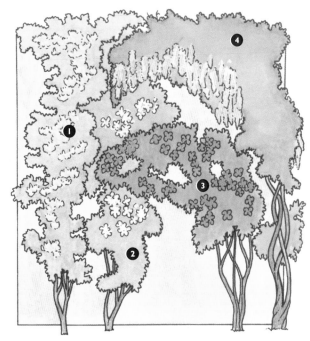

◀ *There are a number of climbers that can be used to frame doorways. Honeysuckle smells lovely but is rather untidy. Clematis montana is very vigorous. Wisteria is best planted in the ground and needs careful pruning.*

❶ Honeysuckle (*lonicera*)
❷ *Clematis montana*
❸ *C. 'Jackmanii Superba'*
❹ *Wisteria sinensis*

containers on steps and paths

*The most dramatic use of containers is to flank formal flights of steps.
Steps may lead from the semibasement of a house to the garden or,
where the garden is on several levels, they can link one area with another.
Containers in these situations make a bold statement.*

Matching the containers
to the garden design

The first thing to consider is the style of
the staircase. A narrow rustic flight built
out of old bricks or wooden railroad
ties in a cottage garden demands small
intimate containers planted to match the
surroundings. A black iron fire escape or
balustrade in a town garden can be
brightened with red pelargoniums in
terracotta pots. Informal steps leading
into the house can also be decorated
using climbing plants, such as clematis,
planted in containers at the foot. The
climbers can be tied in to the banisters,
which often helps to soften what can be
a harsh feature. Large stairways in grand
formal gardens demand classic containers
filled with matching plants, such as white
hydrangeas. They draw attention to the
steps and lead the walker to the next
level. This is particularly true in town
houses where steps lead up to the garden
from a semibasement.

▶ *Bricks make good paths, flanked here by
beds with roses, foxgloves, and heucheras. The
container and statue add an air of mystery.*

Making use of limited space

There are many gardens where space is
limited, but excellent use can be made of
any steps or pathways, such as a flight of
steps outside a kitchen. Culinary herbs
are an excellent choice for such a
position, and many will flourish in shade
or partial shade. The cook has only to
walk from the kitchen armed with a pair
of scissors to have fresh herbs for the pot.

▶ In the summer, ordinary
staircases can be disguised by
containers of colorful annuals:
pelargoniums, petunias, and
verbenas are all good choices.

❶ *Pelargonium* Horizon Series

❷ *Verbena × hybrida*

❸ *Pelargonium* Horizon Series

❹ *Pelargonium* Horizon Series

❺ *Pelargonium* Horizon Series

If you want to brighten a dull passage-way, for example a side passage next to a town house, then this too is possible, but if you are growing flowering plants that need sun, make sure that you rotate the containers so that the plants regularly get bright light. If you just use a few sun-loving plants as accents the task need not be too onerous.

Containers along passageways

Remember that there is likely to be more light in a passageway the higher up the wall you go. The maximum shade is usually at ground level. There may well be a case for using wall pots positioned on the wall, especially if it catches some sun. Another advantage is that space can be left for pedestrians, bicycles, and children's toys. There must also be room to walk down flights of stairs easily, especially fire escapes, and you can only place containers on steps or walkways if they leave excellent access.

Aspect—sun and shade

When you are planning and planting your containers you must always remember the aspect. Containers placed in south-facing positions that are in the sun a lot can get very hot. Grow plants that will flourish in hot dry conditions: any plant, such as lavender or rosemary, that comes from the Mediterranean will do well. Similarly, north-facing and shaded areas need plants that will survive in shade with low light levels. Suitable plants are listed on pages 238–41.

▲ A wrought-iron spiral staircase looks good in a small garden with different levels: lupins, foxgloves and lilies add color in the summer.

▲ Cactus plants can be put outside in the summer months. The blue-gray leaves make a good background for the scarlet pelargoniums.

Containers
for gardens

There are very few gardens that cannot be improved by containers. As a general rule, the smaller the garden, the more important containers become, and in very small gardens they may be the only way to accommodate both plants and people in a restricted outside space.

planning and design

When you look at a new garden you have to think of the practical family aspects. How is the garden going to be used? Is there space for tables and chairs? A basketball area, or a sand box? And all the gardening factors. Especially, what is the soil like and which direction does the garden face?

Soil and its implications

If the whole garden consists entirely of containers, then the type of soil does not really matter. It is under your control. You can choose various composts—acid, alkaline, or neutral—to suit the plants you wish to grow. However, if there is space for a small raised bed around the edge of a patio, and you plan to use existing soil, then you should check its relative acidity or alkalinity. This is done by measuring the pH of the soil, and anyone can do this very easily using a small inexpensive test kit available from garden centers or nurseries. It is very, very important and can save a great deal of heartache and money.

Plant requirements Different plants have different requirements. Some plants, such as camellias and blueberries, will only grow in acid soil, that is soil with a pH below 6.5. If you try to grow them in alkaline soil the leaves will turn yellow, developing chlorosis, and the plants will eventually die. Quite a number of common plants, notably soft fruit, strawberries and raspberries, prefer soil that is slightly acid. Conversely a number of plants, such as brassicas and aquilegias, grow best in alkaline soils and will not flourish when the soil is acid.

Aspect—the unalterable factor

Aspect is all important and you must look to see how much sun the garden gets, not just through the summer, but in the winter as well. Some plants prefer shade and do best when they are sheltered from the sun—the common primrose, *Primula vulgaris,* is a good example—while others need several hours sun each day to flower properly. Some varieties of roses, for instance, will grow happily on a north wall, but others

▲ *The delicately scented wild primrose, Primula vulgaris, prefers partial shade and moist soil. It will not flourish in a dry position.*

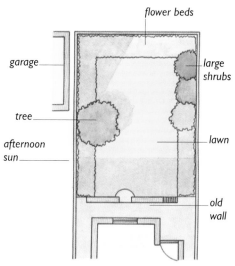

▲ *A north-facing town garden may be in shade for much of the day. It will also be shaded in the evening as shown in the diagram above.*

▲ *A sunny patio is a good place to grow colorful annuals and also a variety of vegetables, such as tomatoes and bell peppers.*

1 Sunflowers
2 Sunflowers
3 Clipped bay tree
4 Petunia
5 Pansies
6 Marigold
7 Lavender
8 Roses
9 California poppies
10 Apple tree
11 Pole beans
12 Tomato 'Tumbler'

prefer to be in sun. If you take care at the planning stage you will not make the mistake of buying plants that do not suit your garden. Check the Plant Lists at the back of the book to make sure you buy plants that will grow properly in the conditions which you offer.

The best starting points

Check the garden area and measure the whole garden exactly. Plot out the garden to scale on graph paper. Decide what you can achieve within the limitations of the space available, check the aspect and also whether the garden is

shaded by surrounding buildings for any significant part of the day. Town gardens surrounded by tall houses may not receive that much sun, even when they face south. Carefully examine the plant list at the back of the book and decide which plants are suitable for your garden, and then buy them from a local garden center or a specialist supplier. Finally, cultivate patience as well as your garden. Gardening is a long-term occupation.

▶ *Measure the garden carefully, especially when planning any major reconstruction. This applies particularly to overgrown and neglected plots.*

Shrubs, trees, and perennials take time to mature. Most new gardens will need several years before they start to reach their full potential.

the vertical dimension

Just think how dull a garden would be without variations in height. There are any number of small trees that can be grown in pots or barrels in small gardens, and even if there is not enough room for a tree, walls and fences can be used to grow climbing plants and shrubs adding color and interest.

Small trees for the container garden

If you want to consider planting small trees then miniature fruit trees are an excellent choice, as are conifers, especially if you have room for two or three containers and choose trees with different colored foliage. Or consider a weeping birch, good varieties are *Betula pendula* 'Purpurea' with purple-tinged bark and dark purple leaves, and *B. p.* 'Youngii' with silvery white bark. Both eventually will outgrow their allotted space but they take time to mature. Small varieties of Japanese maple, *Acer palmatum*, are also very suitable. They really need acid soil and will provide brilliant fall color, making them a real focal point in a small garden.

Planning climbers and wall plants for a container garden

As in all gardening you have to ask yourself a series of questions before you choose the correct plant. Do you want the wall or fence to be covered all year—or just in the summer? If you want permanent cover, then you have to choose an evergreen but how much space have you got? Some climbers are extremely vigorous even when grown in a container, and are unsuitable for small gardens. Is your garden sheltered and warm, or in a cold part of the country? In this case avoid climbers which are not totally hardy. Do you want a brilliant

◄ Cordyline australis 'Variegata' makes a spectacular plant in a large container. Half hardy, they will only flourish in mild areas.

evergreen climbers for year-round interest

1 If you have space then the evergreen clemaris, *C. armandii*, is a good choice. It is vigorous, with large leathery leaves and fragrant white flowers in spring.

2 The variegated ivy, *Hedera colchica* 'Sulphur Heart', known as 'Paddy's Pride', has yellow-edged leaves. Confederate jasmine is scented.

3 Pyracanthus tolerate most situations and have white flowers in spring followed by clusters of red to yellow berries, depending on the variety grown.

flash of colour in the fall? If yes, then choose a climber that has vividly colored leaves, such as a Boston ivy, *Parthenocissus tricuspidata*, but beware, they do need a bit of space and need to be cut back each year to prevent them getting under roof tiles. And are you covering north- or south-facing walls? Make sure you choose climbers and wall plants suitable for these conditions. Once you have asked and answered these questions, you can make a more informed choice.

Evergreen climbers for north- and east-facing walls The coral plant, *Berberidopsis corallina*, is one: it is not fully hardy and prefers acid soil, but it has lovely red flowers. It can be rather difficult to get going. Also consider *Clematis armandii* which is very vigorous, again not fully

hardy, but with wonderful long, pointy, green leathery leaves and a sweet scent from the white flowers early in the year. Only grow it if you have quite a bit of room. Common ivy, *Hedera helix,* may sound a bit dull but there are dozens of varieties with variegated foliage.

Evergreen climbers for south- and west-facing walls The slightly tender Canary Island ivy, *Hedera canariensis* and its varieties, offer white or cream-splashed leaves. Other possibilities include: Confederate jasmine, *Trachelospermum jasminoides*, which needs acid soil; or the potato vine, *Solanum jasminoides*, and its relation, the Chilean potato vine,

▶ *Group pots so that there is a variety of heights. Here a tall "chimney" pot is emphasized by the variegated foliage of the pelargoniums.*

S. crispum—'Glasnevin' is the variety grown most and it has lovely purple flowers, but it is a semievergreen and may well lose its leaves in frosty winters. A firethorn, *Pyracantha*, is another good choice for color throughout the fall.

container-only gardens

It goes without saying that all plants in very small gardens or roof gardens, have to be grown in containers. But if the space is large enough then build a permanent raised bed in the center of the garden, or around the walls. Do this if possible for it extends the range of plants that can be grown.

◄ *Climbing hydrangea,* H. petiolaris, *is a good climber that will flower on north-facing walls. It needs to be controlled.*

Arranging containers in a small space

First you have to buy a number of containers that fit neatly into your garden and do not clash with the surrounding walls. Buying and choosing containers is covered on pages 74–81. Containers should be grouped for the best advantage. Draw the garden to scale on a piece of graph paper, marking in all the essential features such as doors, windows, walls, fences, and faucets. Then transfer this design on to the ground, marking out the areas you have chosen for the containers in chalk on the patio, or use wastepaper baskets to give you an idea of the look. Put them in position and see whether this makes sense. Walk round them and, if necessary, change their position. It is always possible to move containers around, although this should be done before they have been filled with compost. Note that containers work best in groups, in odd numbers,

different sizes, and heights. Also note that it is even more important to mark out the space taken by a permanent raised bed before building it.

Making a framework of plants Every garden needs a framework of plants, and if possible you should plan to plant a number of trees or shrubs that will form the permanent features. Although relatively expensive, fruit trees grafted on dwarfing rootstock are an excellent idea for a small container garden. They require care and attention but will provide spring blossom and fresh fruit in the fall.

Deciduous climbers and wall shrubs

If you can do without permanent color on the walls throughout the year, there are many excellent deciduous plants to choose from. Suitable climbers that will grow in containers include clematis, Virginia creeper, *Parthenocissus*, and common jasmine, *Jasminum officinale*, usually semievergreen in mild climates, but it does require some cutting back after flowering each year to keep it within its allotted bounds.

The best wall shrubs include climbing roses that can provide repeat color and scent throughout the summer and often well into the fall—the climbing form of 'Iceberg' is often still in flower in midwinter given a relatively mild fall. Some roses will also grow on north-facing walls, although they will usually only flower once a year. An excellent wall shrub that really does cover the wall is climbing hydrangea, *Hydrangea petiolaris*. It has clusters of white flowers in summer and dark green leaves that turn yellow in the fall.

Color and form Whatever your priorities, it is important to think of the balance of color and form in a container garden. Choose attractive containers and a selection of leaf colors for maximum variety. You need two or three evergreen foliage plants that give

color in the winter, tall plants or shrubs to break up the shape, for instance bay trees in tubs, and herbs with gold and purple-leaved varieties. Group them to provide interesting contrasts.

▲ Containers of tall plants arranged in rows on walls or staging create a colorful hedge that allows people to see through into the garden beyond. Here a vertical planting of verbascum is complemented by pinks, hostas, veronicas, euphorbias, and irises.

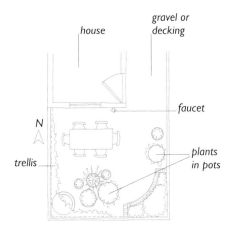

▲ A garden plan showing containers in groups with a small raised bed in the left-hand corner. Access to the table must be a priority here.

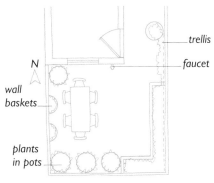

▲ An L-shaped raised bed allows more room in a town garden. Wall pots filled with annuals add height and color in the summer.

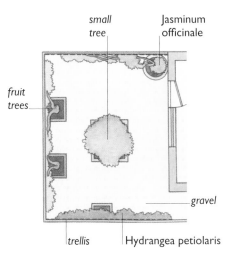

▲ Even a small raised bed placed in the center of the garden allows you to plant a tree, such as a Japanese maple, as a focal point

planting and arranging

When the trees, wall shrubs and climbing plants—the main elements of the container garden—are in place, you have to decide on the remainder of your planting. How much time have you got for gardening? Herbs, fruit, even vegetables can all be grown in containers with a little care.

Do you only use the garden in summer, and if so do you just need colorful summer annuals? Do you want to include spring bulbs in any of the containers, or plant some colorful perennials? Do you want to grow herbs, fruit, and vegetables? Do you want to grow containers of scented plants, or hang pots on the walls with colorful annuals? All of these things are possible options.

Another question that you need to answer before you buy any plants is how long do you want the garden to stay colorful and interesting? It is much easier to fill containers with summer annuals, and then forget about them when the first frosts arrive and the annuals die.

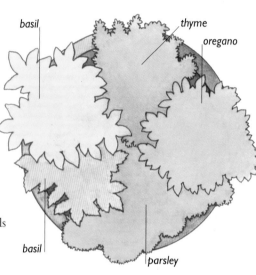

basil   thyme   oregano   basil   parsley

However, summer annuals can be replaced by winter-flowering ones, and with a little care and attention any patio garden can provide interest and color throughout the year. Further ideas for fall and winter color can be found on pages 176–193.

◀ *Pots of semitender herbs make excellent container plants. The small shrubs, thyme and oregano, will both survive the winter out of doors but may need some shelter in severe frosts.*

Planning a container of herbs

Many gardeners use containers to grow herbs, and all patio gardeners should include at least one container of herbs for use in the kitchen. Many herbs, such as mint, are actually better grown in a pot because they are too invasive in the ground; some are also tender and can be brought indoors in the winter, or sheltered from frosts by covering the containers with a horticultural fleece.

Initially, concentrate on the easy herbs that are available throughout the summer—parsley, thyme, basil, and oregano can all be grown in the average container garden, as can various mints such as applemint, spearmint, the larger peppermint, eau de cologne or lemon mint, and Bowles' mint, which is the best for new potatoes. Chives are another decorative herb to give flavor to summer soups, and small shrubs, such as

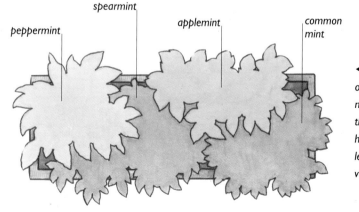

peppermint   spearmint   applemint   common mint

◀ *A mixed container of various mints is much appreciated in the kitchen. They have very different leaf shapes and varying colors.*

◄ *Chives have a delicate onion-like flavor and are good herbs to grow in containers. The flowers are edible and can be used for decoration. Sow parsley in succession through the summer so there is always some available.*

grow raspberries because they need space to spread. Cultivated berries, such as tayberries or blackberries, are a better choice and are excellent grown against a wall, while blueberries should be grown in containers of ericaceous compost. The other easily grown fruit is strawberries, and there are several special planters readily available. The best thing to use is the traditional strawberry barrel, but tower pots add height and variety to the patio design and can be used imaginatively to grow pyramids of strawberry plants that drip with fruit.

rosemary and bay, add a more permanent touch. If you want to be more ambitious try a container or two of scented herbs such as the sun-loving thyme, oregano, marjoram, rosemary, and sage with its many varieties and leaves in contrasting colors of green and purple.

Growing vegetables

You can grow some vegetables even if your patio is quite small. Peas and pole beans can be grown in pots, training them up pyramids of sticks or stakes. This adds height to the garden, and varieties

of pole beans also have yellow or purple pods. Lettuces with their varied colored leaves are also excellent plants for the container garden, and there are now a number of miniature vegetables available, specifically designed for containers.

Fruit can also be grown in containers, but do not try to

▶ *Pole beans can be planted around the edge of a container and trained up a wigwam of stakes. These always provide a good crop.*

top of wigwam

container

bean stake

pole bean plant

Grouping containers in a small garden

One of the advantages of gardening with containers is that you can move them about constantly, creating new color combinations. You can also take say three identical plants, such as trailing lobelia or petunias, and plant them in containers of varying heights to give a different look to each flower. Furthermore, many flowers look quite different when you look up at them in wall pots, instead of looking down on them.

If the garden has a number of containers then some can be positioned on staging so that the plants appear in rows, broadening the band of color. In fact you can use this technique to divide the garden into sections. Some gardeners group a number of containers with vegetables together, while you can also construct a bank of trailing plants to give the impression of a floral waterfall. It is even possible to make a containerized hedge, dividing the garden into rooms

using pots placed on pedestals each with fragrant small shrubs, such as the favorite choice of scented lavender.

Follow the principles of flower arranging

Two basic principles of flower arranging are variation of height and grouping colors to make a harmonious picture. A container gardener can achieve the same

▲ *Trailing nasturtiums are extremely popular annuals and here look as if they were the fire and smoke issuing from the mouth of an ancient cannon. They can be eaten in salads and are excellent companion plants deterring a number of garden pests.*

effect on a grander, bolder scale. Do not make the mistake of trying to achieve height difference with plants, as the traditional gardener would do in a herbaceous border. Let the size of the container dictate the height of the

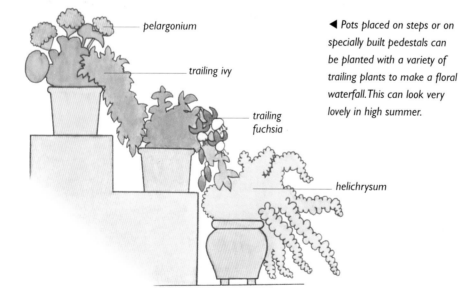

pelargonium

trailing ivy

trailing fuchsia

helichrysum

◄ *Pots placed on steps or on specially built pedestals can be planted with a variety of trailing plants to make a floral waterfall. This can look very lovely in high summer.*

TRAILING PLANTS

Many plants hang down naturally, covering walls and steps, and others have been bred for planting in tubs and baskets. Choose some of these to create a floral waterfall. Small-leaved ivies, such as *Hedera helix* 'Glacier', dark green with white edges, or *H.h.* 'Green Ripple', dark green pointed leaves, are good evergreens. Annuals include: trailing petunias—the Super Cascade hybrids or Surfinia are good choices—trailing fuchsias, and verbenas.

arrangement, using everything from miniature pots to Ali Baba jars. Make groups with odd numbers of containers because they are more effective than even numbers. And make sure that the containers blend together. Brightly painted buckets and large cans are a good idea in the right place, and they can add a dramatic touch of eccentricity, for instance on a town windowsill, but they do not blend well with weathered terracotta or stone troughs placed against old brick or stone walls.

Let the garden develop

However much planning you do, and however carefully you choose the plants and containers for your garden, you will find that your ideas change over the years as the garden matures. It has already been stressed that gardening is an activity that requires patient application, and that plants take time to grow. Only experience will reveal which plants will grow well and which plants do not like your garden. Concentrate on these: the garden will be the better for it.

One of the best phrases to describe certain town gardens is that they suffer from "shrinking lawn syndrome." The gardener just wants to grow more and more plants, the flower beds get larger and larger and the lawn smaller. The same is often true of container gardens. The desire is often to cram in more containers to grow more plants.

▶ *Lavender makes a good small shrub growing in a container. It prefers a warm sheltered position. It should be pruned hard in the spring.*

containers with themes

All enterprising gardeners seek ways of developing interest in their gardens. One good way is to plan various stories, or themes, that can be varied from one container to another. This adds that touch of mystery, an element that is found in all the best gardens.

Ideas for scented containers

One of the best themes to develop in a summer container garden is scent. There are many scented plants, ranging from climbers to annuals, and you can include many of the most fragrant plants in any container garden scheme.

Good scented climbers include *Clematis armandii* and *Wisteria sinensis*, but only grow them if you have a good deal of room. Also note that newly planted wisterias require careful, exact pruning.

Scented climbing roses include 'Golden Showers', yellow; 'Maigold', bronze-yellow; and 'Zéphirine Drouhin', pink—all suitable for a north wall and poor aspect; 'Compassion', pinkish-yellow; 'Climbing Ophelia', blush-pink; 'Constance Spry', deeper pink; and 'Sympathier', deep crimson; while both 'Climbing Iceberg' and 'White Cockade' are lovely, small, white, climbing roses, very suitable for a small town garden, but not so fragrant as the others.

Fragrant shrubs include the floribunda roses—'Margaret Merril', white; and 'English Miss', pink; lavender, blue-purple or pale lavender flowers with narrow gray leaves; *Daphne odora*, evergreen with deep purple to white flowers in late winter and early spring; sweet box, *Sarcococca hookeriana*, which needs acid soil, as do the scented rhododendrons, such as *R. luteum* with its fragrant yellow flowers; *Viburnum carlesii* with its pink buds and white flowers smells very sweetly; and rosemary, *Rosmarinus officinalis*, has fragrant leaves and purple-blue flowers in the spring.

Suitable perennials include scented pinks, such as the old-fashioned *Dianthus*,

◀ *Scented plants can be grouped together even though they flower at different times of the year. Leave the containers in place as permanent features or shift them around.*

❶ Rose 'English Miss'
❷ *Viburnum carlesii*
❸ Rosemary
❹ Rose 'Margaret Merril'
❺ Pinks
❻ *Daphne odora*
❼ Heliotrope
❽ Pinks
❾ Lily-of-the-valley
❿ Wisteria

▶ Herbal and vegetable themes also work well in containers, the varying shades of green contrasting well with each other.

'Mrs Sinkins', with its feathery white flowers, but many modern pinks, available in a range of colors, have a distinct scent of cloves. Lily-of-the-valley, *Convallaria*, is also heavily scented.

For a really striking display of bulbs, plant the white-flowered regal lily, *Lilium regale*. They will need staking, but they perfume the whole garden when the flowers emerge in midsummer.

Scented annuals Many annuals are strongly scented, and top of any list should be tobacco plants, *Nicotiana*; marigolds, phlox, and sweet-scented stocks, *Matthiola*. They all smell delicious when they are in flower in summer. Good scented herbs include: heliotrope, *Heliotropium arborescens*; sweet rocket, *Hesperis matronalis*; hyssop, *Hysoppus officinalis*; bergamot, *Monarda* spp. with its scarlet flowers; sweet cicely, *Myrrhis odorata*; and scented pelargoniums. Flowering medicinal herbs include calamint, *Calamintha grandiflora*;

▶ A group of fragrant flowering herbs and useful vegetables.

California poppies, *Eschscholzia;* cornflowers, *Centaurea cyanus*; and thrift, *Armeria maritima*. All these medicinal herbs will flower in the summer months.

Gray- and silver-leaved plants should also be included in most garden schemes. Among the best are lamb's ears, *Stachys byzantina*; lavender; mugwort, *Artemisia* spp.—there are a number of good silvery varieties; and *Senecio*, now known as *Brachyglottis*. These look good planted in contrast to other colors.

A MINIATURE KITCHEN GARDEN

Vegetables are the ultimate theme for a container garden. It is surprisingly easy to grow many vegetables in containers, and the best ones are described on pages 194–211. Do not think that vegetables are visually dull. Many have delicately colored green leaves, and some have variegated leaves of various colors. A container of vegetables topped by miniature bright red cherry tomatoes can make a real talking point.

1 California poppy
2 Thrift
3 Scented pelargoniums
4 Ruby Swiss chard
5 Chives
6 Variegated mint
7 Heliotrope
8 Bergamot
9 Sweet rocket
10 Cornflower
11 Lamb's ears
12 Artemisia
13 Sweet cicely
14 Pelargoniums
15 Beet
16 Thrift

Containers for patios and patio gardens

Patios are different from patio gardens. Patio gardens are small, paved with brick or stone, enclosed between walls. Patios are convenient seating areas or margins separating the house from the garden. They are a place to grow herbs, or are filled with decorative pots with colorful annuals.

planning and design

The first consideration is space. Measure the size of the patio and draw it to scale on a piece of graph paper. Then mark in the tables and chairs, positioning them so that you can get in and out of the doorway easily. If you have outdoor tables put them in position and check they fit properly.

Once you have established the position of the main furniture, you can consider how you would like to decorate the remainder of the patio. Again space is the key. It is no good filling a patio so full of containers and plants that you cannot walk round it easily, carrying trays, plates, and glasses. It is a question of priorities. What is the main purpose of the patio— a miniature garden, or a seating area? And if the answer to the question is a seating area then that must take priority in the organization and design.

Compatible plants

It is pleasant to decorate the patio with containers full of plants that complement the surroundings and make a colorful outside room, but there are one or two do's and don'ts when you choose the plants. Don't plant roses, euphorbias, or rue where they can be rubbed against. Roses have thorns while euphorbias, and

◄ *Shrub roses and lady's mantle planted in a modern container make a pleasing contrast on a well-designed patio with a raised bed.*

a number of other plants, have irritant properties that can cause a skin rash if they are brushed against, especially when the sun is shining. Check with a nursery before buying. On the other hand, a number of plants release their scent as you brush against the leaves. The scented-leaved pelargoniums is a good example, lemon verbena, another. Scented-leaved plants make it even more pleasant to sit outside in the summer sun.

Creating a barrier

If the patio is large enough, you can make a containerized hedge to separate the patio from the lawn and garden beyond. A line of miniature evergreen conifers will work quite well but they can be a bit dull in summer. They are also expensive plants to purchase. Brightly coloured pelargoniums with trailing ivy and trailing lobelia make a perfect summer barrier, and the containers can be formal or informal.

Some designers might plant a more permanent screen using an arch or a trellis, framed by containers or even a small hedge. This is another excellent idea, and the ideal plants for a miniature hedge are box or lavender that smells so lovely and can be trimmed after flowering. Do not plant a high hedge. Not only would it take light away from the house, but it is essential in all gardens to allow glimpses of what lies beyond.

▶ A mixed container garden designed for a flower show with aquilegias, French lavender, foxgloves and alliums all in flower together.

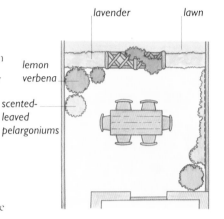

▲ This table has been positioned so that there is room around the table unlike the example on the right where the plants are closer.

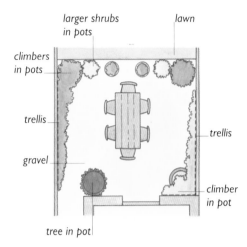

▲ In a small garden you may only just have room for a standard table. Consider using a circular one as this will take up less room.

planning a patio garden

Patio gardens need to be planned with extra care. In a small back yard there may not be room for more than a few containers outside the back door. It is a question of measuring and deciding what is possible, what might be attempted, and then trying to put the plan into practice.

Using containers to make rooms

If there is space then you can consider changing the shape of the garden, cutting it in two, positioning groups of containers so that some corners become round, introducing curved lines and containers of different heights to add more interest and visual variety.

Splitting very small gardens in two
Many terraced houses in towns have a passageway leading down the side of the house. If the line of the house is taken down to the end of the garden using containers, or a dividing line of trellis, it automatically splits it into two. If the garden gets enough sun then you might be able to grow colorful sun-loving plants in one half and shade-loving plants in the other. Another idea would be to divide the garden by a "hedge" of pots placed on staging, or use a series of taller containers. You could grow flowers in one group and herbs, many of which will flourish in shade, in the other. The exact division will depend on the size and shape of the patio and the aspect.

Rounding off the corners

If this is not possible then you can change the shape of the garden by placing containers in curved lines around the boundaries, varying the height. If you put very tall containers opposite the door, and then smaller and smaller ones on either side, the garden will appear wider and be more interesting. Exercise your imagination. A small water feature added in one corner, partly hidden by two containers of hostas, could also transform a tiny space. And containers of individual plants can be placed alongside larger troughs planted with contrasting light green and red-leaved lettuces, or a group of sages, so useful in the kitchen, have lovely varied-colored leaves, especially *Salvia officinalis* 'Purpurascens' and *S. o.* 'Tricolor'.

An oriental touch
Individual pots can be planted with evergreen grasses that will

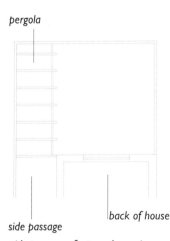

pergola

side passage

back of house

▲ *The side passage of a town house is continued down the garden under a pergola.*

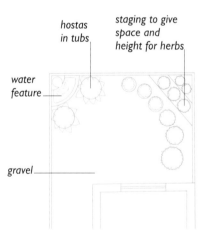

hostas in tubs

staging to give space and height for herbs

water feature

gravel

▲ *Pots placed in a curve create a secret area in the garden. Allow space to walk behind them.*

provide interest all through the year. More importantly, they also add movement when the stems stir in the breeze. Patio gardens in a town may be very sheltered, and any movement of plant or water makes a great difference, particularly in the summer months when the air can be heavy and still.

Covering the wall In the smallest space you may not have room for large containers, but you can cover the walls if you plant a series of wall shrubs, each in a separate container. They can be grown as a hedge or you can grow ivy in containers. This will cover the wall and make an evergreen background for any flowering plants that you have.

Developing a theme

The best gardens, even when very constricted, are those that develop a theme, and this can be achieved in a container garden by planting individual plants in separate containers. If you use annuals you might try a color theme, grading shades of red through rose pink to pale pink and then white or, in the spring, plant containers with bulbs that flower in varying shades of yellow.

You could grade plants by size, taking care to have a number of varieties that flower at the same time, each in an individual pot, or you could tell a story by planting a selection of medieval medicinal herbs. The cook can have containers of miniature vegetables, and you could add a series of scented plants to perfume the air in the evening. All these plantings will create a garden full of interest whatever its size and prove that, with a little imagination, the good gardener is not confined by small boundaries and lack of space.

▲ Chimney pots filled with petunias surround a cordyline in a small town garden.

▼ The color scheme of this garden is nicely restrained with the candelabra primulas, stone edging, and white gravel and seats.

containers on paved areas

Almost every garden has some paved areas that can be decorated with containers filled with plants. As opposed to patio gardens, these areas are part of the garden design and containers and plantings have to fit in with the overall plan. These areas include steps, back yards and garden pools.

Back-door paved areas

Many gardens have a paved area outside the back door, that often leads on into the garden itself. Very often this area is ignored by the gardener and this is a mistake, for there are many uses to which it can be put. The simplest is to plant two or three containers of herbs. Fresh herbs are therefore readily available for the cook, who does not have to go down to the bottom of the garden to cut fresh parsley. It is best if this space is in the sun so the tender herbs that originate from the Mediterranean can easily be grown there. Another practical use is to put house plants, such as small citrus trees or clivias, outside during the summer months. This can benefit them greatly.

If there is a substantial paved area in this position, use containers to divide it off from the rest of the garden to create the impression of an additional room. A line of containers can be planted with evergreens, if you wish, or brightly colored bedding plants, such as winter-flowering pansies in winter, and summer annuals, such as dazzling colored pelargoniums in summer. These cheer up the view from the kitchen window.

Planting beside a pool

Swimming pools and water features can also have containers beside them filled in summer with colorful annuals, such as petunias or pelargoniums. If you are planting containers beside swimming pools, they must be set back out of the way and you have to make sure that they do not contain any plants that

◀ *A specially designed water feature on a paved area surrounded by garden seats. The planting is imaginative and attractive.*

might cause rashes when brushed against by an enthusiastic swimmer.

Special water features often have custom-made beds beside them as part of the overall design, as shown in the photograph on page 42. Here a water trough leads down a silvery chute into a zinc container, and the sides of the chute are designed and planted as mini herbaceous borders with stachys, miniature roses, hostas, and sedums among the plants. Such a plan is immensely stylish and turns an ordinary paved area into something colorful.

Decorating steps and stairways

Often gardens are on different levels. This is a great opportunity for the gardener to decorate plain steps with containers of bright annuals in summer that can match in with the planting in the rest of the garden. If some evergreen plants are included, such as trailing ivy, then they will retain some interest during the winter when the annuals have died

down. It is even possible to erect small pieces of trellis beside many steps of this type and grow climbers, such as ivies and clematis, up the walls. Brick steps beside old houses can be decorated with terracotta pots, each containing a single plant. Match the containers and the plants to the surroundings.

Using neglected areas

Some parts of the garden are often completely ignored: in particular side alleys in town houses. These get little light or sun but they can be used to grow plants in containers that prefer shade, and they give serious gardeners the opportunity to expand their repertoire of plants. Plants for this type of position include ferns, hostas, pulmonarias, and periwinkles.

▲ *In any garden feature it is important that everything matches. Here modern steps are matched by purpose-built containers.*

▼ *A paved area for herbs used to harden off tender plants in summer. Group the containers for a pleasing arrangement.*

containers in courtyards

When courtyards are mentioned one visual image could be of grand palaces in Spain, a vast expanse of immaculate gravel, and rows of trees in formal lines interspersed with containers of flowers or smaller shrubs. With a little planning, you can realize this vision—and many more.

The cloistered courtyard

The effect is cool and peaceful, the main point of attraction being a statue or fountain in the center. The sight and sound of water add to the peaceful setting. Few gardens have the space for this type of design, but many gardens with formal areas can incorporate walkways under arches or pergolas with green climbing plants, such as the golden hop, *Humulus lupulus* 'Aureus', and a formal sundial or small fountain in the center. To create this effect position matching containers at the foot of each leg of the arch, plant the chosen climbers in suitable compost, and train them up. Keep the scheme cool and green, with white as the accent color, and remember that the hard lines of the posts are soon softened as the plants grow.

The formal courtyard

In a formal courtyard the emphasis is on the division of space. As in the knot garden of Elizabethan times, the effect of this type of garden relies on precise geometric patterns and the exact positioning of all the elements within the walls. If the courtyard acts as an entrance, then access must be easy and unimpaired. The dividing lines of the trees and containers should then create the illusion of rooms, for example one large "reception" room being in the center and smaller "anterooms" on either side. This is done by positioning lines of formal evergreens, such as bay trees, *Laurus nobilis*, or conifers, interspersed with containers that can be filled with brightly colored accent plants to complement the scheme and add interest

◀ *A formal courtyard profusely planted with shrubs and flowering plants. The statue of Aphrodite complements the design beautifully.*

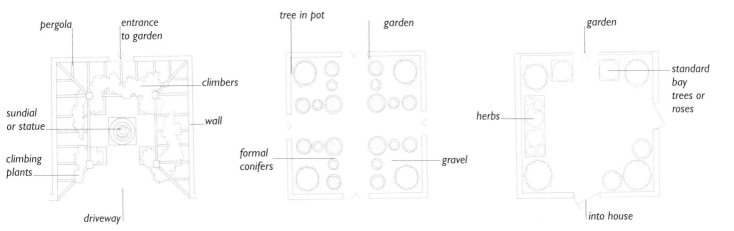

pergola

entrance
to garden

climbers

sundial
or statue

wall

climbing
plants

driveway

tree in pot

garden

formal
conifers

gravel

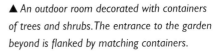

garden

standard
bay
trees or
roses

herbs

into house

▲ A small courtyard covered by a pergola with a statue or sundial in the center. This design emulates the quiet of a cathedral cloister.

▲ Lines of conifers in matching containers divide the courtyard into a series of smaller rooms. This design works best in a large space.

▲ An outdoor room decorated with containers of trees and shrubs. The entrance to the garden beyond is flanked by matching containers.

to the design. These plants can be changed throughout the year, and design of the courtyard will subtly alter.

If you want to try and achieve this effect, plot the elements on paper first, and then simulate the design, using kitchen chairs or any matching pieces of furniture that you have available. Half-close your eyes, and imagine that the chairs are trees or containers filled with plants. This will help you to see whether the design works as a mock-up, before embarking on the expense of buying matching containers, half-barrels or large terracotta pots, and the necessary evergreen trees or shrubs.

The inner courtyard

The third courtyard design can be much more informal. By definition, this is another room in the house that just

▶ A formal knot garden with low-growing box hedges, classical urns, and topiary box spirals. Jasmine has been carefully trained up the arch.

happens to be outside. The decoration can be planned to match the inside of the home, with containers placed in the corners filled with bright plants to give color throughout the year. If the courtyard leads on into the garden then the arch or doorway at the end can be flanked by containers, or small borders

can be filled with herbs for the kitchen, and containers can be used as accent points to provide color in the summer.

Adopt a planting theme. Marigolds and nasturtiums are vividly colored annuals that are also well-known culinary plants. Many medicinal herbs are very colorful when in flower.

Containers for a roof garden

This is the ultimate container garden: all the plants, the soil mix, every pot and trough has to be carried up, through the building, and placed into position. Roof gardens are usually found in towns and cities: the best are quite extraordinary both in design and execution.

practical considerations

The first thing any roof gardener has to do is to get the roof checked by a structural engineer. Containers and plants are fairly heavy, especially when they have been watered, and it is essential that the roof is strong enough to bear their weight. Some roofs may have to be strengthened.

Screens and seclusion

Roof gardens are exposed and you may want to erect screens to provide shelter and seclusion—it is generally best to get professional help to do this to make sure everything is safe. Both screens and plants must be absolutely secure so that there is no risk that they might blow away in a high wind and fall off the roof, injuring pedestrians in the street below.

Flooring

Roof gardens will require flooring. It is a good idea to keep this as light as possible to avoid increasing the weight on the roof. Special light tiles, wooden decking, and gravel are worth considering, and the choice will depend on the type of garden you plan and the number of uses to which it will be put. Gravel is aesthetically pleasing if you are trying to create a cottage garden effect.

Watering

Another extremely important aspect for all roof gardeners is watering. Containers, especially containers on roofs, need to be watered every day in summer and during dry periods. Every roof garden must have a supply of water that is easily accessible, and there is a strong case for installing an automatic watering system. At the very least install an outside faucet for on-site watering.

◀ *Ornamental onions match the color of the painted chair. This is a good idea on a roof garden; the bay tree provides vertical interest.*

One of the most important things when planning and creating a roof garden is not to interfere with the drainage of the roof in any way. Even the flattest of flat roofs will be canted so that rainwater drains away, and the fall of the roof must never be interrupted or problems will build up in the roof itself.

Choosing containers

The first thing to think about is access to the roof. Is there room to carry large containers on to the roof, or is the only access up a narrow flight of attic steps? If the access from the house is restricted then the containers have to be fairly small, or if your design demands a large container, it may have to be built outside, carrying the wood and tools up separately. Keep the containers as light as possible and choose lightweight materials such as fiberglass and tufa, rather than stone and terracotta. Remember though that roof gardens are often miniature in scale, and every element is subject to close inspection; take care to make everything as attractive as possible.

Aspect Finally look at the aspect of the roof garden. As with any garden, this is the most important feature, and the one that is unalterable. Many roof gardens are sunny and open, but some may be overshadowed by taller buildings or the walls of the house. Before you decide on the garden you want and the plants you plan to grow, check that there is plenty of sun—there may be less than you think. If not, plan to grow plants that will flourish in shade.

◀ A group of modern containers based on classical designs. All containers acquire the patina of age outside in the garden.

▶ A large balcony surrounded by walls that is in shade for most of the day. Choose climbers that flourish without the sun.

▲ A collection of ornamental grasses with broad-leaved hostas for contrast. The blue stars could be replaced by painted rocks or tufa.

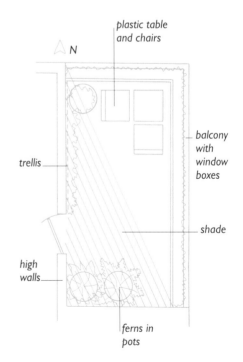

plastic table and chairs

N

balcony with window boxes

trellis

shade

high walls

ferns in pots

Planning the space— the outdoor room

Large roof gardens present a number of
opportunities. They can be planned as
one large open space or, more effectively,
as a series of rooms, each one
contributing something different. If the
roof can be divided in two, then one half
can be used as a seating and eating area
with tables and chairs, surrounded by
containers of flowers or scented plants.
This can be separated from the second
half of the garden which may be more
formal, with containers of roses or small
shrubs, or be used as a miniature kitchen
garden with vegetables and herbs.

When there is space, roof gardens
can be divided in a number of ways. The
division may be just a line of containers
separating one area from another, or
more formal. Fixed divisions can be
made by erecting trellises, by planting a
screen of trees in tubs or creating a line
of miniature espaliered fruit trees. Roof

▲ *A row of lavenders in containers make a small hedge. This idea can be copied on roof gardens using lightweight materials.*

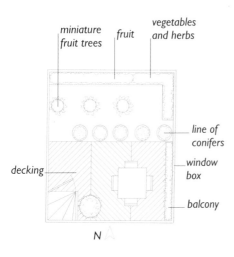

▲ *A large roof garden divided into two by a line of conifers. The containers around the sides are used for growing vegetables and herbs.*

gardens do allow the gardener to grow
freestanding trees, and pyramid fruit
trees, such as apple and plum, can be
grown without training them against a
wall. A line of evergreen conifers planted
in containers would make another
division, while some gardeners use pots,
placed at different levels, planted with
small shrubs, such as lavender, to make a
sweetly scented, eye-level hedge.

All this requires careful planning and
you may well need to construct special
containers on site, to make the best use
of the space available.

The small roof garden

More often than not roof gardens are
restricted in space. If this is the case aim
for originality and charm. Use unusual
containers, such as metal buckets, and

paint them in matching colors, and also
choose plants that look attractive, and be
prepared to alter the planting scheme
throughout the year. If there is room for
just a few plants and containers choose
plants with calm, pale colors rather than
brilliant red and dark blue that have
more impact. You do not want to
overwhelm a small space with very
bright colors which in any case make
small areas appear even smaller. Pale
colors, such as white, pale pink,
lavender, and gray recede and make a
small roof garden appear a bit larger.
Sometimes the roof garden may be more
formal, for example a large balcony

outside a bedroom which is accessible through French windows. The planting here should complement and embellish the space and the most effective schemes are simple, perhaps just one plant in a special container, such as a white hydrangea, or a passionflower, *Passiflora* spp., climbing up a miniature trellis.

Watching the details The most successful roof gardens need to be planned extremely carefully. Every detail must be as perfect as possible. Make sure that any trellis fits in with the surroundings, and that matching trellises are exactly the same design. Also check that the containers are grouped properly, and that all the plants blend together so that plants and containers decorate the garden to the best advantage. For example, if you plan to use growing bags on a roof garden to raise tomatoes, sweet peppers, or beans, make sure that the bags are hidden in specially constructed troughs to conceal the brightly colored plastic. Finally, be as ambitious as you can. Some roof gardens are urban oases of quiet, overhung by mature trees, with fruit and shrubs, white painted trellises and walkways wandering through areas of containers filled with plants of many colors, each with a different tone of green leaf. Such roof gardens always evolve over time, but an ambitious plan never did any harm.

▶ *Fruit trees grafted on to dwarfing rootstocks are good plants for containers and provide both fruit and the lovely blossom of spring.*

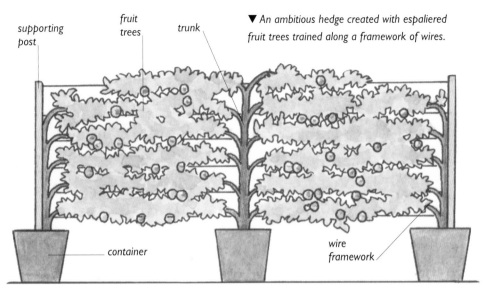

▼ *An ambitious hedge created with espaliered fruit trees trained along a framework of wires.*

supporting post

fruit trees

trunk

container

wire framework

practical planting

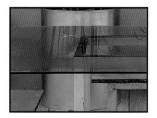

The first practical consideration is size and the second is aspect. How big is the garden, do you need to erect screens, is the garden totally open or is it bounded by walls on one or two sides? You may need professional help erecting screens: anything on a roof must be absolutely secure.

Plants for screens

If you have erected screens or trellises to hide the garden from view, then you need to plant climbers that will cover the screens. Ivy is often the most suitable evergreen climber, and the Confederate jasmine, *Trachelospermum jasminoides*, is excellent but it prefers the shelter of a sunny wall. Ivies cling on with their suckers, and may need tying in and encouragement of a plank or two to get them going up a trellis.

The choice of deciduous climbers is larger and all clematis are suitable, except perhaps the evergreen *C. armandii*. It is very rampant and also needs shelter. Winter jasmine, *Jasminum nudiflorum*, and weeping forsythia, *Forsythia suspensa*, both need tying in and pruning after flowering, but you can also plant one of the climbing roses to be trained along a trellis or against a wall (roses and clematis mix well together). Virginia creepers, *Parthenocissus* spp. and honeysuckles are too rampant, but one of the ornamental grape vines, *Vitis vinifera* 'Purpurea', or the hop, *Humulus lupulus*, are suitable.

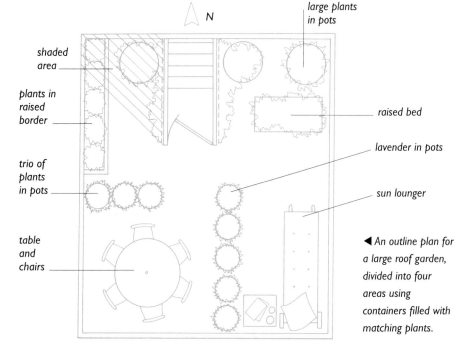

◄ An outline plan for a large roof garden, divided into four areas using containers filled with matching plants.

Annual climbers, such as morning glory, or nasturtium can also be used.

Making internal divisions

If the roof garden is large, you may want to divide it into two or three rooms. These divisions may be formal physical barriers or just a line of pots containing identical plants to suggest separate spaces. There are a number of small or large hedging plants that are suitable.

For a small dividing hedge lavender is ideal. It is evergreen, smells delicious and has lovely blue or white flowers in summer. Lavender hedges need to be planted in fairly tall containers to achieve this effect. The same goes for box, although it can be used as a low edging plant in closely positioned containers to emphasize a formal division.

A line of matching evergreen conifers makes another excellent

◀ A mature roof garden of the most ambitious kind shows what can be achieved over time. Evergreen shrubs, dwarf conifers, and the weeping birch insure that the garden remains interesting even during the winter months.

▼ A minimalist garden design using aluminum containers and a glass table top. The plant element is restricted to a few bamboos.

dividing line. Try *Juniperus communis* 'Compressa', slow-growing, vertical, and suitable for containers, or try *J. c.* 'Hibernica' or *J. scopulorum* 'Skyrocket'. These two have a similar, upright shape but grow more quickly. *Picea glauca* 'Albertiana Conica' is another good small slow-growing conifer with smoky blue foliage. In a mild climate the evergreen or semievergreen *Abelia* x *grandiflora* makes a good flowering hedge, and is ideal for a sunny or partially shaded position. There is also a dwarf form. It will need fairly hard clipping in spring, as does lavender and box.

You can achieve the same effect with fruit trees which can be trained to make an excellent dividing barrier. They will need a framework of wires to which the branches can be tied, but it is quite easy to tie them in correctly. They have lovely blossom in late spring and fruit in the fall. Trees grafted on to suitable miniature rootstocks are available from most nurseries. Do check their pollination requirements. Some fruit trees may need two or even three varieties growing nearby to achieve pollination, and some are what are called self-fertile and don't need this.

The importance of height

Make sure that the plants vary in height. Use clipped bay trees, *Laurus nobilis*, planted in individual containers, or grow matching standard roses in tubs. Also note that you can place containers on stands, and pole beans and peppers can be trained up stakes. There are a number of suitable climbing plants that will grow in shade, even roses. Hide the parapet walls with ivy planted in containers all along it, or try the climbing *Hydrangea petiolaris* or the similar deciduous climber, *Schizophragma hydrangeoides*—both have clumps of white flowers in summer.

containers for balconies

There are three approaches to gardening on a balcony. If the balcony is small then you may be restricted to one or two formal plants in matching containers, or you can cram in as many plants as possible to create a riot of color. The third approach is to treat the balcony as a small herb garden.

Aspect—colorful annuals in the sun

The style of planting and the type of plant you can grow greatly depends on the situation. If the balcony is in the sun for much of the day then you can grow colorful annuals that love the sun. Everyone has an image of a Swiss chalet with wooden balconies filled to the brim with red and white alpine pelargoniums, with ivy or lobelia trailing over the edge. This style of planting may not be to everybody's taste, but if you want to copy this effect then, above all, you need a balcony that faces south. You also need special containers designed to fit exactly along its length. You should rotate the plants throughout the year, changing the summer bedding plants for winter-flowering pansies. You may find it a help to include a few permanent evergreen plants, such as trailing ivy, to provide a framework. Finally, note that all containers need to be watered at least

DOING YOUR OWN THING

The essential in this type of gardening is to please yourself, experiment, try out various plants, and as in all gardening on a small scale, be ruthless when a plant does not live up to your expectations or grows too large for its place. One of the beauties of container gardening is that when a plant does outgrow its welcome it can be uprooted easily, thrown away and the container refilled with compost and another, smaller version planted for the next few years. Be ruthless about this. Nothing is worse than seeing a small garden dominated by one tree or shrub that has outgrown its space, however attractive it may be.

◀ *Petunias mixed with alpine pelargoniums smother a balcony in summer. Massed plantings using one color are most effective.*

once every day because the compost will dry out quickly in the sun. Annuals also need to be deadheaded regularly.

The informal balcony

Where there is room, pack in as many containers and plants as possible. As in all gardening some planning is essential. Place the chairs, benches, and tables and then add the containers. They can be filled with a variety of evergreen, perennial and annual plants, and the small scale will provide its own interest. Try to include some climbers.

If the balcony is large and almost a roof garden, you can grow any of the plants listed in that section. Another climber you might consider is the deciduous *Actinidia kolomikta* that has green leaves that quickly turn pink and white with age. It is a bit rampant and may require some restricting. It also has fragrant white flowers in summer. If this is not possible then include some hanging baskets filled with colorful annuals to provide the vertical dimension. Include pots of spring, summer, and fall bulbs. Regal lily, *Lilium regale*, is a wonderful plant for a container with an overpowering scent, and agapanthus lilies are beautiful in late summer. Smaller containers should be included with miniature plants, such as houseleeks, *Sempervivum* spp., or cactuses placed outdoors for the summer months.

▶ *A really beautifully designed balcony planted to make a cool impression in summer using mainly white and yellow flowers.*

the small formal balcony

A typical balcony is small with wrought iron outside the large window of a town house. Here space is severely limited and the planting must be restrained to match the style of the house. The best idea is to include two matching containers and plants to frame the window.

▶ *A design for a formal balcony with the doorway or French windows flanked by matching evergreen trees. If there is room then you can add a trellis and a climber, such as ivy or winter jasmine.*

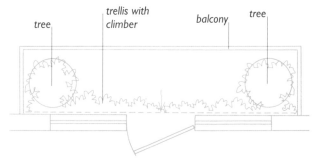

tree   trellis with climber   balcony   tree

Good formal small trees for this situation would be the evergreen bay, or camellias (if the balcony is shaded). Camellias can be pruned quite hard to maintain their shape, and this is best done after flowering is over in late spring. An alternative is clipped box, trained into a ball or spiral. It is worthwhile buying trained shrubs from a specialist supplier for this type of planting because you are aiming for an instant effect, and it takes a number of years to train box properly. The box can be complemented in

ESSENTIAL ASPECT

Some balconies face north and are in the shade for most of the day, even in high summer. You need to choose plants that will provide some color in this type of situation because the sun-lovers will end up long and lanky if they get too much shade, and produce few flowers. The following plants are suitable for any balcony that is in shade for much of the day.

◀ *Containers of different heights grouped in a roof garden. The cordyline palm adds height and red-striped phormium gives fall color.*

summer with low containers filled with white daisies or petunias, and possibly one or two blue trailing lobelias. This is not the place to indulge in flashy colors and take care, also, to choose containers that blend with the style of the house.

A kitchen garden balcony

Balconies that face the sun can support a number of vegetables, planted in growing bags or special containers—pole beans, tomatoes, and sweet peppers are all favorite choices. They need regular watering and care throughout the summer. It is best to concentrate on vegetables that mature relatively quickly, and provide some bright color and interesting form in a small space.

Herbs on balconies

Herbs that originated from the hot climate of the Mediterranean like dry, sunny conditions and will flourish if your balcony receives plenty of sun throughout the day. If you do have a sunny balcony and want to produce fresh herbs then you can include rosemary, with its light blue to purple flowers in spring, sage, thyme, chives, basil, and dill.

If you live on the other side of the building then herbs that will flourish in shade include parsley (although it can also be grown in sun), chervil, most mints, and oregano. Stick to the rules to start with but also experiment, you may well be surprised at the result. All sites are different, and there are an infinite variety of microclimates, especially to be found in towns and town gardens.

▲ A kitchen garden balcony of vegetables and herbs can look attractive with different colors.

❶ Pole beans
❷ Carrots
❸ Tomato 'Tumbler'
❹ Tomato 'Tornado'
❺ Applemint
❻ Mint
❼ Basil
❽ Parsley
❾ Thyme

SUITABLE PLANTS FOR SHADED BALCONIES

Climbers and wall shrubs

Coral plant, *Berberidopsis corallina*—prefers moist acid soil. Not fully hardy.

Clematis—many large-flowered clematis, such as 'Hagley Hybrid', 'Jackmanii Superba', 'Nelly Moser', 'Comtesse de Bouchaud', and 'Guernsey Cream', will grow on a north wall, as will all *alpina* and *macropetala* varieties.

Weeping forsythia, *Forsythia suspensa*

Climbing hydrangea, *Hydrangea petiolaris*

Winter jasmine, *Jasminum nudiflorum*

Roses—'Königin von Dänemark' ('Queen of Denmark'), 'Madame Legras de Saint Germain', 'Maigold'

Schizophragma hydrangeoides

Tropaeolum—the annual climbing nasturtium.

Shrubs

Box, *Buxus sempervirens*

Camellias

Ivy, *Hedera*

Hydrangeas

Calico bush, *Kalmia latifolia*—'Elf' is a small variety with white flowers; all need moist acid soil.

Bay, *Laurus nobilis*

Rhododendrons—several small varieties are suitable for a container.

Skimmia japonica 'Rubella'

Perennials and annuals

Lady's mantle, *Alchemilla mollis*

Begonia rex hybrids

Ferns—most are suitable.

Fuchsias

Hostas

Busy Lizzy, *Impatiens*, New Guinea Group

Primrose, *Primulas*

Violas

walls and trellises

The container gardener with limited room has to seize every opportunity to make the best use of the available space. The most obvious extension to a small garden is extending the walls upward by erecting a trellis. Climbers can be grown up the trellis to give the garden more seclusion.

How plants climb

Climbing plants operate in three main ways. The serious climbers—ivy, Boston ivy, or Virginia creeper and climbing hydrangea, *Hydrangea petiolaris*—all cling to the wall by suction pads or aerial roots. Pull any away from the wall and you will see the small spots left by the pads. These climbers prefer a flat surface and do best grown against a wall. They need no support. The next group are the clingers—clematis, everlasting pea, *Lathyrus* spp., passionflower, and vines, *Vitis* spp. These wind their leaf tendrils or, in the case of peas, passionflowers, and vines, special climbing tendrils, around anything they find on their way up. They need something to hold on to whether it be netting, trellis, wire, or pea sticks. The last group are the twiners—wisteria, pole (stick) beans, and summer jasmine—that wind their stems around poles or trellis, whatever is to hand.

▶ *Colored trellis can look very striking, especially if a climber with bright flowers is trained up it: purple looks good with blue.*

There are also a number of climbers that need help on their way up. These plants, such as bougainvillea, *Solanum crispum*, roses, and winter jasmine, *Jasminium nudiflorum*, throw out long shoots that

need to be tied in. There are also rambling roses that climb using their thorns to hold on to their host trees. Ramblers are vigorous and are unsuitable for growing in a container garden.

planting a climber in a container

1 Put broken crocks in the base to prevent the compost being washed away when the container is watered. Add more stones or gravel to aid drainage.

2 Fix a small purpose-built trellis to the wall behind the container and then fill the container with suitable compost and firm the plant in position. Water well.

3 Tie in the shoots of any climber, here some variegated ivy, to get the climber started. As the plant grows tie the shoots until the suckers take hold.

Using trellis to the best advantage

Ordinary trellis is ideal for any of these climbers and can even accommodate ivy and Virginia creeper with some judicious help. If you plan to grow climbers against a garden or house wall, and you do not wish to cover it with ivy, then you will need to erect a frame of trellis against it, either to tie in the shoots or to let the plant use it as a climbing frame. The best way to do this is to secure wooden battens against the wall so that the trellis is not fastened to the wall itself. This also allows air to circulate behind the plant. If you then fix the bottom of the trellis to the battens with hinges and secure it to the top with hooks and eyes, you can unhook it and lower the whole trellis to the ground, including the plant, when you need to repaint or repair the wall. It is worth doing this properly.

The best containers for climbers

If you are planning to grow a climber as a permanent feature in the garden you should try to give it as large a container as possible. No one wants to try pulling a climber away from the trellis every two years so that it can be potted on.

Ideally climbers should be grown in permanent containers or trenches around the walls, and if you want to grow dense permanent climbers, such as ivy or a climbing hydrangea, this is absolutely essential. Even some of the smaller climbers, such as clematis, need their roots to be cool and moist if they are to grow properly and this is best achieved in a large container mulched with stones. Half-barrels are ideal for growing clematis in because they are not subject to such extremes of temperature as terracotta or stone are in winter months.

▲ The blue flowers of the ceanothus are lovely in early summer. They can be tied against a wall on a suitable trellis arrangement.

planting tips for climbers

If you are growing a small climber you can buy specially made trellis panels that have two legs at the bottom designed to fit into a container. These can be used with ordinary terracotta pots, and the trellis can be bedded in with the compost. Tie the climber to the trellis when you have planted it.

If you want to grow a climber standing on its own on a terrace or patio, choose one of the lower growing varieties of clematis and plant it in a half-barrel.

Secure some lengths of pipe vertically around the inside of the barrel, and then push long canes into the pipes. Secure them at the top to make a wigwam.

Plant the clematis deeply and tie in the shoots to individual canes. Use a rich compost and make sure that there is adequate drainage for the roots.

▶ *Hops are good, vigorous climbers that will quickly cover a pergola. Cut them right down in the fall. Only the female plants have flowers.*

▼ *Pyracanthus make excellent evergreen wall shrubs and their colored berries last all winter. They need careful pruning in spring.*

◄ Chaenomeles, *usually called just japonica, is another good wall shrub. The flowers usually emerge on bare branches before the leaves.*

OTHER WALL PLANTS

If you have room, then you can consider the merits of some of the wall shrubs that can be planted in containers and trained against a wall. One of the best is firethorn, Pyracantha, evergreen with clumps of white flowers in spring followed by bright red, yellow, or orange berries in the fall, depending on the species. They respond well to hard pruning and are easy to shape against a wall. Their only disadvantage is the long sharp thorns on the branches. Japonica or Japanese quince, Chaenomeles, is another common shrub often trained against a wall. It is deciduous and flowers early in the year, generally in pink or red, although some white varieties are available. These are followed by edible fruits. Fruit trees are also excellent plants to grow against a wall and if you can offer a warm, south-facing position you can grow some of the tender kinds such as peaches or nectarines. Finally, all gardens are brightened by climbing roses. They have to be tied in to any trellis or wire frame, but the scent and flowers they provide are one of the highlights of the summer.

A brief guide to climbers

A surprising number of climbers can be grown against a north-facing wall although not all are suitable for growing in containers. They include: the chocolate vine, *Akebia quinata;* the coral plant, *Berberidopsis corallina;* some, but not all, kinds of ivy; the crimson glory vine, *Vitis coignetiae;* and the perennial flame creeper, *Tropaeolum speciosum.*

Evergreen climbers include: ivy; the coral plant, *Berberidopsis corallina; Clematis armandii; Clerodendrum splendens★; C. thomsoniae★; Eccremocarpus scaber* (usually grown as an annual in temperate climates); blue passionflower, *Passiflora caerulea; Stephanotis floribunda★,* and *Trachelospermum jasminoides.* A good number of evergreen climbers come from tropical or semitropical climates

and need some form of protection over the winter. The climbers marked ★ are not hardy and should either be brought inside, or at the least given the shelter of a warm south-facing wall. Check the precise requirements of each plant before purchasing and planting.

A number of climbers provide superb fall color. The main climbers grown for their foliage are the Virginia creepers, *Parthenocissus* spp., and the decorative kinds of vine, *Vitis* spp. The best foliage climbers include: *Actinidia kolomikta,* pink, white, and green leaves; the golden hop, *Humulus lupulus* 'Aureus', golden-yellow leaves; Boston ivy, *Parthenocissus tricuspidata,* red to purple leaves in the fall; and *Vitis coignetiae* and *V. vinifera,* both of which have leaves that turn dark red, then purple in the fall.

Not all climbers are suitable for growing in containers: among the most suitable are: bougainvillea, that needs a hot climate; *Clematis alpina* and *C. macropetala;* many different kinds of ivy; common jasmine, *Jasminum officinale;* Chilean bellflower, *Lapageria rosea;* and the passionflower, *Passiflora caerulea.* Climbing annuals that give instant effect include: *Eccremocarpus scaber;* morning glory, *Ipomea tricolor;* and black-eyed Susan, *Thunbergia alata.*

window boxes

Attractive window boxes can be marvels of ingenuity, both in design and color. Successful window box gardening takes thought, time, and care. Each one is rather like a semipermanent flower arrangement and many of the rules that apply to flower arranging also apply to window box gardening.

Practical aspects

There are a number of practical things to consider. First, the window box must fit on or beneath a window and it must be securely fastened in place. It will be fairly heavy when full of plants and compost, and anyone planning a window box overhanging a street must be certain that it is retained securely in position. This is usually done by securing metal brackets to the wall. (If you are not an expert get professional help.) In this type of position make certain that the window box has safety chains which can be secured to the wall or the window frame.

Window boxes must also blend in with the building. Normally they are made of wood or plastic, and can be painted to match the color of the paintwork around the window. They must also be able to drain freely. The bottom must have a number of drainage holes and if it is placed flat on a windowsill, it should be supported on and raised by wood battens to facilitate good drainage. If this is not done then the plants will suffer as they become waterlogged, and the base of the window box will rot if it is made of wood.

Window boxes, indeed all containers, need watering frequently and they need feeding at least once a fortnight. They do not contain a large amount of soil mix, and therefore the plants will need additional encouragement if they are to grow properly. This is particularly true when you are growing vegetables and fruit.

▲ *This window box includes variegated ivy, small tobacco plants, verbena, helichrysum, and pansies in a carefully controlled design.*

MAKING A WINDOW BOX

If you cannot buy a window box that will fit your windowsill, the solution is to build your own. This is not difficult as long as you have some basic carpentry skills and the right tools. The most important thing is to measure the window space and wood accurately. There is nothing more aggravating than finding the window box is a bit too long, and it is quite easy to do this if you forget to add the thickness of the wood on both sides.

Secure the sides and the bottom firmly using battens to hold them in place. Use good screws and do not just nail one piece of wood to another. Treat all the timber with wood preservative before you start (using proper preservative that will not damage the plants) and drill drainage holes in the bottom. Then, when the box is complete, line it with polyethylene, holding this in place with staples (use a staple gun). Finally, cut out matching holes in the liner to marry up with the drainage holes, and the box is ready for planting. A window box treated in this way should give good service for many years.

▶ *Careful planning has created this brilliant yellow window box using broom (genista), ivy, and chrysanthemums.*

assembling the window box

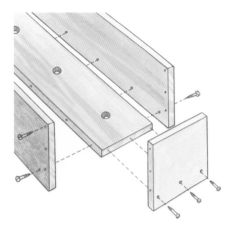

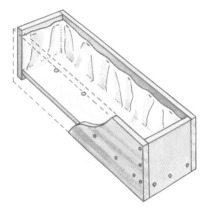

1 Measure the space and cut all the timber to size. Drill holes for the screws or, preferably, use battens to hold the sides and bottom in place.

2 When you have screwed the window box firmly together, line it with heavy-duty polyethylene to prevent the timber rotting. Staple the lining in place.

3 If the window box is freestanding fix it to the wall with brackets as shown. Make sure these are really secure and attach safety chains to the sides.

a variety of window boxes

Window boxes can be used in many ways. Most are planted with colorful annuals, but there are many other schemes that can be adopted. Some of the most effective window boxes are planted to give color during the cold, gray months of winter when few flowers are in bloom.

A colorful window box for winter

Many people imagine that gardens come to a full stop at the end of the fall but this certainly is not true of window boxes. There are many plants that will provide color in the winter months, and they can be used to enliven the darkest days of the year. There are two main groups of plants that flower in winter and are suitable for window boxes. The first is the winter-

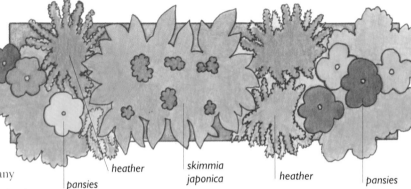

heather | skimmia japonica | heather | pansies
pansies

◄ A simple design for a window box that will give color through the winter. Make certain that this container is filled with ericaceous compost otherwise the heathers will die.

flowering heathers, *Erica carnea*, and the second the winter-flowering pansies, varieties of *Viola* x *wittrockiana*. Another colorful addition for a winter box are the bright red berries of the small evergreen

Skimmia japonica reevesiana. These are a wonderful scarlet that remain on the plant for many months. Heathers, too, are evergreen, although their leaves are a bit insignificant and the flowers are mainly pink or white.

If you are planting violas in a container with heathers for the winter, it is probably best to choose a white heather, such as *E. carnea* 'Springwood White,' *E.* x *darleyensis* 'White Glow', or the slightly larger *E.* x *d.* 'White Perfection'. They will not clash with any brightly colored violas. 'Springwood White' also has the advantage of a

◄ Erica x darleyensis 'Ghost Hills' has a mass of lovely pink flowers that last from the winter to early spring. They need acid soil.

slightly trailing habit, so it hangs down and helps to soften the edge of the window box. Although some heathers will tolerate alkaline conditions most really prefer acid soil, and you need to insure that the window box is filled with ericaceous soil to guarantee success.

Window boxes of spring bulbs

There are a number of bulbs that grow well in window boxes but that favorite spring bulb, the snowdrop, *Galanthus* spp., is not really one of them. Snowdrops like to naturalize under trees and in grassy places, and they do best when they are planted "in the green," i.e. dug up, split, and replanted at the end of their flowering period. You cannot plant

snowdrop bulbs in the fall and expect them to do very well, and no self-respecting window box gardener can afford the straggly foliage that takes some time to die down. Crocuses, on the other hand, work well. Plant them in the container in the fall and they will flower the following year at the end of winter. They like a sunny position, and are a welcome sight when they open their petals wide in the spring.

Miniature kinds of daffodil, *Narcissus* spp. also flower well in containers. You can plant a number of crocuses and daffodils in the same container with the narcissus bulbs below the level of the crocuses, and then one will flower after the other. If you add some good

▲ *A formal balcony in spring planted with daffodils and forget-me-nots, with ivy trailing over the front to soften the railings.*

evergreens, such as trailing ivy to provide contrasting foliage, the arrangement can be most successful. Other bulbs that will succeed, providing you plant them deep enough, are small tulips, the low-growing cultivars from Division 1 called Single Early Tulips, and those from Division 14, the Greigii Group. Choose ones with good contrasting colors.

Finally, buy the bulbs from a specialist supplier with an extensive catalog, and never buy a cheap mixed group of daffodils from a supermarket or garden center. They will flower at different times and look dreadful.

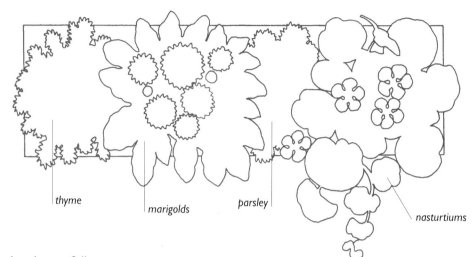

thyme   marigolds   parsley   nasturtiums

◀ *A plan for a small window box filled with an edible mixture of flowering annuals and herbs. Raise the parsley in separate pots and insert these into the window box, for the seeds take a long time to germinate. Use the marigolds for tea and food coloring and the nasturtiums in salads.*

Window boxes full of summer annuals

It is inevitable that the finest and most colorful window boxes are planted with annuals in the summer. Annuals are wonderful plants for all containers, and they are especially effective when they are planted in a small space giving concentrated color. You should also match the color of the window box with the arrangement. White works well with all colors, while a neutral shade of green provides a quiet foil for most plants and their blooms.

Alternatively, paint the window boxes a bright color, in which case a white, or a varied tonal planting would look best. If possible plant the boxes with flowers in bloom because few gardeners are so expert that they can judge matching color tones exactly, before the flowers begin to emerge.

The planting principle is the same as in flower arranging. Plant blocks of color like reds and pinks, or lilac, blues, and white. Use strong colors sparingly in quiet arrangements, or unreservedly fill the window box with brilliant tones. Add taller plants for height and trailing plants to hang over the edge. The choice is entirely personal. For a choice of summer annuals see pages 226–33.

The edible window box —herbs and flowers

Many people use their window boxes to grow herbs for the kitchen, and even gardeners with large vegetable plots often have a window box near the kitchen door, ready for a quick supply of ingredients. Before planning a window box of herbs you need to check which way it faces because some herbs do best in the sun and some in shade. A number of attractive plants can be included and the planting need not just be varying

◀ *A window box of tomato plants, lettuces, carrots, strawberries, and mini-cauliflowers makes a talking point on a town windowsill.*

◀ *Blue and white arrangements make a cool statement in summer. Petunias, white daisies, and variegated ivy are the main ingredients.*

shades of green. Try some flowering herbs, especially the trailing nasturtium, *Tropaeolum*, that can be used in salads and can be planted with a few marigolds (the flowers can be used as a food coloring and the leaves can be made into tea). Chives have attractive light purple flowers but there might be a bit of a color clash if they are planted with the orange and yellow flowers of the first two plants. And purple-leaved basil, sage, variegated mint, and the curly-leaved parsley can all be included in a small herbal window box.

A window box of miniature vegetables

Miniature vegetables are a good idea. These are now readily available, and a variety can be planted in a vegetable-only window box. Beets, carrots, cauliflowers, leeks, lettuce, onions, corn, turnips, and zucchini are just some of the mini-vegetables available, and many have contrasting leaf colors and shapes. The seed can be sown in patches and the seedlings thinned to produce the most attractive effect. The good thing about mini-vegetables is that they mature more quickly than larger ones, and in less

than three months you should be able to visit your window box and cut plenty of lettuce and scallions for salads, and pull beets and carrots as well.

Mixed window boxes of fruit and vegetables

If you want to add variety and colour to the vegetable window box include one or two plants of the small tomatoes that have been developed for the container gardener. 'Tumbler' and 'Patio' are both good varieties and they can even be grown in a hanging basket. You can also include the dwarf sweet pepper 'Jingle Bells' or a miniature cucumber, although this will not provide the flash of brilliant red color.

Add one or two strawberry plants if you want; there are varieties specially bred for the container gardener that flower and fruit over a long period, or if you prefer old-fashioned plants, grow a few wild strawberries. The small berries are most enticing and you won't be able to buy them in the stores either.

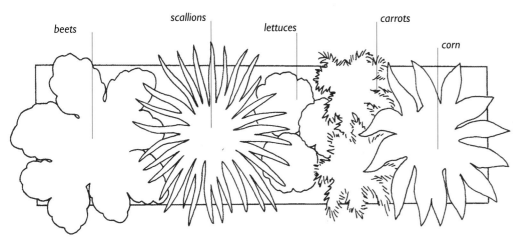

beets   scallions   lettuces   carrots   corn

◀ *Mini-vegetables have been developed for window boxes and containers. They enable the gardener to provide fresh organic crops for some special meals in season, and are well worth the effort of planting and harvesting.*

hanging baskets

Hanging baskets are one of the glories of summer and brighten porches, city streets, and balconies. They are not all that difficult to manage and maintain, but you do have to take care when choosing the plants if you want to achieve the best effect.

A blue, red, and white basket

For a 40cm/16in diameter hanging basket you will need: six trailing plants such as…

Helichrysum petiolare—trailing variety, heart-shaped leaves, densely gray-wooly above, lighter underneath. Off-white flower heads.

Hedera helix (ivy)—use small-leaved variegated varieties such as 'Adam', 'Asterisk', or 'Glacier'.

Plectranthus forsteri 'Marginatus'—trailing, variegated green and white leaves, and *P. australis*—small bright green leaves; or

P. oertendahlii—white-veined leaves with rosy-purple undersides.

Also use…

3–6 trailing *Pelargonium* 'Roulette', with crimson and white striped flowers.

1–2 Pelargonium 'Pulsar Scarlet' for the top of the basket, or red dwarf plants from the 'Video Mixed' Series.

6–9 *Petunia grandiflora*—a white variety.

6 Lobelia 'Sapphire'—violet blue with a white eye or 'Crystal Palace'—blue.

Larger or smaller baskets may require more or fewer plants, bearing in mind that it is best to overcrowd the basket for maximum effect. Plant the trailing foliage plants around the rim of the basket to trail down the sides, and plant the colored plants in bands. They will grow through the trailing green-leaved ivy, *Hedera*, and make an increasing impact throughout the summer.

A yellow and orange hanging basket for maximum impact

For a 40cm/16in diameter hanging basket you will need…

6–9 trailing *Tropaeolum majus* (nasturtium), either Double Gleam Hybrids or Alaska Mixed.

6 *Lysimachia congestiflora* (loosestrife)—clumps of yellow tubular flowers with red centers.

6 *Bidens ferulifolia*—small yellow star-shaped flowers that cascade down the sides of the basket.

6 *Tagetes* (marigold)—French or signet marigolds are best for baskets—look for Disco Series and Gem Series in shades of orange, gold, and yellow. 'Naughty Marietta' has yellow flowers with maroon markings.

▶ *This is another red, white, and blue design using ageratum and begonias for a blue and red effect. Start planting at the base of the basket and push the plants through the wire from inside to the outside. Keep the plant as intact as possible.*

❶ Begonia (red)
❷ Ageratum (blue)
❸ Petunia (white)
❹ Lobelia (blue)
❺ Ivy

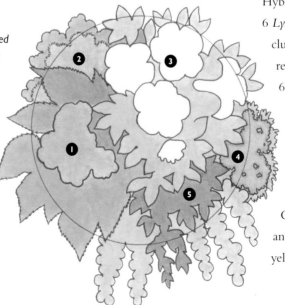

▲ *Hanging baskets can be used as part of the overall garden design. The main plants used in this fragrant garden are scented geraniums.*

▶ *Deep pink and white busy lizzies make a simple two-colored basket. Other similar baskets echo the planting in the garden.*

A hanging basket for the winter months

Almost all hanging baskets are planted for summer display, but you can contrive an attractive mixture of plants that will give color throughout the winter provided you can keep the basket in a relatively frost-free environment. The basis for a winter basket is hardy evergreen plants that provide a green backdrop. The plants to include are…
Hedera helix 'Glacier' or *H. h.* 'Pin Oak' (both ivies)—if the basket is in an exposed position make sure you choose varieties that are fully hardy.
Polypodium vulgare—an evergreen fern.

Vinca minor, lesser periwinkle—evergreen, with trailing shoots and flowers from early in spring to the fall.
Viola x *wittrockiana*, winter pansy—either choose mixed colors or plain blue or white varieties. They provide color for months over the winter.

Simple baskets for summer color

Some of the most effective hanging baskets are those where only one plant is used, often in a variety of colors. The best annual for a tonal basket is the petunia. There are three types: grandiflora, the one with the largest flowers up to 12.5cm/5in across;

multiflora, with each plant carrying many flowers, single or double up to 7.5cm/3in across; and milliflora, smaller plants carrying many flowers. Most petunias are in shades of red, pink, purple, and white. Plants from the Celebrity Mixed Series, the Celebrity Bunting Series (darker colors), and Celebrity Pastel Mixed Series, produce matching displays with a random variety of color. Single color petunias, such as 'Sonata' in white and Supercascade in rose-pink, are also good. The grandiflora petunias in the Picotee Series and Razzle Dazzle Series produce flowers in vivid colors, often bicolored, with ruffled margins.

tonal baskets

Some gardeners prefer to create quieter displays with varying shades. There are an infinite number of plants and color schemes that can be used in this way. Concentrate on one color, such as pink or pale blue, or plant a variety of complementary colors in the paler shades of the color circle.

A pink and purple hanging basket

Use lavender, *Lavandula* 'Munstead', deep purple, or the pink, *Dianthus* 'London Delight', light rose with a deeper eye. Use some of the half-hardy fuchsias, such as, 'Auntie Jinks', white and purple; 'Micky Gault', white with cerise pink centers; or 'Leonora', soft pink; the bright pink busy lizzie, *Impatiens* New Guinea Hybrid, for the center of the basket. Include some gray-green trailing foliage, *Hedera helix* 'Glacier' or *Helichrysum*

petiolare 'Roundabout', to hold the elements together.

A blue, purple, and silver basket

A similar color scheme, but even quieter, could be obtained using purple-blue pansies from the *Viola* x *wittrockiana* range as the main accent, with purple-flowered *Salvia officinalis* 'Aurea' that is small enough for a hanging basket, with *Hedera helix* 'Glacier', helichrysum, and gray-leaved *Senecio cineraria* 'Silver Dust'.

A hanging basket of vegetables

This is an unusual idea but it can work well and provides a talking point. Make sure that all vegetables are fed regularly, at least once a week, during their growing period. This is particularly important for the trailing tomatoes that form the highlight of any display.

Salvia officinalis

Senecio cinerari 'Silver

Helichrysum petiolare 'Roundabout'

Hedera helix

Viola x wittrockiana

▲ *A blue and white basket is always effective and creates a calm atmosphere. Always use water-retaining granules when planting baskets.*

Lettuce—choose a selection of the loose-leaf varieties, such as 'Red Fox' with red and green leaves; 'Lollo Biondo' with pale green leaves; 'Lollo Rosso' with red frilled leaves; and 'Red and Green Salad Bowl'. Plant them in the sides of the baskets with the darker colored leaves at the bottom, and the light green 'Lollo

Fuchsia

Lavandula 'Munstead'

petunias

Dianthus

Hedera helix

Helichrysum petiolare 'Roundabout'

◀ *A basket of pink flowers contrasted with the blue lavender. Lavenders need careful placing to show the flowers properly.*

A HERBAL
HANGING BASKET

Plant a smaller hanging basket with herbs because they are attractive and useful in the kitchen. Herbs do not produce the vibrant colors of annuals but they have attractive variegated leaves. Also use nasturtium, *tropaeolum*, as trailing plants because they are attractive and edible. The leaves add bite to any salad and the flowers add decoration. The main choice should include…

Thyme—*Thymas herba-barona*, the herb traditionally served with roast beef, will hang down; *T. vulgaris* 'Aureus' and 'Silver Posie' have gold and silver-edged leaves.

Sage—*Salvia officinalis* 'Icterina' has variegated yellow and green leaves; *S. o.* 'Purpurascens' has red-purple young leaves; other varieties are available with different colored leaves.

Chives—delightful lilac flowers.

Parsley—the curly leaved form.

Finally add a few yellow marigolds, the French marigold *Tagetes patula* 'Lemon Drop' is excellent, or the old medieval "pot" herb, the orange marigold, *Calendula officinalis*.

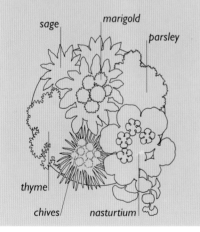

Bciondo' around the rim to give a good contrast between the different greens. Then add three plants of the cherry tomato 'Tumbler', that has been specially bred for growing in hanging baskets, and add one or two basil or oregano plants to give a herbal touch if there is room.

▲ *Strawberries and parsley go well together with their contrasting leaf shapes and green colors fringed with white alyssum.*

Practical considerations

Container gardening is much the same as any other form of gardening. Seed is sown, plants grow, mature, flower, set seed, and die. The main thing to remember is that the plant roots are more restricted, and therefore they need feeding more often than plants in open ground.

large containers for impact

The choice of container is not something to be rushed. Really large containers made from terracotta or reconstituted stone are extremely expensive, and antique containers even more so. Large containers can be used as accent points, drawing the eye, for plants of special interest.

Using tall pots

Very often the choice of container is dictated either by the height of the plant you wish to grow or the overall garden design. In a garden that is full of containers you will need varying heights. The tallest, the large Ali Baba type jars, may well be difficult to find and are expensive. Sometimes a search around antique or junk shops reveals some surprising treasures that are cheaper and more interesting than those available in garden centers. Take time to find the right one that suits your garden. Very often you find old Victorian pots used for indoor plants or umbrella stands that look perfect in a container garden.

Care in planting One of the things to watch out for when planting large containers is the shape of the neck. Old chimney pots are both popular and decorative, as are Ali Baba jars, but they, and all other containers with narrow necks, are unsuitable for any permanent planting. The problem is that when you plant a shrub in a container the roots expand over time. The only way you can then pot on the shrub into a larger container is to break the top of the jar. Always put permanent plants in an open container where they can be removed relatively easily.

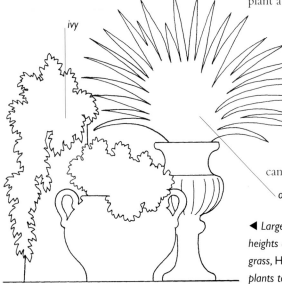

ivy

ornamental grass

◀ *Large pots grouped together to give different heights and shapes. Trailing ivy, the decorative grass, Hakonechloa, and thyme would be good plants to include in this type of arrangement.*

▼ *Large containers and brightly colored pots make their own statement in a garden. Plan with care or they may overwhelm the plants.*

blue-glazed pot

square planter

ornamental urn

Terracotta pots

The most common material for garden containers is terracotta (which means "cooked or baked earth"). The beauty of terracotta is the large variety of styles and shapes that are available. You can form attractive groups of terracotta containers, either using pots of the same basic design in a variety of sizes, or using a number of

how to age a terracotta pot

1 Modern terracotta pots are often brightly colored and look garish and out of place in the garden. They can easily be aged so that they blend in.

2 Paint the surface of the pot with yogurt, or a mixture of yogurt and sour milk. This attracts algae that will discolor the pot.

3 After a few weeks the pot will be covered with algae and will look as if it is several years old. Leave the inside of the pot unpainted.

different shapes such as egg pots, half-pots, third-pots, and various shapes and styles of seed pans. They can be interspersed by some "long Toms" that are both taller and narrower.

Many designs now on the market are copies of older-style pots that were available in the 19th century, and some of the more elaborate urns are based on classical designs. To give new pots an ancient look, either paint them in softer colors or age them by applying yogurt or sour milk. This attracts algae and the pot soon looks suitably aged. Another alternative is to buy the colored terracotta pots that are now available in a range of soft, muted shades.

▶ *A classical container filled with a mound of sempervivums. Some varieties have red leaves and carry upright flowers in summer.*

other types of container

Many different types of container can be used and the garden designer should not be confined to standard pots available at garden centers. Old tin baths, kitchen sinks, stone troughs, all make excellent containers and add interest to a container garden. Insure that all plants can drain freely.

Troughs

The most expensive and heaviest troughs are made from lead, and they definitely are not suitable for roof gardens. Copies of traditional lead troughs are now made from fiberglass, and traditional stone troughs are available made from reconstituted stone or hypertufa. Be absolutely certain where you are going to position any trough in the garden before buying it though, and put any large container in position first before filling it with compost and planting. Containers are much easier to move around when they are empty. This particularly applies when you are arranging a group of containers in a container-only garden. Place them all in position and move them around until you are completely satisfied with the arrangement. Leave the pots in position overnight and check the grouping again in the morning before finally filling them with compost and plants.

Strawberry planters

One of the favorite containers for the patio is the strawberry planter, and many gardeners have visions of ripe fruit dripping down the sides of the pot. They are readily available in all garden centers but in truth it is difficult to cultivate a huge crop using them, and the greatest

◄ *Strawberries ripening in a traditional strawberry planter. These need to be turned each week to give the plants equal sun.*

care needs to be taken if you are to succeed. The first and most important thing is to buy a perforated central plastic pipe. Put this in position because it enables you to water the bottom of the container as well as the top. Add some stones or pot shards to hold the pipe upright and provide additional drainage. Then fill the strawberry planter with a well fertilized, loam-based soil mix—strawberries are greedy plants and need all the encouragement they can get. Plant the strawberries as you fill up the container, pushing the plants through from the inside—choose a variety especially developed for growing in pots. Firm in all the roots and then water well. If you really want to be successful with strawberries you should pick off the flowers in the first year to build up the strength of the plant.

Keep the planter watered throughout the summer and turn it every week so that all the sides get an

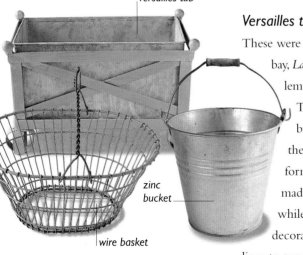

Versailles tub

zinc bucket

wire basket

▲ Many different containers can be used in gardens, both formal and informal. Punch holes in the bottom of buckets to allow drainage.

equal amount of sun. Feed the plants with liquid fertilizer every two weeks after the flowers appear in the spring. Protect from birds if necessary.

Versailles tubs

These were traditionally used for clipped bay, *Laurus nobilis*, and orange or lemon trees in conservatories. They have a pleasing shape but are only suitable where there is space to design a fairly formal garden. They can be made from wood or plastic, and while the wooden ones are more decorative they require a plastic liner to prevent the wood rotting over the years. They are also heavier and much more expensive, but look the part.

▲ Proper lead containers are both heavy and expensive. Fiberglass copies of classical designs look just as good. Line them with polyethylene.

Unusual containers

A number of unusual containers can be used and there is plenty of choice. Old sinks and tin baths are good contenders but check that they fit in with the garden design and are suitable for your planting. Sinks, in particular, are often used for low-growing alpine plants. Old cattle troughs are another idea if you have room, as are smaller discarded water cisterns. They do weigh quite a lot though, so don't fill them before you have to move them and be sure that you can make drainage holes in the base before putting in rubble and compost.

smaller containers

The smaller the space the more care has to be taken to choose containers that fit the garden design and match the plants. Often the small containers in a grouping get ignored; take care to see they blend with the others. Wall pots, too, are most important and can extend the garden upward.

Small containers for small spaces

When it comes to choosing small containers there is a considerable choice, and with a little imagination the gardener can achieve great effects in a tiny space. Often in small gardens there is only room for a few plants, and each can be matched individually to the container. Small pots can be grouped together with small plants, such as primroses, *Primula* spp. or violas, while larger flat-bottomed bowls can be filled with rosette-shaped *Sempervivum*s that rejoice in the common name of houseleek.

The important point is to focus on your favorite plants—small lavender bushes, spring bulbs, herbs, and colorful annuals. Then collect a number of similar terracotta pots in varying sizes, plant them up and arrange them to suit the space. There may even be room for one or two climbing plants, such as a clematis, that can be trained up the wall of the house if a larger pot can be found to accommodate their root systems. Clematis like their roots to be cool, so shade the pots of clematis from the sun if

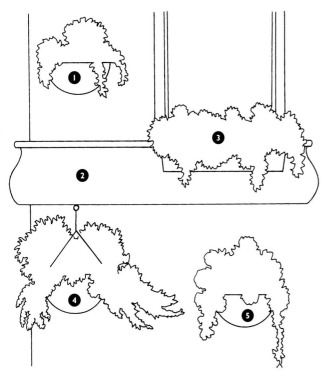

◀ *When the gardener is restricted to a small space such as a balcony then there is often scope to add hanging baskets and window boxes to extend the number of plants that can be grown. Make sure that these plantings match each other in style or the effect may be incongruous.*

❶ Wall pot
❷ Balcony outside window
❸ Window box
❹ Hanging basket
❺ Wall pot

ANTIQUE WALL POTS

Plain wall pots are most suitable for many situations but there are a number of shapes available, either copied from classical designs or from ancient civilizations such as the Aztecs and Mayans. These can look very good on old walls in the right surroundings. They include shell wall pots, masks, lattice designs, honeypots, and gourds. All wall pots dry out quickly in summer so it is essential to include water-retaining granules when planting and to water them at least once a day, if not more.

▶ *Ordinary terracotta pots secured to a garden fence with wire rings, planted with bright busy lizzies to make everyone sit up and notice.*

you can. Even if you do not have a lot of space many lovely effects can be created with a bit of imagination.

Wall pots and hanging baskets

Container-only gardeners should always be aware of the vertical dimension. There is enormous scope to extend a garden upward, given a suitable wall, or even some firm trellis, using a variety of wall pots. These are half-pots with flat backs that fit against a wall and hold plants that trail over the edge. If you fill these half-pots with colorful annuals they make a series of vivid splashes. Used with imagination, the keen gardener can paint a series of abstract pictures using the flowers and plants.

There are many kinds of wall pots, including honeypots, decorated and plain shells, and fluted and rounded terracotta, emulating the styles of full pots. If you have a number of terracotta pots in the garden of varying shapes and designs, try to match the half-pots to the full ones, integrating the design. Also make sure that they are firmly secured to the wall, and that you can reach them easily with a hose extension for watering. Being that much more in the sun they will require watering as frequently as hanging baskets. Finally, when planting wall pots insure, as far as possible, that the plants will flower at the same time. That way you will obtain the maximum effect.

Hanging baskets

Most hanging baskets are plain, made from wire, and the two most common sizes are 40cm/16in and 30cm/12in diameter. You can buy ornate filigree metal baskets if you want but the plain ones are generally better as the metalwork is soon obscured by the plants. Make sure that the hook and beam on which the basket hangs is strong and secure. Hanging baskets weigh a surprising amount when they are in full growth and have been watered. For care and planting details see pages 92–3.

Both wall pots and hanging baskets are especially useful for balconies. Unless the balcony is very large, it is unlikely that there will be room enough for large containers or a raised bed big enough to accommodate climbers. In this situation, carefully positioned wall pots and hanging baskets provide color and interest.

79

containers for large plants

It stands to reason that large plants need large containers, especially if they are going to grow successfully. Much thought should be given to purchasing larger containers, as they are often expensive, and it is important that they fit into the style that you have decided on for your garden.

Containers for large plants

If you want to grow large plants, you have got to think big. In fact all large plants, trees, fruit, and shrubs will need as

◄ *Canna lilies contribute to a garden planned to give the feeling of a tropical forest. Heat and sun are necessary for success.*

large a container as you can provide if they are to flourish and attain anything like their potential proportions. They are best grown in raised beds or in special large containers to match the overall design of the patio, roof garden, or terrace. All containers need good drainage at the bottom, and an automatic watering system is a great help.

The next key factor is style—you have to think carefully about how a large expensive container will fit into the garden, and how the container will relate to the type and shape of the plant. Trees or shrubs with a spreading habit look best in wide-brimmed pots, and formal clipped topiarized trees need formal containers to look their best. Very often large containers are made from terracotta, but other materials, such as stone or glazed earthenware, are also suitable provided they can accommodate the root system of the plant. Also, keep

the containers and their contents in proportion. It is always possible to pot on a tree into a larger container as it grows, while a small plant alone in a large pot will look bare and isolated. It is best to fill the space around the main plant with low-growing herbs or annuals to keep the planting in proportion.

Half-barrels

Half-barrels make good containers and can accommodate quite large trees. They look natural and suit almost any surrounding. You may be able to find old barrels in a junkyard, but good copies are now made specifically as plant containers. If you are lucky enough to get some barrels they need to be cut in half. Do this carefully with a saw, marking the circumference with a chalk line to guide you. Then fill the barrel with water and leave it overnight so that the wood swells. You may have to soak the barrel for even longer if the wood has become extremely dry. Then make drainage holes in the bottom and line the barrel with a thick plastic liner, holding it in place with staples. Make holes in the liner at the bottom to fit the drainage holes. Trim the plastic neatly before filling the barrel with hardcore and compost.

Positioning tall pots to the best advantage

Tall pots make excellent features on a patio garden and hardly need any plants to make them attractive. Ali Baba pots, in particular, are very decorative on their own but be careful if you are planning to plant up a very tall pot. There are few plants that work well and you should aim for some trailing nasturtium, *Tropaeolum*, or something equally simple.

Very large containers need to be placed carefully in the garden, and care has to be taken over the color of the pot and the background that it is against. The design of a garden is composed of many things and background color and planting are often overlooked.

The shape of the container often dictates the type of plant. Trees suit Versailles tubs while trailing nasturtiums fit Ali Baba jars.

DRAINAGE FEET

Although it does not matter in every case it can be very important to keep the base of the container off the ground. This particularly applies to window boxes and any container made from wood or MDF. Raise them using wooden battens or tiles. Special feet are available for most terracotta pots and they should be placed underneath to let the water drain away freely. Half-barrels should always be placed on bricks.

▶ Foliage plants look good in spectacular containers. Here the blue-gray leaves of the agave tone in with the color of the jars, and the spiky leaves contrast well.

building raised beds

Raised beds are an excellent idea in all container gardens where there is sufficient room. They enable the gardener to create a permanent display and increase the range of plants that can be grown. They are also extremely useful for disabled gardeners who cannot reach beds at soil level.

Planning and measuring

Begin by making sure that there is enough space around the edges of the bed to allow adequate access. Plan out the size of the bed on paper and then calculate the amount of material needed. Raised beds can be built from bricks, stone slabs, decorative blocks, or cinder blocks, whichever you prefer. Cinder or concrete blocks are the cheapest, but they will need rendering and painting if they are going to look satisfactory. Stone and stone slabs are rather difficult to handle, and decorative blocks are not really satisfactory. Bricks, old or new, are probably best and fit in with most designs, but there will be a number of gardens in parts of the country where stone is the predominant building material. Any raised bed there would have to be built from stone because brick would look quite inappropriate.

Having decided on the material you then have to mark out the area accurately with string, making sure that all the corners are square—assuming you are building a square bed. Then dig out a trench, 30cm/12in wide and 30cm/12in deep, for the footing that supports the walls. Fill this with concrete, make sure that it is quite level and leave overnight. If you are building your raised bed on a solid foundation, such as a patio, you then need to break up the base to allow the water to drain through properly into the subsoil. If you do not do this all you will do is create a miniature swimming pool filled with earth or compost, and all the plants will eventually rot and die. Do

◀ *A simple wooden trough is the easiest form of raised bed, here devoted to vegetables and herbs. The leaves make a pleasing contrast.*

making a raised bed

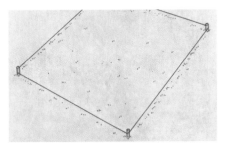

1 Measure the area and mark it out with pegs and string. Make sure that the corners are at right angles. Break up the base to allow free drainage.

2 Dig out a trench around the sides of the raised bed 30cm/12in high and 30cm/12in deep. Tamp down some hardcore in the bottom and then fill the trench with cement.

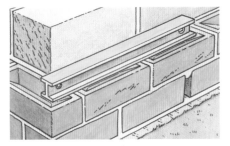

3 Leave the cement overnight to dry. Protect in wet or frosty weather. Start by building an inner wall of cinder blocks. Lay these on a bed of mortar at least 12mm/½in thick.

4 Check the levels with string and a level and insert wall ties at intervals to give the walls extra strength. It is best to build from the corners outward.

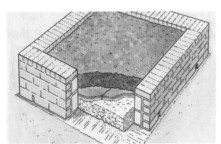

5 Finish off the walls by laying bricks across the cinder blocks and brick walls as shown to make a neat finish. Fill the bed with compost and allow this to settle before planting.

this part properly so that the container can drain freely and well. And take particular care, if you are doing this on a patio, not to obstruct or damage any of the main services or drains.

If you are constructing a traditional brick bed, now build an inner wall using cinder blocks. Lay each block on a 12mm/½in-layer of mortar with one end butted against the next side of the bed using a dab of the mortar. When the inner walls have been completed, check that they are level and then build the outer wall using bricks. Build the outer wall out from each corner, and then set a string guideline between the corners and infill the corners with bricks insuring that they are totally level. Insert some metal wall ties at intervals to add to the strength of the wall. When the walls are finished lay a final course of bricks lengthwise across the inner and the outer wall as shown in the picture on the left. Add a good layer of rubble or stones to the base to assist drainage, and then fill the bed with good soil mix or good quality garden soil.

▲ *An extremely glamorous patio designed in the style of Charles Rennie Mackintosh with raised beds that complement the colors used.*

building permanent trenches

A raised trench in any container garden is wonderful for all elderly or disabled gardeners confined to a wheelchair; special long-handled tools are available that enable anyone to reach the center of the bed. They also allow anyone to grow a selection of more permanent plants.

A number of patio gardens can be improved if there are permanent trenches or beds positioned around the side or sides of the garden. The principles of building a trench around the perimeter of a small garden are exactly the same as building a raised bed in the center, but there are one or two extra questions that you should ask yourself, and one or two additional factors to be taken into account. The first question is width. There is no point in building a permanent bed around the walls of your garden if you cannot reach the back easily to prune and tie in any plants and shrubs growing there.

You then have to decide on the height. Should it be relatively high, the same height as a raised bed accessible from a wheelchair, or just one or two bricks high, holding a small bed in place around the edge of the garden? And which way does the garden face? A raised bed in the center of the garden is relatively unaffected by aspect, but a bed against a south- or southwest-facing wall is very different from one against a north-facing wall. For example, a south-facing wall will support a number of fruit trees from peaches to pears that can be trained against it on a framework of wires. On a north-facing wall, if you are lucky, you may be able to grow a Morello cherry, but they make large trees and grow too big for the normal container garden.

If you do plan to use an old garden wall as the back of the raised trench, is it in good enough condition to stand the additional weight, or are the bricks and mortar old, crumbly and unable to cope

◄ *A raised trench enables the gardener to grow a good selection of more permanent plants, such as larger shrubs and trees.*

making a permanent trench

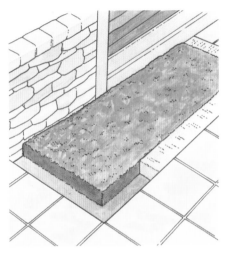

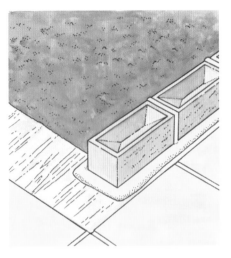

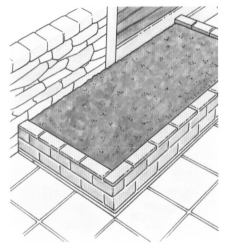

1 Measure the space for a permanent trench and then remove enough topsoil around the walls to lay the cement footing for the walls.

2 Lay the bricks once the footing is dry. If the trench is built against a freestanding wall, as shown, you need only build three walls.

3 Always leave a gap if the trench is built against the wall of the house so that there is no chance of damaging the damp course.

with damp earth and winter frosts? If the wall is in really poor condition then you may need to rebuild it before starting. Alternatively, you may have to build a retaining wall in front of it, leaving a gap for the air to circulate. This also applies to the walls of the house or apartment. Never, ever, build a garden trench right

up against the house walls because it will interfere with the damp course and cause problems. Always leave a good gap.

Design

Now check the design and plan everything before you start. Two small beds may look better than one large one. There may even be room for small freestanding beds in the middle of a terrace or roof garden. They should be made

from wood or plastic because bricks would normally be too heavy. Natural materials, wood, and brick always look attractive, but all surfaces can be painted and this may work better.

Work out the size of the bed and the number of bricks and slabs you need. But remember, however easy it may look, bricklaying is quite a skilled profession. Call for an expert if you have any doubt in your ability to do a good job.

PLANTS FOR RAISED TRENCHES

The main benefit of making a raised trench or bed in or around the patio is the increased range of plants that this allows you to grow. Fruit trees trained on a framework of wire make excellent use of wall space and small climbing roses are another excellent wall-covering plant in a small garden, and they can be used as ladders by large-flowered clematis in summer.

climbing roses

smaller shrubs

◄ *Choose suitable climbing plants for the back of a raised trench and then place smaller shrubs in front. Climbing roses are excellent but evergreen climbers and shrubs are available for color over winter.*

paths, steps, and trellises

The design of the patio or garden must be considered as a whole. This entails looking at the flooring, the seating areas, steps, trellises, and pergolas. Any reasonably confident handyman can build any of these features, but it is best to consult a specialist manual before starting.

Flooring—paving stones, blocks, and bricks

There are many attractive flooring materials available for any patio. Natural stone crazy paving is one of the best, but it is very expensive and difficult for the amateur to lay correctly. It may be better to consider one of the modern concrete look-alikes. They mimic the qualities of natural stone but are more regular, easier to lay and provide an attractive surface.

Another good flooring material that looks most attractive and is extremely flexible is brick. It can be laid in various patterns including herringbone, circles, and quadrants. In fact different patterns can be used to delineate and highlight particular areas of the patio.

There are a large variety of brick and paving blocks available at various prices that can be used. Anyone wanting to relay the surface of a patio or garden is advised to consult a specialist manual and follow the instructions carefully. It is essential that there is a really good foundation of hardcore and sand, and that adequate allowance is made for good drainage. All external flooring must also allow rainwater to drain away from the walls of the house, and if you are laying or relaying a patio butting on to the lawn, it is advisable to dig out a soakaway at the edge of the patio that can be returfed when the patio is complete. If you do not do this the edge of the lawn will be extremely damp and sodden whenever it rains.

◄ *An old brick path in a small garden that blends with the terracotta container. Note how closely the bricks have been laid together.*

laying a brick path

1 Brick paths are best laid on a sand base. Spread the sand evenly and make sure that the surface is level before putting the bricks in place.

2 Brick paths are more interesting if the bricks are set out in a variety of patterns. Make sure that they are placed close together and check the level.

3 When the path has been laid brush a weak mixture of sand and cement lightly over the bricks and then water it in. Keep the bricks as clean as possible.

Gravel paths and walkways

Gravel and cobblestones are two other materials for patterning the surface of the patio. Gravel can be used as a garden surface in a small town garden where a grass lawn would be inappropriate. If you want to make a gravel garden just lay 25mm/1in of gravel directly on top of the soil; you can plant directly into the soil beneath. Apply a simazine-based weedkiller to the gravel areas in the summer to stop any weeds germinating. When laying a gravel path it needs to be excavated more deeply, and depending on the amount of traffic, you may need to put down a layer of hardcore before spreading the gravel on top. Cobblestones can be used as decoration.

Wooden decking If the shape and design of the garden allows, consider putting down wooden decking as a sitting or walking area. Wood is a most sympathetic material, and timbered flooring on a balcony or raised terrace always looks exactly right. Although not quite as permanent as paving, good quality timber that has been properly treated with preservative will last for a long time. The same applies to trellises, archways, and pergolas. They can all add interest to the design of a patio garden.

▶ *Old railroad ties have been used to surround a novel water feature, flanked by painted wooden decking.*

using extraordinary containers

In any formal garden odd and unusual containers look out of place. Elegant balconies and balustrades need formal terracotta and stoneware pots. In a small private garden you can let your imagination run riot, and any number of unusual containers and vessels can be pressed into use.

Found containers

If buying new containers is too expensive look out for all kinds of pots, baskets, and buckets in out-of-the-way places. Most can be painted, and all they need is adequate drainage holes. Tin baths; discarded sinks; troughs used for animal feed, and old buckets that can be painted to fit in with the design and color of the garden, are all useful.

Another good idea is old car or tractor tires. They may not be hugely elegant but they are extremely useful, and many professional potato growers produce record yields by adding tire upon tire,

▲ *Old chimney pots can be found in junkyards. They allow the container gardener to present brilliant annuals in a new way.*

◄ *The dark green leaves and bright orange fruit of the calamondin make a glorious contrast with the polished steel bucket.*

topping up the compost as the potato plant grows. If they are painted white, grouped together and sensitively covered with some trailing plants they will not look too outrageous.

Temporary containers

Try to find containers that will last for a good length of time, but if that is not possible several objects can be used for a while and then discarded when something better turns up. Wooden boxes can hold soil mix and plants for a period even if they will eventually rot away. Plastic crates are another idea: cover them with plants, or paint them to match your garden color scheme. Garbage cans, tin or plastic, can also be used, preferably brightened with a coat of paint. Catering-sized food cans, if you can get hold of them, are another good idea.

Smaller containers

When you come to smaller plants and containers there is more scope. China and pottery are tricky. One of the essential things with all containers is adequate drainage and this means making holes in the base. It is very difficult to make a series of holes in the base of jam jars or mustard pots although they can be used for some plants for short periods. Great care has to be taken to make sure that any plant grown in this type of container does not become waterlogged, for inevitably the roots will rot and the plant will die.

Among the best small containers are cans of various shapes and sizes. Holes

can easily be punched in the bottom and they can be painted to disguise their origin; any number of small plants can be grown in them. Another good idea is to use wicker baskets of varying sizes lined with polyethylene. These do look attractive in an informal setting, but they should be used with care for, however meticulous you are when planting and watering, inevitably some water will get on to the wickerwork and it will eventually rot—move them inside when it rains.

▲ *A galvanized garbage can is used here to present foxgloves with clematis and grasses. The wild garden effect contrasts sharply with the materials used as containers and background.*

USING YOUR IMAGINATION

The great thing with all container gardening is to use your imagination. Lovely gardens can be made using the most unpromising receptacles and if painted the effect can be extremely exciting and unusual.

tufa and hypertufa

Tufa is porous limestone rock, light in weight, that can be used for growing small plants, and it is most often used in an alpine garden. Tufa can be used in a bed on its own, or positioned in groups in troughs. Not only does tufa look attractive but it retains water well.

Using tufa

Buy some tufa rocks and then chisel out holes in them about 2.5cm/1in diameter and 7.5cm/3in deep. Make the holes about 10cm/4in apart. Put some sharp sand in the bottom of each hole and then insert small alpine plants or rooted cuttings. Then fill in any gaps with compost, firming around the plants gently with a pencil or small dibble. Wedge some pieces of rock in the hole to keep the plant in place, and keep watering the tufa well until the plants have become established. It is important that at least half to one-third of the tufa rock is buried below the surface of the soil, and that holes are made at a variety of angles so that plants grow down all the sides of the rock.

Hypertufa can be used to make realistic troughs that can also be used as window boxes. Alternatively, with suitable molds, it can be fashioned into rocks and stones.

Hypertufa is made by mixing 2 parts peat, 1 part cement, and 3 parts coarse sand. Mix as you would cement. Check the color and add paint if you want the mixture to be a certain hue.

It is possible to make all types of shapes using hypertufa. To do this it is probably easiest to make papier mâché molds. Put strips of wire over the molds to give them some strength and then cover with hypertufa, adding it bit

HYPERTUFA ROCKS

If you have fashioned a number of hypertufa rocks they can be placed in an alpine garden. See that they are firmly embedded in the soil or compost. Chisel away some holes in the rocks and then fill them with compost. Keep the compost topped up through the year because it will tend to shrink away. Plant small alpines or trailing plants in these holes and they will soon cover the rocks.

◄ *The pink flowers of the winter-flowering heather* Erica carnea *'Springwood Pink' are most welcome in the winter months.*

making a hypertufa trough

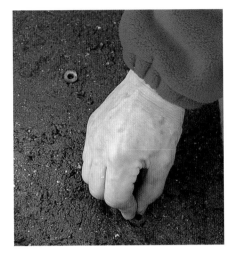

1 To make a trough you now need two boxes, one smaller than the other. Cut squares of wire netting to fit the sides of the smaller box. Coat the boxes with oil to stop the hypertufa sticking.

2 Put a layer of hypertufa in the bottom of the large box, add the wire and a sandwich layer of hypertufa, repeat around the sides. Press a sawn up broom handle into the base to make drainage holes.

3 Cover and then leave for about one week for the hypertufa to set properly. Finally, remove the boxes. Roughen the surface and then paint with liquid manure to encourage algae.

by bit until you have achieved the effect you wish. Hypertufa can also be used to cover up old troughs and even glazed surfaces, although it is best to score them with a tile- or glass-cutter first to help the hypertufa stick.

▶ *The finished hypertufa trough planted with heathers and mulched with gravel. This is light enough to be moved easily around the garden and looks perfectly natural.*

hanging baskets

Most hanging baskets are filled with bright annuals that make a glorious impact in summer. Practically all hanging baskets have to appear against a strongly colored background, such as a brick wall, and they have to compete. The background for a hanging basket is not a muted green.

Planting a hanging basket

Choose the biggest basket you can because they work best when they are fairly large. Place the basket on top of a large bucket to hold it level when planting. Traditionally the basket was lined with sphagnum moss, but preformed liners are much more environmentally friendly although they do not look so attractive. Fill the liner with multipurpose mix, adding water-retaining granules to help the basket stay moist during the summer, and slow-release fertilizer. Now make slits in the liner at regular intervals. Water the plants well and then push them through the basket from the inside. Plant the bottom row of annuals on their sides so that they hang down as they grow. Continue in this way until you reach the top of the basket, and then plant around the rim so

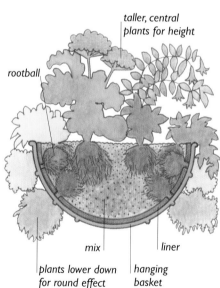

taller, central plants for height

rootball

mix

liner

plants lower down for round effect

hanging basket

▲ Cross-section of a small hanging basket showing the plants in full growth. Cut slits in the liner when planting.

◄ A delicate hanging basket that relies for its effect on the lemon-yellow petunias surrounded by brachyscome, sutera, and lysimachia.

that the plants will hide the edge. Finally, put some upright plants in the middle. Add more mix as required, water the basket well and mulch with moss to minimize moisture loss. The plants will soon fill out the basket and will quickly hide the liner.

Keep the basket in a frost-free place, such as a conservatory or porch, until you can put it outside safely. You can buy self-watering baskets that have a reservoir of water at the base, and they are useful if you do not have the time to water the basket more than once a day.

General points for hanging baskets Use soilless multipurpose mix. This is the best for annuals and bedding plants that are only grown for one season. Put the mix on the compost heap or throw it away at the end of the summer when the baskets are dismantled.

Plant all baskets thickly. Aim for the maximum color impact and fill in any gaps that may appear in the summer. Water the plants and the container when planting is finished, and never let the container dry out. It is essential that hanging baskets are watered every day, and they should be watered twice a day in very hot weather in summer. If they do dry out it can be difficult to resurrect them. Try putting the basket in a large bowl of water, or the bath, and leave it there for several hours.

Feed the hanging basket regularly with a liquid fertilizer and add slow-release fertilizer granules to the mix when planting; you can also add foliar feed to the water with advantage. This helps to keep the plants healthy.

Deadhead the flowers regularly—this applies to all annuals and all containers, and never let the plants set seed because if they do they think their work is done. Check the baskets for disease, spray when necessary, and mist the plants regularly when the weather is hot to prevent the spread of spider mites.

▼ *A vivid hanging basket of trailing nasturtiums topped by begonias. The canna lilies extend the line of color along the garden.*

WATERING

It is worth repeating that hanging baskets need constant watering during the summer when the soil mix can dry out very quickly. Rather than climb long ladders, have the basket on a pulley system or use a long-armed attachment to make the job easier.

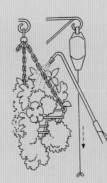

growing bags

One of the most useful (and most hideous!) containers in the small garden is the growing bag. Growing bags really are excellent. They are simple to use, contain the right type of soil mix for plants such as tomatoes and cucumbers, and can be used to grow other shallow-rooted vegetables.

Concealing growing bags

There are two ways of hiding growing bags. The first is to make a special container the same shape as the bag and put the growing bag inside it. The second method that is useful on a patio is to leave a special space in the floor of the patio so that the growing bag can be put in, level with the patio itself. This does not necessarily conceal the growing bag to start with, but when the plants grow it becomes much less noticeable. Another idea is to make small pockets of soil in the patio when it is laid out. Plant ground-covering plants, such as creeping thyme, around the growing bag trench and then train them over the surface.

Stake supports

It is now possible to buy special wire holders that go with growing bags into which three stakes can be inserted. They hold the stakes in exactly the right place

◄ *Tomatoes in a growing bag trained up a fence, with a few pot marigolds planted in front to deter butterflies and aphids.*

► *Tomatoes and bell peppers in growing bags against a south-facing wall. With careful feeding these can produce prolific crops.*

and make tying in the plants much easier. The holders are extremely neat and helpful, especially if the bag is positioned away from a wall.

Plants for growing bags

The traditional plants for growing bags are tomatoes. Depending on the climate, these will grow well outside: 'First Lady', 'Oregon Spring', and 'Celebrity'. 'Taxi' has good yellow fruits while 'Whipper-snapper', 'Sun Cherry', and 'Sun Gold' are popular cherry tomatoes. Many gardeners like to grow peppers and cucumbers, and they and eggplants can be grown provided the patio gets the sun. 'Ace' ball pepper ripens to green in 50 days and to red in 70. The eggplant 'Little Finger' can also be grown while, of the outdoor cucumbers, 'Little Leaf' or 'Jazzer' are good.

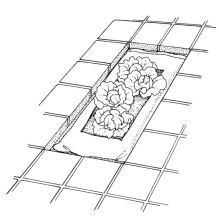

▲ *To conceal growing bags make a shallow trench in the patio the same dimensions as the bag. The plants will soon cover the edges.*

▲ *Low-growing plants, such as thyme or Campanula carpatica, can be planted around the bag and trained over the surface.*

GROWING PLANTS IN GROWING BAGS

The beauty of using bags is that they initially save the gardener a lot of time. That is because they contain a nutrient-enriched soil mix, originally peat based, now more often peat substitute, such as coir. There are adequate nutrients in the mix to establish all the plants. As they mature, these nutrients need replenishing and it is necessary to feed all plants with a liquid food, such as tomato fertilizer, every week or 10 days. The other essential is watering. The bags need to be watered every day like most containers, particularly in hot weather. Make sure that you buy one of the special pipe and water holders now available. They allow the bag to be watered along the whole of its length and make sure an even distribution of nutrients when the plants are fed.

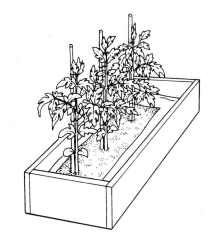

▲ *Growing bags can be hidden in containers. This is a good idea on roof gardens and small patios to keep them looking neat and tidy.*

Gardening basics

All gardening depends on three things—the soil or growing medium, light, and water. Soil is essential, and is acid, neutral, or alkaline. Some plants grow best in one type of soil, some in another. The light or aspect is almost as important, and for the same reason. Some plants only grow well in full sun, others only grow well in shade or partial shade. See which way your garden faces and plant accordingly. As for water, all normal plants in temperate zones need a drink, so see that they get it.

soil and soil mixes

It is a good idea to use proper potting mix for all containers; this has a number of advantages. It is clean, sterile, and contains the nutrients necessary for plant growth. It is also light, easy to handle, and has no unwanted weed seeds (at least to start with). It is, however, quite expensive.

Using topsoil

A cheaper growing medium is topsoil. Sterilized topsoil can be bought from garden suppliers or specialists. Any specialist firm will advise you on the amount you will require, given the cubic volume of the containers you are going to fill. One of the difficulties about using topsoil though is that it usually arrives by truck, and if you live in a row house in a town, you have to be on hand to barrow it up and take it through the house. You also have to clean up the street properly afterward otherwise the neighbors may complain. Technically there should not be much difference between topsoil and soil mix. Topsoil, even when sterilized, will contain the seeds of some weeds but these are pretty unimportant. What you must do though is test the topsoil to establish whether it is acid, alkaline, or neutral. This is easy to do using a simple chemistry kit which is available from all gardening centers and nurseries. You can also test for the nutrients at the same time if you wish, but this is not so important.

Testing your soil The basic soil test will establish the pH of the soil. Neutral soil, suitable for growing most plants, has a pH of between 6.5–7, acid soils have a lower pH and alkaline soils a higher one.

TESTING YOUR SOIL

It is vital that you test your soil to see what kind you have in your garden. This is particularly important to do before you start planning your planting and buying expensive plants. Both of these kits are very easy to use and will tell you what kind of soil you have in a matter of minutes. It is always possible to make alkaline soil more acid, or acid soil more alkaline, so don't despair if your soil is strongly one or the other. The first pH-testing meter consists of a probe, which you push into the ground, and a display that tells you what kind of soil you have. To use the other kit, you must mix a sample of your soil with the chemicals provided to find out the type.

1 Testing the acidity or alkalinity of soil is easy with a pH-testing meter. This device is essential for gardeners who are red/green color blind.

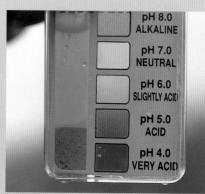

2 Lime-testing kits, in which a soil sample is mixed with water and chemicals, are inexpensive and easy to use. Check the color indicator against a color chart.

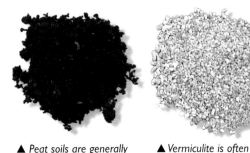

▲ Lime can be added to acid soil for alkalinity.

▲ Peat soils are generally acid, for acid-loving plants.

▲ Vermiculite is often added for better drainage.

▲ Multipurpose mix can be bought everywhere.

▲ Use bulb-fiber mix for indoor bulbs.

Some plants prefer acid soil, such as camellias or rhododendrons. You can always make acid soil more alkaline by adding lime over the winter (sprinkle it on the surface and let the rain and weather wash it in) or, conversely, alkaline soil more acid by adding peat, sulfur chips or sulfur powder (flowers of sulfur).

Types of soil mixes

There are three main types of soil mix and the beginner is often confused over when and how they should be used.

Seed starting mix—this is specifically for growing seeds. Seed mixes may be loam-based (i.e. with soil) or be peat (or peat-substitute) based. They are very fine so that the medium is in direct contact with the small seeds, and they contain few nutrients, because small plants do not require many. If seedlings are kept in the original seed mix for any length of time after germination though, they will need feeding as the original nutrients will soon be exhausted.

Universal or multipurpose mix—these are the most popular mixes and can be used to germinate seeds and grow most plants. They contain rather fewer nutrients than potting mixes, and the plants should be fed rather more frequently than those grown in them, but this is really a minor consideration. They are probably the best medium for general gardening, but they should not be used for containers where you plan to grow large permanent plants.

Potting mixes—these are loam-based or peat- (or peat-substitute) based. Loam-based soil mixes are based on the John Innes formulae developed by the John

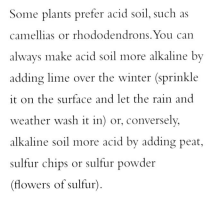

▲ Low-growing azaleas make good container plants, although most will eventually outgrow their position. A number are sweet-smelling.

◄ Rhododendrons make spectacular plants early in the summer. They need acid soil. Take care when watering them in hard-water areas.

9 9

Innes Horticultural Institute in the 1930s. This is not a trade name but a recipe. The number refers to the amount of nutrients present in the soil. For example, John Innes No. 3 has three times the amount of nutrients of John Innes No. 1. Loam-based mixes retain water and nutrients better than any peat-based mixes, and therefore are more suitable for any permanent plants in containers such as fruit trees, wall shrubs and any permanent climbers. They are not suitable for acid-loving plants, such as camellias or rhododendrons, for these

▲ *A grouping of formal containers topped by a lacecap hydrangea. Hydrangeas need a good supply of water during the summer.*

◄ *An ambitious evergreen arrangement in a blue-glazed pot using* Fatsia japonica *and ivy. This is suitable for a shady garden.*

▶ *Healthy strawberry plants in a planter with the young fruit forming after the flowers. Strawberries are greedy plants and require regular feeding throughout the summer.*

need special ericaceous mix. Loam-based mixes are rather more difficult to find than peat-based ones and more difficult to handle. Peat-based potting mixes are lighter, easier to use, cleaner, and more satisfactory for general gardening. They are ideal for small and medium-sized containers.

Special mixes—besides the three basic types of mix described above, there are a number of other mixes. They include ericaceous mix for acid-loving plants such as rhododendrons; orchid mix for growing orchids indoors; alpine and cacti mix; bulb fiber (specifically formulated for forcing bulbs to flower indoors in the winter; and hanging basket mix that includes water-retaining granules to help the baskets retain moisture during the summer. In addition, you can always make your own mix using sterilized soil or potting mix, adding grit and vermiculite to improve the drainage, and slow-release fertilizer granules to supply the nutrients necessary.

Standard potting mix is made using 7 parts sterilized loam, 3 parts peat or peat substitute and 1 part washed sharp sand, with some balanced fertilizer as required. Mixes for cuttings need to be free draining and is best made using equal quantities of peat substitute and sand, with some slow-release fertilizer granules added to provide the necessary nutrients that the cuttings need.

TOOLS FOR THE CONTAINER GARDENER

The container gardener has one major advantage over the ordinary gardener—the range of tools required is very limited: no spade, fork, lawnmower, hedge trimmer or shears for edging the lawn. What you will need though is a hand fork, two trowels (one wide one and one narrow mainly for transplanting young plants), a hand rake, a good pair of pruners (the "parrot-beak" type are the best), a watering can with a long arm to reach over the bed, a sprayer (you will not usually require a very large one), and a garden basket or trug and possibly a garden sheet to make collecting garden waste much easier. You will also need a hammer, masonry drill, vine eyes, tensioning bolts, ring eyes, screws, various nails and Rawlplugs if you plan to construct a wire frame around the walls to train fruit trees or tie in roses and other

climbing plants. Nonessential items include a pair of hand shears, a pruning saw, a garden knife, a sieve and one or two pairs of gardening gloves. Heavy duty gloves are essential if you need to prune roses except the climber Zéphirine Drouhin, which has no thorns.

watering can

atomizer spray

fork

small trowel

trowel

pruners

aspect and position

Look at your garden and see exactly how much sun it gets each day. Does it face north or south, east or west? South and west are best but many successful gardens face north or east. Which direction do the walls face—a south-facing wall enables you to grow a number of trees and tender shrubs.

Check on the sun

In an urban garden it may not be enough to see which way the garden faces. You may well be surrounded by office or apartment blocks, terraces, and tall buildings that shade the garden even when it should be in sun. And then how much sun does it get in the winter? Most roses, for example, need at least three hours sunshine a day for six months of the year if they are to repeat flower. That said there are a number that will flower in poor conditions, and even some that can be grown against a north-facing wall. You just have to check which plants will grow best in your situation.

Check the orientation

If a garden or street has been built running north–west or south–east, the gardener will feel that the garden actually faces north or south and plant accordingly. This can be a great mistake. In fact the side wall is the best spot and should be treated as a south wall because it will receive more sun during the day. Once you are aware of this you can plant shade-loving plants such as primroses on the opposite side of the garden, and they will flourish in the partial shade.

Temperature and shelter

Almost as important as the aspect is the temperature in the garden, especially in the winter and early spring, and the amount of shelter it provides. A small town garden may be an unlikely candidate for a frost pocket but if you are unlucky then the whole garden, or just parts of it, may be liable to frosts in the winter and early spring, when all around is frost free. Before the middle of winter frosts often have little or no effect because most plants are dying back, and have reached their dormant stage. It is only in the spring, especially after an unaccustomed mild spell early in the year has started plants and shrubs into premature growth, that a sudden hard

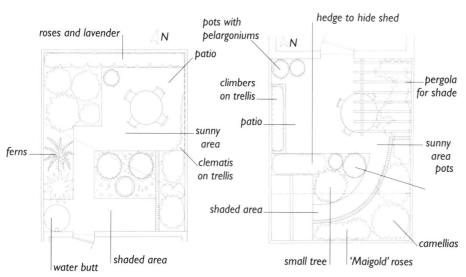

▲ *South-facing walls enable the gardener to grow a number of climbers and trees that relish the sun, such as peaches and lavender.*

▲ *When the main part of the garden is in shade, choose plants with care. Camellias in tubs are good plants for shady areas.*

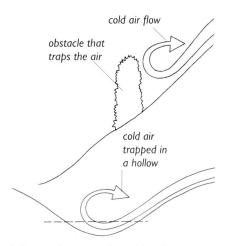

cold air flow

obstacle that
traps the air

cold air
trapped in
a hollow

▲ *Frost pockets occur when cold air flows
downhill and becomes trapped in a hollow or by
an obstacle such as a dense hedge. Frost pockets
seldom occur in gardens on convex slopes.*

frost matters, and then it can do major
damage if they are left unprotected.

If your garden is seriously bothered
by late frosts then you must take care to
avoid semitender plants. The most likely
candidates are a number of early
flowering trees or shrubs, such as
camellias or the beautifully fragrant,
half-hardy wintersweet, *Chimonanthus
praecox*. Fruit blossom too, especially on
early flowering peach and apricot trees,
can suffer badly. If this is a rare
occurrence you may be able to cover the
plants when a late frost is forecast, but if
it is a common occurrence, only grow
plants that are fully hardy. Otherwise you
will be doomed to disappointment.
Strong, cold winds are another factor.
These can be a problem on roof gardens,
and you need to supply adequate shelter.

▶ *Containers of lavender and pelargoniums for a
hot, sunny position in a rustic garden. The white
daisies help to emphasize the bright colors.*

choosing and buying plants

Do not buy all the plants for your garden in one go. Since garden centers tend to stock plants flowering at that particular time, you need to visit on a regular basis, right through the year, to make sure your garden will have a continuous succession of flowers.

Ordering plants from specialist nurseries

The best plan of action is to make a list of the plants that you plan to grow and check if there are any specialist suppliers near you. Garden centers really only sell a very small selection. For example, if you want to grow a climbing rose against a north wall, then it is unlikely that a garden center will stock a suitable variety. If there is a specialist nursery near you, they will provide a good choice, if

not buy one by mail order. Specialist nurseries are used to sending plants through the mail, and they nearly always arrive in good condition.

Bare-root plants Always plant at the right time of the year, and this particularly applies to trees and shrubs. Generally they are best planted in the fall when their growth is dying down but there is enough warmth and moisture in the soil to let the root system establish

itself. Also, roses and fruit trees are best bought as bare-root and not container-grown plants. This may sound a strange piece of advice especially if they are to be grown in a container, but plants raised in containers inevitably have a restricted root system and the bare-root kind, planted at the right time of the year, do better in the end. No reputable supplier would send out bare-root plants at the wrong time of the year. If you cannot plant trees or shrubs as soon as they

▲ *Always soak bare-root roses for a good half an hour before planting.*

▶ *A container-grown shrub for repotting. If the roots are congested, tease them out gently to allow the plant to establish more quickly.*

HEELING IN PLANTS

If you are unable to plant bare-root plants when you receive them, heel them in. Dig a trench with a sloping side, lay the plants in the trench as shown and then firm soil over the roots. These can wait until you have time to plant them.

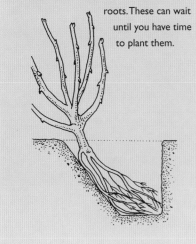

▲ *Garden centers are fun to look around and the plants in flower may well give you some new ideas. Check out each plant before buying it.*

▼ *The climbing form of the rose 'Iceberg' makes a graceful nodding plant. The honeysuckle helps to make a scented screen.*

arrive, dig a small trench in one container, lay the plants in it at an angle of 45° and cover firmly with soil until you do have time to complete the job properly. They are unlikely to come to any harm if they are not left for too long. But do not let them dry out.

Checking the plants If you plan to buy the plants at a garden center or nursery, there are a number of things to look for. Check the leaves for signs of pests or disease, avoid plants that have moss growing on the surface of their container because they have been in it for too long, check that few roots have grown out of the holes at the bottom for the same reason, and make sure that the plant is healthy with a good shape and equally spaced branches. It is worth taking time over each purchase to get what you want.

planting—potting and repotting

Don't be put off by technical planting terms. Potting up means transferring a young seedling into its first pot; repotting means taking the plant out of the container and then replanting it in the same container with new soil mix; and potting on means transferring a plant to a larger container.

◄ *When a plant outgrows its container, pot it on into a container that is approximately 5cm/2in larger than the present one.*

The general principles of planting

All plants must be planted in containers large enough to accommodate their root systems. The container should be 5cm/2in larger than the rootball of the plant. To plant a shrub remove it from the original container and gently tease out the roots if they have become congested, and trim off any damaged roots. Put a good layer of pot shards, broken tiles, or stones at the bottom of the new container to provide adequate drainage, and then add a layer of soil mix. Put the plant in the container, making certain that the soil level is the same in the new container as it was in the old. Check the soil mark on the plant to do this accurately. Add the mix around the sides of the pot making sure that it is pressed firmly against the roots. Firm the soil with your hands or a dibble, but do not ram the mix down too tightly. Lift the container, if you can, and rap it down

repotting a plant

1 Put a handful of pot shards or small stones in the bottom of any container. This prevents the soil mix draining away when the plant is watered.

2 Remove the plant carefully from the old container. Check the soil level. The plant should be replanted at the same depth in the new container.

3 Tease out the roots if they have become congested and trim away any that are damaged. This helps them to spread out into the new mix.

on a hard surface two or three times to shake out any air pockets. Finally, water thoroughly and top up the level with soil mix as it settles. To save moving a heavy pot into position, site it where you need it before starting.

Potting on Young plants need to be transferred from small pots to larger pots, depending on their rate of growth. This should be done carefully. Transfer a growing plant to a pot just larger than the existing one, say by about 5cm/2in. This helps to keep the plant growing at a steady rate—if you potted on into a much larger pot, the roots would spread out too quickly, upsetting the growth balance. If a plant is slow growing the roots will not fill the large container quickly enough, while quick-growing plants tend to produce too much foliage and not enough flowers and fruit.

◄ *Agapanthus lilies make good container plants with a color range from white to deep blue. They usually need staking.*

REPOTTING

Large raised beds, especially when they contain permanent trees or shrubs, cannot easily be emptied. What you must do in these cases is remove as much of the topsoil as possible and replace it with fresh mix and add a balanced granular fertilizer. In smaller containers the soil should be emptied and replaced every other year, or every year when the plant is growing well. Remove the plant from the container and shake the root system clear of old soil, put the plant in a bucket of water for an hour or more, then follow the planting steps above. When repotting you can tease out the root system and trim away any damaged roots.

planting—general tips

As a general rule planting in container gardens can be done at almost any time of the year. Fall is still preferred but if you do repot in high summer, make sure that the plant is kept really moist to start with so that the roots have the best chance to grow into the new potting mix.

Planting bare-root trees and shrubs

There are some plants that do better, even in containers, if they are planted as bare-root specimens in the fall. This particularly applies to roses and fruit trees. Order your roses for fall delivery from a reputable rose grower and plant them out when you receive them. They make better plants than container-grown roses bought and planted in the spring. The same goes for fruit trees. Try and choose a specialist nursery that is used to sending larger horticultural specimens through the mail. It is best to buy one-year-old trees as bare-root plants, or at a pinch two-year-old trees (the latter take time to become established and are more difficult to train).

▶ *Small apple trees can be grown quite happily in containers. Use an appropriate soil mix from a garden center and feed them regularly.*

PLANTING BULBS

Bulbs absorb their strength through their foliage so never cut it off after flowering—let it yellow and fade naturally. Although this may mean untidy containers, you will get better flowering results in the long run. One solution to the straggly leaves, if cost be no object, is to throw them all away and plant new bulbs each year. If you only have room for one container of bulbs, try planting a number of different ones in layers, one below the other. All bulbs should be planted two and a half times their depth—plant the largest daffodil, *Narcissus*, bulbs at the bottom of the container with smaller crocuses and chionodoxa on top. The bulbs will grow up through each layer and flower one after the other.

planting bulbs

  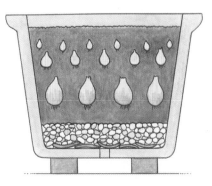

1 Put a good layer of gravel in the bottom of the container to aid drainage before starting to plant the bulbs. Use specially prepared bulb fiber.

2 Plant the largest bulbs first. Space them out evenly but put them closer together than you would if you were planting them in open ground.

3 Plant them in layers as shown above. After flowering, any bulbs grown in containers can be planted out in the garden for the following year.

Planting vines

Vines can be grown in containers, and bare-root specimens should be planted in winter when they are dormant. Add a good quantity of granular fertilizer and

▲ *Planting a container with pansies. Position the plants at regular intervals around the rim and firm the plants in with your fingers.*

make sure that the vine is well watered during the initial growing period. Vines bought as container-grown specimens can be potted on from one container to another at any time before growth starts. Be sure that you have erected a suitable framework of wires and posts up which the vines can be trained.

Planting annuals and small bedding plants

When planting small annuals take care that the roots are not damaged. Make sure the young plants are well watered, ease the plants out of the seed tray, and then firm the soil mix gently around their roots in their new container. When you have finished planting out summer annuals, water them lightly with a weak solution of liquid fertilizer.

PRICKING OUT SEEDLINGS

If you have sown your own seeds, you need to prick out the seedlings into larger containers when they have germinated. Wait until they have two pairs of leaves and then ease them out of the seed tray using a small knife or a pencil. Always hold the seedlings by the first pair of leaves (the seed leaves), and not by the stalk. Handling them in this way does not damage the plant. Harden off the seedlings by placing them outside for part of the day when they are large enough, and plant out when there are no more frosts.

how to prune

Nothing in gardening causes as much bother as pruning. In fact pruning is not difficult. The elementary principles are easy to learn, and once you understand them, the whole subject loses its mystique. The most important thing is to try and prune each plant at the correct time of the year.

Pruning principles

The two basic pruning principles are: first, that some plants flower and fruit on wood produced in the current year, while others flower on last year's growth. Second, pruning stimulates growth; cutting a single branch back to a bud (usually) means that two branches will grow from the cut. The purpose of pruning is to stimulate the correct growth to produce the optimum amount of flowers and fruit.

The basic pruning steps for most plants that you are likely to grow in a container garden are listed below.

Climbing roses—if you are growing roses against a wall in a container garden the best ones to plant are some of the modern climbers with hybrid tea-shaped flowers that grow fairly slowly. Other suitable roses include climbing varieties of some hybrid tea and floribunda roses, such as the climbing variety of the very popular 'Iceberg' or 'Climbing Ophelia'. Most of these roses are repeat flowering.

On planting, trim away any damaged roots, then train in the shoots, cut back any damaged growth and cut out weak sideshoots. The following summer tie in the sideshoots as growth develops, and train the shoots into a fan. Deadhead the roses after flowering. Early in spring or late winter the following year, cut back all the flowering laterals (side-shoots) to 15cm/6in from the main branches, and tie in any shoots to form a framework. Repeat this on an annual basis. As the main shoots become exhausted they can be removed, one at a time, to within

◄ *Box needs to be clipped two or three times a year to preserve its shape. Take care pruning rosemary: it will not regenerate from old wood.*

▶ *Vigorous climbers, such as the golden hop and ornamental vines, should be cut back hard in late winter and as needed in the summer.*

5cm/2in of the ground. This stimulates new growth from the base that should always be tied in as it develops.

Summer-flowering jasmine is a vigorous plant and may have to be cut back to keep it within bounds. It is not wholly suitable for container gardens but it is widely grown. It should be cut back after flowering. Thin any old weak wood, and cut out up to one-third of the shoots if necessary. Tie in new growth as it develops—if it is too long it will need to be shortened. Be fairly ruthless.

Winter jasmine, *Jasminum nudiflorum*, should be pruned after flowering in early spring. Cut back all the shoots that have flowered by one third. Cut out completely any shoots that appear weak, damaged, or dead. Tie in the shoots. Hop, *Humulus*, is a vigorous climber. Cut back hard in the spring to within 60–90cm/2–3ft of the ground if it needs

to be kept within bounds. Ivy, *Hedera*; the climbing hydrangea, *Hydrangea petiolaris*; and all forms of Virginia creeper, *Parthenocissus*—are all climbers that adhere to the wall by suckers. None of them requires specific pruning. Clip the ivy and the climbing hydrangea to keep them within bounds after flowering. Cut

back the Virginia creeper or Boston ivy hard in the spring before growth has started, especially if it threatens to get into gutters or under roof tiles. This should be avoided at all costs for the shoots will pull away tiles and damage any roof. It is quite easy to pull the old shoots away from the wall by hand.

▲ *Summer prune all roses by removing dead heads before they develop into hips. This helps to build up the strength of the plant.*

▲ *On an upright rose remove weak and crossing branches and tie in shoots as they develop. Cut back flowered laterals as shown.*

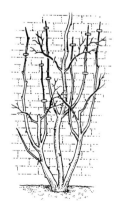

▲ *On new climbing roses tie in laterals as they develop. Remove crossing branches. Cut back flowered laterals to 3–4 eyes, about 15cm/6in.*

Pruning clematis and vines

Clematis—it is probably more difficult for the amateur gardener to prune a clematis correctly than any other group of plants. The problem is not one of pruning, but identification. There are three groups for pruning and they should be treated in different ways.

Group 1—this group flowers on wood made the previous year. In an ideal world this group should not be pruned at all, but as the plants need to be confined within their allotted space they have to be thinned after flowering. Cut out any old and dead stems, and cut back all growth. This will probably mean that

there are fewer flowers next year but that cannot be helped in this case.

Clematis that need to be treated in this way are all the *alpina* and *macropetala* kinds; all *montana*s (if you cannot identify any of these you will have to ask a knowledgeable neighbor, but as a rule all these clematis flower in late spring and early summer and have small flowers); some small-flowered hybrids and species (as a general rule those that flower early in the year or in winter); a few large-flowered varieties (those that flower before midsummer); and almost all double and semidouble large-flowered varieties. If you do not know

▲ Clematis montana *is difficult to prune successfully. Cut it back after flowering to keep it within its allotted bounds.*

the name and type of your clematis, and cannot obtain any information from anyone, then you should leave the clematis unpruned for a year and make a note of the month in which the first flowers start to appear.

Group 2—these varieties can be left unpruned, but it is best to cut out old and dead wood in late winter and then cut the remaining stems down to a strong pair of buds. Do not be seduced by mild weather early in the year and do

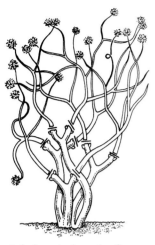

▲ *Group 1 clematis, those that flower on the new season's growth, should be cut back hard in spring to a pair of buds.*

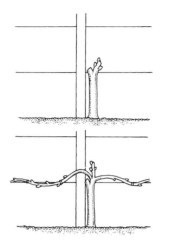

▲ *The first and second years of a newly planted vine. Cut back the leader to three buds in winter and tie in the shoots. Trim the sideshoots.*

three buds will produce three shoots and they should be tied in vertically as they grow. Pinch out any other side-shoots. That winter train the two lowest shoots horizontally on to a wire, cutting each one back to about 90cm/3ft or 12 buds. Cut the central shoot back to three buds. The horizontal shoots will produce laterals that are then trained up the wall, or over the top of a pergola as they grow, and the three shoots from the main stem are tied in vertically as before. When summer is over cut away the horizontal laterals that have born fruit, and repeat the process the following year.

this too soon, which may result in damage by late frosts. Clematis that should be pruned in this way include some large-flowered varieties, and some small-flowered hybrids and species (those that flower from midsummer onward). *Group 3*—these clematis flower on new wood produced in the current year and they should be cut back to 25–50cm/10–20in from the ground in late winter or early spring. Cut the plants back to a strong pair of buds.

Clematis that should be treated in this way include a number of the large-flowered varieties (those that flower first after midsummer); almost all the herbaceous, semiherbaceous and sub-shrubs; all the *viticella*s; a good number of the small-flowered hybrids and species (again the ones that first come into flower after midsummer). Rest assured that if you do not prune clematis they will still flower perfectly well. The only

trouble with most of them is that the base of the plant will become bare and the flowers will appear amidst a straggly and unsightly tangle of foliage at the top. **Vine, *Vitis*—**these are popular plants to grow on patios and are frequently trained over pergolas to form shady arches in summer. Ornamental vines, such as *Vitis* 'Brandt' or *V. coignetiae* should be pruned in midwinter to make sure that they remain within their allotted space. Formal pruning is not required, but do prune when the plant is dormant otherwise they bleed sap excessively.

Grape vines are best pruned on what is called the Double Guyot system. This may sound frightfully technical, but it just means cutting the main stem right down to three buds. The first year these

▶ *A mature vine in a container trained over a pergola. Reduce the number of leaves in the summer to allow the sun to ripen the grapes. Protect from birds.*

Pruning shrubs and fruit trees

Herbs and shrubs—trim all shrubby herbs, such as thyme, sage, and marjoram, to keep them neat in their container in early spring, otherwise they do not need specific pruning. The same applies to the winter-flowering heathers, *Erica carnea* and *E.* x *darleyensis*. Clip them over when flowering has finished in spring to keep them neat and tidy.

Rosemary should have any misplaced shoots cut back in the spring, but beware, rosemary will not regenerate if it is cut back into the hard wood. Trim new growth lightly. If a branch dies, cut it back to the joint or base, whichever is appropriate. Prune lavender hard in mid-spring each year to keep the bushes within bounds and stimulate new growth. Cut all flowering shoots right

back including at least 2.5cm/1in of last year's wood. Do not prune after flowering because this only stimulates fresh growth that may be damaged in a hard winter. Lavender may regenerate from old wood, and if you have a very old and unsightly plant it is worth trying cutting it back really hard in spring just to see what happens.

Apples and pears—in a container garden they should be trained as cordons or grown as espaliers against a wall.

Cordons are generally single-stem trees, although double or even triple cordons can be created. Apple and pear cordons are generally planted at an angle of 45° and trained to a height of 1.8m/6ft. This produces a stem 2.4m/8ft long. All cordons should be pruned in the summer (little winter pruning is necessary). Cut back all laterals to three buds beyond the basal cluster (the cluster of leaves nearest the main stem). Tie in the leader but do not prune it until it has reached 1.8m/6ft in height. Mature cordons may need some of the fruiting spurs thinned in the course of time.

Espaliers are trees with branches radiating horizontally from a main stem. Before planting the tree erect a horizontal wire framework with each wire 38–45cm/15–18in apart. To create an

◀ *Low-growing shrubs in containers may have to be clipped after flowering to keep them looking neat and tidy.*

CREATING A FAN-TRAINED PLUM TREE

Buy a feathered maiden (a whip with side-shoots), and plant it in the fall. In late spring cut back the central stem to the uppermost of two strong laterals growing on opposite sides of the stem. Train these horizontally against the wall, the top side-shoots should be about 60cm/2ft above the ground. Tie these shoots in and then cut them back by one half to an upward-facing bud. They form the first ribs. During the summer select two new shoots from each branch growing upward and one shoot growing downward, spaced evenly along the rib. Tie these in and pinch back any other side-shoots to 1–2 leaves. Rub out any shoots growing inward toward the wall or outward. The following spring cut back the new ribs by between one half and one-third, and during the summer select three new shoots from each of these. Continue this process on an annual basis until the tree has taken up its allotted space.

espalier, plant a whip (a young single-stem tree) in the fall. In the spring cut back the stem to a bud about 60cm/2ft above the ground, making sure that there are two further buds below the top one. The tree will produce three shoots in the summer. Tie in the top one vertically and the two side-shoots at an angle of 45° to stakes attached to the wires. In the summer prune any other shoots that emerge to three leaves from the basal cluster.

The second year cut back the leader again to three good buds in the spring and take down the first two side-shoots from 45° to the horizontal. Tie these shoots on to stakes attached to the wires. Then repeat this process each year until

creating an espalier

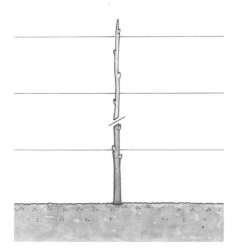
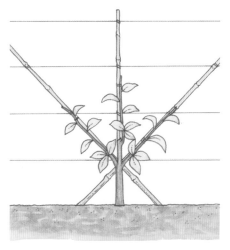
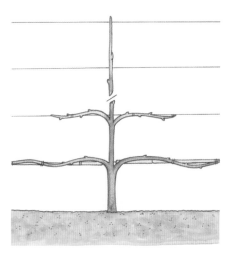

1 Plant an unfeathered maiden and cut it back to about 45cm/18in from the ground. Make sure it has three good buds with the lower two facing each other.

2 As the shoots grow during the summer, tie in the three shoots. Keep the leader vertical and tie in the two main sideshoots at 45°. Secure to stakes.

3 In early winter, lower the sideshoots to the horizontal. Tie them in and cut them back by one-third. Cut the main leader to 45cm/18in and repeat 1 and 2.

the tree has reached the height and spread that you wish, at which point the extension leaders should then be stopped and the lateral shoots treated as if they were cordons.

▲ *Trim shrubby herbs to keep them neat in their allotted containers.*

▶ *This unusual pear is 'Mrs Seddon' with dark purple fruit. Pears can be grown against a wall.*

staking and supporting

Many plants need support during their growing periods, and a number need a permanent framework of wire or trellis to make sure that they grow well and can be trained to best advantage. Always put permanent supports, such as a wire frame, in place before planting any tree.

Erecting a wire framework

If you have a wall and can grow plants up it, you may want to erect a wire framework to which you can tie in espaliered apples or pears, or other trained trees that make a container garden so satisfying. First of all check the condition of the wall. See that it is sound, that the bricks are properly bedded in, and that the wall needs neither repointing nor rebuilding. Both are fairly expensive tasks but do not attempt to put up a wire frame on an unsound wall, for tensioning bolts put quite a strain on the wire and the bricks may well pull out of the wall.

You will need a mortar drill, plastic Rawlplugs, screw eyes, a hammer, screwdriver and tensioning bolts, as well as strong 3mm/⅛in wire. Check where you want the framework to go. Allow 38–45cm/15–18in between the rows of horizontal wires, then drill proper holes in the bricks and tap in the Rawlplugs so

securing a wire framework

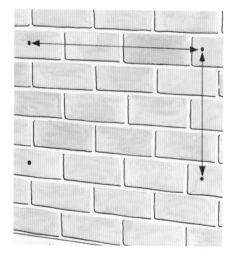

1 Mark out the area of the wall you want to cover with the frame. Allow 45cm/18in between the rows. Use sturdy 2mm wire for the main strands.

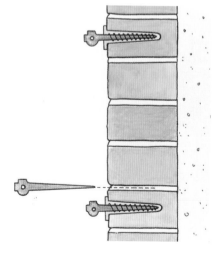

2 Drill holes in the brick and insert plastic Rawlplugs. You will need a proper masonry drill for this. Insert the retaining screws so that they are vertical.

3 Alternatively, hammer vine eyes into the mortar. This is not so secure a method. Secure the wires to tensioning bolts and tighten. Tie stakes to the wires.

erecting a trellis

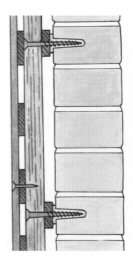

1 Measure the height of the trellis and then secure uprights to the wall with Rawlplugs and screws. Check them with a level to insure they are vertical.

2 Fix each length of trellis to the upright. This can be done with screws or metal brackets. Check they are level and fix a cap to the post to prevent rot.

3 When fixing a trellis, use battens to insure good air circulation. Fix the bottom of the trellis to one with hinges, and then the trellis can be lowered.

that they are level with the brickwork. Screw in the screw eyes. Position them about 60cm/2ft apart. Thread the wire through the screw eyes and secure it firmly at one end. Attach the tensioning bolt at the other end, attach the wire to the bolt, and then twist it until the slack has been taken up and the wire is taut.

Erecting a trellis

If the garden wall is not very tall you may want to erect a trellis around it to give more vertical gardening space. It is worth doing this job properly or it might get damaged in a high wind. If you are able to dig a hole, or series of holes, in

▶ A trompe l'oeil trellis used to create the illusion of space in a small town garden. This can be combined with outdoor mirrors.

the ground around the wall you can either cement in the posts or, much better, cement in small preformed concrete foundation posts with holes so you can screw the wooden posts in position behind them. Although tempting, it is not really a good idea to set a wooden post in concrete in the ground. However carefully you shape the concrete to allow the water to run off, and however well you treat the timber, eventually it rots and you are left with a concrete plug that is difficult to remove.

If you cannot cement concrete foundation posts into the ground it is better to fix the timber posts directly to the wall. This can be done with large screws and plastic Rawlplugs. Decide on the height you want your trellis to be. Check the length of the wall and the number of pieces of trellis that you will need, then buy all the materials—upright posts, trellis, and long screws. Drill three or four holes in the uprights at intervals. Put the posts against the wall and check that they are vertical. Then tap a long nail or screw through the holes to mark the wall behind the post. Drill holes in the wall using a mortar drill and tap in the Rawlplugs. Match up the holes in the post with those in the wall: hopefully they will fit exactly. Secure each post in place using long screws. Attach the trellis to the post using special fitments or screw them in place if you prefer. If you are securing a trellis against a wall, make sure that you leave a gap between the wall and the trellis to allow air to circulate behind the plant and let you tie in shoots properly. Never, ever, however tempting it may be, secure a shoot by pushing it through the trellis, or behind a wire. It will always need pulling out and retraining which is often impossible after a year or two.

Staking trees and standards

It is essential to stake all trees and standards when they are planted, even if they are growing in containers. Insert a stake before planting and make sure it is upright. When the tree has been planted, secure the trunk to the stake using proper tree ties that do not damage the bark. If you need to secure larger trees do this is by using guy ropes attached to ring bolts inserted in the patio floor. Again make sure that they are firm, and protect the trunk of the tree from chafing by running the wires through a length of old hosepipe or a rubber protective tube.

Supporting perennials Perennials can be supported in a number of ways. The best method is to position a ring stake above each plant early in the year, letting the

◀ *Sweet peas trained up a wigwam of specially constructed wickerwork. The more flowers you cut, the more the plant produces.*

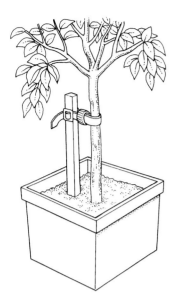

▲ On a windy patio or roof garden even the small trees are better staked. Secure the stake to the side of the container before planting.

▲ Special small trellises are available that can be secured to the back of wooden troughs and containers. These are suitable for small climbers.

▲ Bulbs, such as agapanthus, can be secured by inserting short bamboo stakes around the pot and joining these with circles of garden twine.

plant grow upward through the mesh at the top. Another method is to surround the plant with stakes and make rings of garden twine to contain the plant as it grows. Pea sticks or twigs are the third method and they are pretty unobtrusive.

Staking container-grown plants

A number of plants that are regularly grown in containers need supporting as a matter of course. Among these are regal lilies, *Lilium regale*, and agapanthus. The best method is to insert a ring of small stakes around the rim of the container and then tie garden twine in rings around them. The plants will then be confined within the circumference of the string circle and will not flop over.

Supporting climbers All climbers except those that climb by suckers need support. Climbing roses in a container

need to be tied to a framework of wire, and pillar roses can be tied to pergolas to give height and color to the garden. Clematis need a trellis through which they can twine and annual climbers, such as sweet pea, *Lathyrus odoratus*, need a frame of netting or wire that they can cling to with their tendrils. Vines in particular need a permanent frame in place before planting, and in a small patio garden in a mild climate that attracts sufficient sun, they can be trained over a pergola to great effect. If you are growing a small climber in a wooden container you can attach a small piece of wooden trellis to the back to make an effective frame. These can be bought from garden centers. Otherwise you have to make certain that containers of all climbers are positioned close to the wall so that they can easily reach the wall or trellis in order to climb up it.

Don't forget that climbing plants, such as ivy, need a surface to cling to. They will not climb up a wire fence and the solution is to tie planks of wood to the fence to allow the ivy purchase.

SECURING CONTAINERS ON A ROOF GARDEN

One of the problems with containers is that they may blow over in high winds, especially if they are on an exposed roof garden and are top-heavy with trees or shrubs. To avoid this it is most important to insure that all containers are supported securely, and this equally applies to any screen or trellis put up around a roof garden for shelter and screening. Common sense must be the guide. If you have a really large tree in a container, it may be necessary to secure the container with guy ropes or wire fastened to ring bolts on the roof or walls of the garden. If you are not confident in your ability to do this yourself, you must get professional help.

watering

Watering is all important for the container gardener. All plants need water, and containers dry out extremely quickly, especially on hot summer days. This is particularly true of terracotta pots and tubs where the porous clay allows water to evaporate more quickly than through plastic or stone.

In the summer, in hot sunny weather, a large container may lose up to 5 litres/1.3 gallons a day through transpiration (water evaporating from the leaves of the plants) and evaporation through the sides of the container. Evaporation from a terracotta container can be restricted if you take the trouble to line the insides of the container with plastic sheeting when it is planted.

Hanging baskets and wall pots are subject to an even greater degree of water loss, and in the case of wall pots this can be exacerbated by the heat generated by the sun on the wall itself. Touch the south wall of your house on a hot sunny afternoon and see just how hot it feels. The baskets also contain relatively little soil mix and dry out all the sooner. It follows that you have to water a

container garden at least once a day during the summer, and hanging baskets and wall pots may require watering twice a day. If you cannot do this, then there is little point in trying to create a successful container garden. That does not mean to say that you have to water *every* single day. When the weather is dull and rainy additional watering is unnecessary, but if you go away on holiday when there is a hot dry spell and you have not arranged for the plants to be watered, do not be surprised if most of them are dead when you return from your trip.

Making watering as easy as possible

If you do not want to install an automatic watering system then you can take certain steps to make the chore of watering much easier. If you are going to water by hand install an outside faucet—this is essential on a roof garden when you do not want to traipse through the house carrying heavy watering cans. Buy a proper watering can with a long arm that will easily reach to the back of any bed. Use it to water specific containers

▲ *Water hanging baskets with a special long-armed hose attachment.*

▲ *A rose attachment to a garden hose speeds up watering in summer.*

▲ *Delicate plants can be watered with a watering can and a fine rose.*

▲ *A lilac-colored pergola with matching containers contrasts with the bright orange nasturtiums and canna lilies.*

▶ *A selection of bright flowers and herbs in individual pots line a stairway in France. The colors contrast with the plain steps and walls.*

and plants at times when general watering may not be required. Also buy a hose attachment for the faucet, a reinforced plastic hosepipe that will last longer and a range of nozzles. Watering using a hose is far quicker and easier than filling a watering can time after time. If you have a number of hanging baskets get a long-arm attachment for the hose that enables you to reach all the baskets

and wall pots in the garden. And finally, invest in a feeder attachment. They allow you to supply the plants with diluted foliar feed when you water.

How to water Make sure that each container is watered thoroughly, but do not overwater or the plant will become waterlogged, and may even start to rot. Fill it to the brim and let the water drain

down through the soil. You should check on the condition of the soil mix as well as the plants before you start, for if the plants are wilting they may be lacking in nutrients, or the soil mix may even be waterlogged. Feel the soil about 2.5cm/1in below the surface, and if it is dry to the touch then the container should be watered. Water regularly but do not overwater.

Watering systems If you have a large container garden, or you know that you are unable to water the garden regularly in the summer, then consider investing in a computer-controlled automatic watering system. They operate on a 24-hour time clock and are installed with a time switch to turn them on and off. The most sophisticated systems can be attached to sensors that switch on when the soil is too dry. If you install one of these then all your problems are solved. There are three main systems—overhead sprinklers, trickle hoses, and the capillary system. Each system has its advantages and disadvantages.

Overhead systems are probably the cheapest to install. They have a series of small sprinklers that can be directed on to the plants. However, they use the most water and much of it may evaporate quickly in hot dry weather. Watering systems are so sophisticated now that you can even get special systems to water hanging baskets, and minisystems are available to water window boxes. It is worth investigating them thoroughly because they are enormously helpful. And do not forget to incorporate some water-retaining granules in the soil mix you use for hanging baskets, wall pots and window boxes because this cuts

down on the amount of water that the soil mix needs, and helps to prevent it from drying out during very hot weather in the summer months.

Trickle hoses are often more expensive than overhead sprinklers, but they are more effective because they allow water to seep into the soil where it reaches the roots of the plants directly. And they do not use so much water. There are even very small trickle hose systems for window boxes and containers on balconies.

▼ *A greenhouse full of half-hardy flowering plants ready for placing outside in the summer. Hanging baskets benefit from this treatment.*

◄ *Capillary matting draws up water through the bottom of the container.*

◄ *Trickle hoses can be expensive but are very effective.*

◄ *Sprinkler systems can be computer controlled so your garden gets watered even when you're not there.*

▲ *Hanging baskets need plenty of water during the summer months to stop them drying out. Use a long-handled device to reach the basket.*

Capillary systems draw up water through the bottom of the container. They are mainly used by nurseries and in greenhouses. The amateur gardener can go some way to imitating a capillary system by placing containers full of plants in a larger bowl, and then filling the base with gravel. If this gravel container is filled with water the plant will draw up the water it needs in a gradual manner and the soil will not become waterlogged.

A warning If you live in a hard water area and want to grow a number of acid-loving plants, such as camellias, heathers, *pieris sarcococa*, or rhododendrons, in ericaceous soil mix, you need to take some precautions when you water to alleviate the effect of the lime in the water. The best solution, that is not always possible, is to install a water butt so that you can water the plants with rainwater taken directly from the roof.

If you cannot do this then add some flowers of sulfur or sulfur chips or some sequestered iron to the container to help acidify the soil and keep the pH at the correct level.

It is important to test the soil at intervals to check its acidity, which can change. Acid-loving plants that grow in a mix that is too alkaline soon develop chlorosis, where the leaves turn yellow, and if this is not corrected then the plants will soon die.

REVIVING PLANTS

If a plant appears totally dead and dried out, then it is worth plunging the pot in a bucket of water and leaving it there until the soil has reabsorbed the water. Sometimes the plant will revive. This is certainly worth trying with small plants in small containers that can be moved about easily.

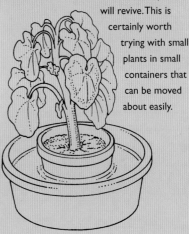

feeding and maintenance

All plants require nutrients to thrive and grow. In a garden these are present naturally in the soil, but in a container this is different. Not only is the volume of the growing medium far less, but frequent watering washes the nutrients away. They need to be replaced.

▲ *An ambitious fruit and vegetable garden with a traditional strawberry pot and a raised bed. The contrasting leaf colors are most attractive.*

The basic nutrients

There are three main nutrients in all soils that are needed by all plants. Each has a different function. They are nitrogen (N), phosphorus (P), and potassium (K). Nitrogen promotes good leafy growth, phosphorus enables the plant to develop a good root system, and potassium helps the plant to produce flowers and fruit. In addition to the main nutrients there are a number of other nutrients or trace elements required by plants, such as magnesium (Mg), calcium (Ca), and manganese (Mn), but they are only required in tiny amounts and can safely be ignored by container gardeners.

Organic versus inorganic It has to be said that it is very much easier for the container gardener to use inorganic fertilizers than to rely on organic alternatives. There are two main reasons for this, availability and bulk. In a standard garden there is always room for a compost heap, and if there is a lawn, grass clippings provide the essential ingredients for organic compost.

A container gardener has neither of these things, although a small wormery might be a possibility, feeding the worms on suitable kitchen waste.

Compost, in a garden, has two functions. It provides much of the nutrients necessary for healthy growth, but more importantly it gives any soil bulk and helps to improve the structure. Containers, filled with prepared compost, do not require such help and do not have room for the additional bulk. Inorganic alternatives are available in compact pelleted form or in bottles of liquid fertilizer. Both can be applied easily when required. The organic alternatives of bonemeal or fish, blood and bone are perfectly satisfactory but may attract unwelcome predators.

Basic steps

When putting a permanent plant in a container you should incorporate a general fertilizer. The easiest to use is in granular form: an inorganic balanced NPK formula, 7:7:7, that contains equal proportions of nitrogen,

feeding a plant correctly

1 When planting a shrub or tree add some bonemeal or general fertilizer to the soil mix. Follow the manufacturer's instructions on the packet.

2 Slow-release fertilizers can be added in spring in pellet form. There are various types that work in different ways. One application lasts through summer.

3 Liquid fertilizers and foliar feeds can be added when plants are watered. These should be used when the plant is in growth, and then every 2 or 3 weeks.

phosphorus, and potassium and provides all the plant's requirements. Do not use the organic alternatives of bonemeal or fish, blood, and bone if you live where there are urban foxes. They will arrive

each night and dig up your plants time after time, looking for bones and old fish.

Vegetables, such as tomatoes, peppers, or eggplants, all need high nitrogen feeds to start them into growth, followed by a

high potassium (potash) feed when the plants are bearing fruit. Tomato feed is high in potash and is excellent for all plants as well as tomatoes.

General feeding It is a good idea to apply slow-release fertilizer granules or pellets to all permanent containers at the start of each year. Follow the manufacturer's instructions. Very often plants in containers will require no additional feeding, but if the plants do show signs of wilting, they can be watered using a foliar feed absorbed through the leaves of the plant, or be given liquid fertilizer. Foliar feeds are extremely economical and effective. When using all liquid and foliar feeds be sure to follow the manufacturer's instructions carefully or you may damage the plant.

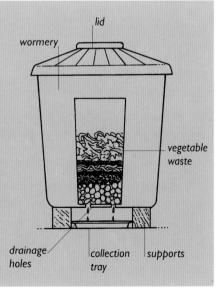

HOW TO BUILD
A WORMERY

You can buy a ready-made wormery or make your own using a plastic garbage bin with a faucet to drain off excess moisture or drainage holes and collection tray. Drill air holes around the top and make sure the lid can be fastened securely. Fill the bin with 10cm/4in gravel and then put a divider (old carpet is good) on top. Add 10cm/4in of multipurpose soil mix and shredded newspaper, then at least 100 red brandling worms (from angling shops). Add kitchen waste in thin layers, about 5cm/2in. Cover with damp newspaper. When the food scraps are full of worms you can add more.

lid

wormery

vegetable waste

drainage holes

collection tray

supports

basic pests and diseases

Pests and diseases are inevitable. The best cure is constant vigilance and what is known as good garden hygiene. If you walk around your garden every evening you will soon spot any unwelcome pests, and if they are sprayed straight away the infestation is much easier to control.

Start by creating as healthy an environment as possible. As a first rule try to insure adequate ventilation. If you have a large number of plants in an enclosed space then diseases will flourish. It is difficult to do this if you are growing a number of plants in a small space (a balcony or patio). Make sure though that the center of each plant is open, and that air can circulate. This applies to fruit trees and shrubs.

Common pests

Ants—they cause more damage than is commonly realized. They feed on the honeydew excreted by aphids and will carry them from plant to plant. They cause damage to the roots of plants by tunneling underground and will eat newly sown seeds. If you find a nest destroy it immediately by pouring boiling water over it. Then dust affected areas with a recommended insecticide, or apply a residual product that forms a lasting barrier.

Aphids—there are many kinds of aphids but they all suck the sap from the plant and weaken it. Some plants such as roses, *Philadelphus*, and broad beans are particularly prone to infestation. Pinch off all the infected plant parts and spray with a contact or systemic insecticide, or organically with a solution of dishwashing liquid. This may not be so effective as nonorganic kinds.

Birds—particularly troublesome when it comes to fruit or vegetables, although they are unlikely to cause so much damage in a container garden as they do in a traditional kitchen garden. The only thing that really works is to net everything at risk and to keep the plants netted.

Caterpillars—companion planting will go a long way to avoiding these pests. If you grow vegetables that do become

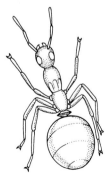

Ant

Spider mite

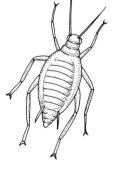

Aphid

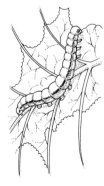

Caterpillar

Pigeon

▶ *Tomatoes make good companion plants as they help to deter cabbage white butterflies from laying their eggs on brassicas.*

infested with caterpillars, pick them off by hand and spray with a suitable pesticide. Sadly, this may be too late.

Leafminers—these are small insect larvae that feed inside the leaves of plants. Eventually the whole leaves will be destroyed. Pick off infested leaves and spray with a suitable pesticide as soon as you see any signs appearing. Spraying may have to be repeated every two weeks if the infestation is bad.

Japanese beetle—these shiny green beetles are about ½in long and chew the leaves and flowers of many plants. The larvae are grayish white with a dark brown head and feed on roots and tubers. Pick them off by hand whenever you see them, dropping the beetles into a jar of water and detergents; then spray the plants weekly with neem until the beetles are under control.

Spider mite—tiny creatures the size of a pin head, with several species. They are serious pests and do considerable damage to plants such as tomatoes, grapes, chrysanthemums, and house plants. Spray the plants with water to keep the atmosphere moist. Outdoors, spray infested plants with a strong jet of water to knock mites off leaves. Repeat daily for three days. Many species are resistant to pesticides.

Sawfly—they cause serious damage to fruit, including apples, pears, and cherries. Spray with an insecticide.

Slugs and snails—these well-known creatures can be a major problem, especially in moist, damp areas. There are various methods of control. Trap them under an upturned half grapefruit skin, or sink a shallow pot half filled with sweet liquid in the soil into which they will fall and drown. Deter them by cutting up plastic bottles and putting collars of plastic around young plants, or surround the plants with a circle of grit—this will work because slugs do not like to slide over sharp surfaces.

Squirrels—birds, especially pigeons, may be bad but squirrels are far worse. There are two ways to deal with squirrels. One is to erect a permanent wire barrier over everything that matters, because netting simply is not strong enough to keep them out. The other is to obtain a humane squirrel trap.

Whitefly—the nymphs of these small creatures attack plants out of doors, but they also attack house plants. They are easily seen hanging off the flowers and foliage off the plant they have decided to attack. Spray with an insecticide.

SPRAYING—ORGANIC OR NON-ORGANIC

This is a vexed question and the approach you take to spraying and pest control depends entirely on how strictly you adhere to organic principles. There are organic alternatives to most normal garden pesticides but you have to decide whether they are sufficiently effective for the extra work they may involve.

Remember that tomatoes and marigold, *Tagetes*, will deter many butterflies from laying their eggs, particularly on brassicas, and if you grow them together you may avoid infestation by their caterpillars. This is known as companion planting.

Common diseases

Black spot—common on roses. Spray weekly with garden sulfur before the disease appears.

Canker—shrunken scars that appear on the shoots of woody plants especially apple, pear, and plum trees in summer. Cut off the infected branches immediately and dispose of them, and paint the wound with fungicide paint.

Damping off—a fungal disease of seedlings that makes them collapse and die. It is usually caused by damp soil that is too cold, or overcrowding. To control, water the seedlings regularly with a suitable fungicide, throw away any trays of seedlings that are affected and disinfect all your seed trays.

Botrytis—caused by cold, damp conditions and affects fruit such as

◄ *Crowded plum trees can sometimes be prone to botrytis. Thin out the crop to prevent overcrowding. Remove infected fruit immediately.*

Powdery mildew affects many plants. Spray with garden sulfur.

Whitefly affects indoor and outdoor plants. Spray with insecticide.

Canker affects fruit trees. Cut off and destroy affected shoots.

Black spot is prevalent on roses. Spray with garden sulfur.

▶ *Organic sprays are available for most garden pests and diseases, and it is up to the individual gardener to find out which one works best.*

strawberries. Spray susceptible plants early in spring with garden sulfur, and keep plants as dry and well ventilated as possible; removing infected leaves will help prevent the disease spreading.

Fungal diseases—they cause mold, mildew, and wilt, and thrive in humid conditions. All fungal diseases are difficult to control and improved ventilation is the best prevention. The same applies to leaf spot.

Downy mildew—caused by various species of fungi but they are not the ones that produce powdery mildew. They are more prevalent in damp weather and cause white growths to appear on the underside of the leaves and blotches on the surface. It can affect many bulbs, garden perennials, and vegetables such as lettuce and onions. Once present the

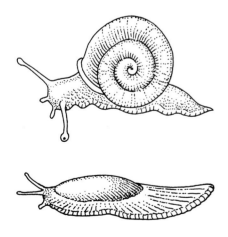

Slugs and snails can be trapped or controlled with slug pellets.

disease is difficult to control. Make sure that all plants are properly watered, and avoid overcrowding and overhead watering where possible. Spray affected plants with copper sulfate early in the morning on a bright, dry day.

Powdery mildew—a common fungal disease that can affect many garden plants. The symptoms are a white powdery coating that appears on the leaves and the stems of plants. The white coating later thickens, turns brown, and small black dots appear on the surface. Spray susceptible plants with garden sulfur before the disease appears, and avoid watering leaves.

Viruses—there are several kinds that affect many plants, but they all show roughly the same symptoms. The leaves become mottled and distorted, and they may also develop yellow or brown

blotches. If you are certain that your plants are suffering from a viral disease, then you should pull them up and destroy them straight away. There is no effective chemical control for this problem but some plants are sold certified virus-free. Keeping aphids under control helps because the disease is spread through the sap of the plant which the aphids feed on. Advice may be available from professional organizations.

DEFICIENCIES

As if the gardener's life was not complicated enough, many soil deficiencies, such as chlorosis and nitrogen deficiency, cause plants to behave in much the same way as if they had some disease. The container gardener can be thankful that soil deficiencies are unlikely to affect plants in containers.

overwintering

Containers get too hot and dry in summer, and in winter they get colder than the surrounding garden. Plants in containers may therefore need special protection in hard weather: containers on roof gardens can be a particular problem for they are more likely to be buffeted by stormy winds.

Growing and protecting tender plants

If you have room you can grow tender plants in containers provided you can give them shelter indoors in the winter. Most plants require a cool light area free of central heating. A north-facing room that is unused and can be kept reasonably cool is ideal, or failing that use a cool porch, but remember that some plants do not like drafts. If you want to grow semitender plants in containers and have the facilities to winter them indoors, consult a specialist plant encyclopedia. This should provide accurate information about the minimum temperature they require and the conditions they prefer. A number of attractive flowering shrubs and climbers suitable for containers that will need protection include lemon tree, *Citrus limon*, *Abutilon* 'Nabob' or *A.* 'Souvenir de Bonn', and the many varieties of *Hibiscus rosa-sinensis* or even one of the bougainvilleas, although all bougainvilleas will eventually outgrow their allotted space. There are also a number of smaller plants, such as streptocarpus and cyclamen, that will flower out of doors in mild climates in summer if they are kept in a sheltered spot.

Protecting plants out of doors

If you do not have the facilities to keep containers inside then tender plants need

◄ *Grasses and bamboo covered in snow in midwinter. Shake any heavy snow off the branches of fir trees or they may break.*

▶ Spring crocuses surrounded by old fallen chestnut leaves after a slight frost. Such a frost is unlikely to do much damage in the garden.

protection outside. Traditionally they were wrapped in straw or bracken and covered with burlap. Tender perennials can be protected by a good layer of straw or bracken that is removed in the spring. Secure some netting over the top to prevent it blowing away.

Wrapping plants in garden fleece is also excellent because it allows light and moisture to penetrate, although it is flimsy and liable to tear if subjected to strong winds and sharp corners. And being fairly thin it will not provide complete protection for tender plants in a really hard frost. Another idea is to wrap the plants in bubble wrap. This gives excellent insulation and allows some light to penetrate, but it should not be kept on any longer than is strictly necessary because it does not allow the

plant to breathe and can lead to disease. A surprising amount of protection can also be obtained by wrapping plants in netting, and this is most suitable if you want to protect a half-hardy fruit tree, such as a peach or nectarine, growing against a wall. Two or three layers of netting will generally give perfectly adequate protection when late frosts threaten the emerging blossom in early spring. There are two other things worth

remembering when it comes to protection. The frosts that occur in spring and hit the new young growth do the real damage. Frost before Christmas seldom kills anything. And second, cold strong winds, especially from the east, can do just as much damage as frosts. This is where netting really helps because it filters the wind, reduces its speed and often prevents damage to the leaves. It is particularly important on roof gardens.

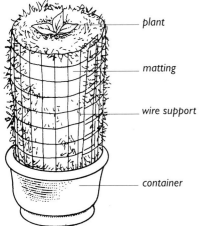

▲ Plants in circular containers can be covered with matting or straw held in place by a wire frame. Alternatively, wind fleece around the plant.

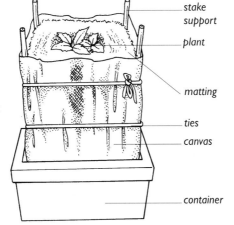

▲ Plants in square containers can be protected as shown. Do not leave covering, such as plastic sheets, on plants for longer than necessary.

LOOKING AFTER CONTAINERS

Plants are not the only things that require protection. Terracotta pots may well crumble and crack if they are subjected to extremes of frost and rain. They can be wrapped in plastic bubble wrap. Cracking can often be prevented by securing the top of the pot with wire under the rim and twisting it tight.

raising plants

The container gardener may well not have sufficient room to contemplate raising plants. Even the simplest form of propagation, sowing seeds, requires a certain amount of space, or, at the least, some vacant window ledges. It can be very easy to get carried away.

Sowing seed—general advice

Before you start consider how many plants you actually can use, how many varieties you want to raise, and how much time you are prepared to give to raising and tending seedlings. If you have room then this can save a good deal of money, for a packet of seeds costs very little and produces more plants than you need. Don't be too ambitious.

Scarification and stratification

Some plants have specific requirements before their seed will germinate properly. This involves two processes, scarification and stratification. Scarification applies to certain large kinds of seed with a hard outer coating. In the wild it would remain in the ground over winter and the outer coating of the seed would gradually rot, allowing the seed to absorb water and start into growth. Without this process the seed needs to have its outer

◀ *It is much cheaper to raise your own bedding plants for the summer by sowing seed in spring. Nicotianas and petunias are easy to grow.*

propagating seeds

1 Cover drainage holes with crocks and fill tray with seed mix. Water it and let the moisture drain off. Seeds like warm, damp conditions.

2 Seeds should be sown thinly over the seed mix surface. With fine seed, it is helpful to use a sheet of white paper as shown to scatter the seeds thinly.

3 Seed trays with plastic tops and ventilation holes help to keep moisture at the right level. If using plastic wrap, remove once the seeds germinate.

coating chipped or weakened to allow growth to take place. This is usually done by rubbing the seeds with sandpaper or by chipping them with a knife. You can do this with both stick and pole beans to accelerate their germination but it is not strictly necessary.

SOWING SEED

At its simplest sowing seed merely involves buying seed trays and seed starting mix, and spreading the mix evenly in the tray. Water it so that it is reasonably moist and then sprinkle the seed over the surface, covering the tray with a sheet of glass or clear plastic, and then leave it somewhere light and warm until the seed germinates. Read the instructions on each packet carefully because these basic requirements often vary from plant to plant.

Stratification is when the seed germinates better after a period of either hot or cold. The gardener with space and time can usually overcome this, but two good very ordinary examples from the vegetable garden are parsnips, where seed should be sown very early in the year when the ground is still extremely cold, and parsley, a notoriously slow germinator, where success can be virtually guaranteed if you pour boiling water on to the seed mix before you sow in the spring.

You can achieve both these effects artificially by either keeping the seed in a plastic bag mixed with peat substitute and sand in a heated closet, if the seed needs a period of warmth, or in the refrigerator if it needs cold. Few kinds of seed need either treatment.

Light and darkness

Some seed requires light to germinate, in other words it germinates on the surface of the compost. The sprouts of alfalfa and mung beans are good examples, but some kinds of seed need to be kept in the dark and covered with soil mix. Read the instructions on the seed packet.

Once the seed has germinated it needs to be kept in good light on a windowsill, out of direct sunlight. Keep the soil moist and turn the seed tray every day to stop the seedlings growing at one angle toward the light. The first leaves that appear are the seed leaves, which are followed by the true leaves, and when there are two pairs of them the seedlings can be pricked out into a larger container filled with general purpose or potting mix.

sowing seed—handy tips

Fine seeds should be sown as thinly as possible. Take care and time when sowing to achieve this. There isn't any point in filling a seed tray with a large number of seeds, for when they all germinate, the tray is too congested, the seedlings don't grow properly, and it is difficult to prick them out.

Sowing larger seeds

They are much easier to sow and generally include vegetables, i.e. peas and beans, although clivias have lovely dark brown seeds that in two year's time make excellent and unusual presents.

If you plan to grow vegetables in your container garden then it is a good idea to sow them separately, and you should plan to operate on the two-for-one principle. Sow peas and beans, for example, in degradable cardboard pots or modules, two seeds at a time and discard one if both germinate. Then plant the pot or module directly into the container in early summer when all danger of frost has passed. The plants will then grow without suffering any check.

Watering Try to water seed pans and small seedlings from below, rather than from above. It is very difficult to get a fine enough rose spray, and the heavy drops of water damage the seedlings and can even wash out the roots. Stand the trays in a tray of water and the seed mix will absorb sufficient water to keep the seeds moist and the small plants growing.

Temperature

Every seed has a temperature at which it will germinate, and it is particularly important to stick to this. It will be stated on the seed packet. Nearly all vegetables require a soil temperature of above 7°C/45°F for a week before they germinate, and a number of annuals require temperatures from 13°C–21°C/55°–70°F. Read the instructions carefully on the packet before you sow anything.

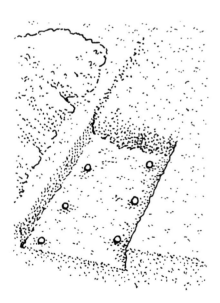

▲ *Larger seeds, such as peas and beans, can be sown in shallow double trenches. Space them out according to packet instructions.*

SOWING SEED DIRECTLY INTO THE CONTAINER

Some plants are difficult to handle when they are small and should be sown directly where they are to grow, even in a container. This applies to a number of vegetables such as carrots, beets, and chives. Thin the seedlings when they appear. Hardy annuals are often sown in this way in the kitchen garden, and if you have a container devoted to hardy annuals you can follow this practice. Draw shapes on the surface of the container, and then sow individual plants in each section. Sow the seed thinly. Borage, flax, California poppy, *Eschscholzia,* and poached-egg plant, *Limnanthes,* can all be sown in this way for a summer display.

Aftercare

The worst thing that can happen to a tray of seedlings is the fungal disease called "damping off." This usually happens when seedlings are too crowded within the seed tray, or when the soil itself is too cold and too wet.

Spray the seedlings from time to time with a fungicide as a prevention, and take care to keep all containers that you use as clean as you possibly can. And do not forget to turn the seed trays on windowsills every day or the plants will grow lopsided toward the light. Put them outside as soon as possible, shade them from direct sunlight to start with, and water them with a diluted liquid fertilizer every week.

▲ Growing peas in a container is most satisfying; train the plants up a wigwam of stakes. Choose a snow pea variety.

▼ It is a help when raising annuals from seed to stick to one color, as this can then be matched with other plants in beds and pots.

135

propagation—taking cuttings

There is something very satisfying about taking cuttings and propagating your own plants. It is actually very simple and the principle is invariably the same—cut off a portion of the parent plant, dip the cutting in hormone rooting powder, and replant it in moist cutting mix.

Softwood cuttings

They are taken in the spring when the new shoots are fully formed and are just starting to harden. They are usually taken from the tips of new shoots but with some plants the cuttings are taken from new basal shoots, growing from the base of the plant. Make the cut just below a node (a leaf joint), and then reduce the number of leaves and the leaf area by cutting some of the leaves in half. Cuttings require some leaf growth but find it difficult to support a large leaf system. Dip the cutting in hormone rooting powder and push the cutting into moist cutting mix. It is important to keep softwood cuttings in a moist environment, preferably a propagating frame because they lose moisture quickly.

Semiripe cuttings

They are taken in late summer from new wood produced in the current year.

▶ *Pelargoniums are easily raised from cuttings and can be overwintered on windowsills or in a cool greenhouse. This is a great money saver!*

► *Osteospermums are easily raised from softwood cuttings taken early in the year. The variety 'Whirligig' has wheel-like petals.*

Choose a nonflowering shoot if available. Cuttings 5–10cm/2–4in long are about the normal length. Trim them just below a leaf joint and remove the lower leaves. Remove the top leaves to reduce moisture loss. Dip the cutting in rooting powder and insert it gently into the cutting mix.

Some shrubs and herbs root best from semiripe cuttings taken with a "heel" of the old wood. Pull the shoot

VARIOUS SORTS OF CUTTINGS

There are various types of cuttings—root, basal, stem, leaf, softwood, semiripe, and hardwood. These variations on a theme apply to different plants. Some plants, such as hydrangeas, lavateras and osteospermums, root best from softwood cuttings taken early in the year. Others, including almost all evergreens and roses, are best propagated by semiripe or hardwood cuttings taken in the fall. (See the text on these pages on how to take softwood and hardwood cuttings.)

away from the plant in a downward direction and it will come away with a heel of wood. Trim this if necessary.

Stem cuttings

Most hardwood and semiripe cuttings are stem cuttings taken from a straight length of shoot. The normal length is around 5–12cm/2–5in. Trim each stem to length just below a node, and strip away the lower leaves to allow the shoot to be inserted in the soil. Also remove all flowering shoots and buds because they reduce the effect of the root-producing

hormones that cuttings rely on. Geraniums, *pelargoniums*, are normally propagated from stem cuttings, as are a number of other plants. In fact, geraniums are a good example of those plants that need to be left in the open air overnight to form a pad at the foot of the stem. In some plants this helps rooting, in others it helps to prevent the cuttings rotting. If you have difficulty in getting geraniums to root then this is worth trying. Dip all the cuttings in hormone rooting powder, or a hormone rooting solution.

taking cuttings and division

Division Many plants, especially perennials that have spreading rootstocks, can easily be propagated by division in spring. This is something that all gardeners should practice because some plants, such as delphiniums, form large clumps of roots where the center dies away. Such plants should be split and only the healthy outer sections of the roots replanted. Primroses, hostas, irises, and pulmonarias should all be divided in this way. There are two schools of thought about how this should be done. Some plants, such as primroses, can simply be pulled apart and the various portions replanted. Other fibrous-rooted plants have to be split by cutting through the rootball with a spade, or pulling the plant apart, using two forks back to back. This is hardly something that the everyday container gardener will have to do, but if the case does arise, it is best to split the rootball cleanly with a spade or a sharp knife.

Leaf cuttings

This is the simplest form of propagation and is normally used for house plants, such as streptocarpus and African violet, *Saintpaulia*. Some plants root best when a whole leaf is used, pinned out flat on the soil, with a few small cuts or nicks made in the veins on the underside of the leaf. This encourages the plants to form calluses and the roots spring from them (begonias are often propagated in this way). Another common house plant

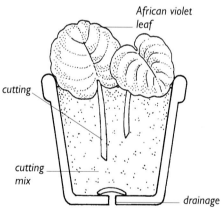

African violet leaf

cutting

cutting mix

drainage

▲ African violets are easy to propagate by leaf cuttings. Pull off a number of leaves and insert them in the mix around the edge of the pot.

◀ Make sure the base of the leaf is touching the surface of the cutting mix. New leaves will show in a few weeks.

dividing plants successfully

1 Some smaller plants, such as primroses and pulmonarias, can be divided easily by hand. Dig up the plant when flowering is over and pull it apart.

2 Large perennials can be divided with two forks, as shown. Put the forks in back to back and lever the plant apart. Or, just cut the plant in two with a spade.

3 Irises can be divided, cutting the new rhizomes away from the old clump. Dust with fungicide powder and cut back the leaves by two-thirds before replanting.

propagated by leaf cuttings is the African violet. Pull off whole leaves including the stalk and push them into cutting mix around the rim of a pot. Some of these may not take but others will. Streptocarpus is best propagated by cutting the leaf into strips and then planting them in the mix, edge down.

Layering This occurs naturally in many plants, and the method can be used to propagate a number of plants that are difficult to raise from cuttings, such as rhododendrons. Strawberries propagate themselves by sending out runners that root. They can then be severed from the parent plant and potted up separately. Blackberries propagate themselves by tip-layering where the tips of shoots bury themselves in the ground and

develop roots. This is the principle behind layering. Peg a branch of a plant or shrub down, burying part of it in the ground. You can nick the stem lightly to promote rooting if you wish. Serpentine layering is where a long branch is pegged down in waves with the crests above ground. This can produce several plants from one stem.

General points when taking cuttings
Choose shoots without flowers or flowering buds if possible: nonflowering shoots produce roots more quickly. Use a sharp knife and make your cuts cleanly between or just below a node. Keep all cuttings moist and use a propagating frame for softwood cuttings. Leave hardwood cuttings in the ground for one year. They are generally slow to take.

HARDWOOD CUTTINGS

They are taken in the fall from new shoots that have completed their first year of growth. Cut the shoots into lengths 25–30cm/10–12in long. Trim them at the top above a pair of buds and at the foot below a pair of buds. Remove a sliver

of wood from the base of the cutting. Insert the cuttings in a trench with coarse sand or grit in the bottom to aid drainage, 7.5–10cm/3–4in apart, to at least half their depth. They may take a long time to develop—leave them undisturbed for one year unless they have obviously failed.

training and topiary

Topiary is important for the container gardener. In formal gardens clipped shapes complement the garden design. In patios and on roof gardens topiary shapes can be used to divide the garden into different areas, and give height to the garden.

There are not all that many plants that are suitable for topiary. The most impressive is yew, *Taxus baccata*, but it requires a good deal of space to show off its best attributes and only flourishes in large formal gardens where fantastic tortured shapes can be created over the years. This kind of skill and patience is usually outside the scope of the normal gardener. Box, *Buxus sempervirens,* and bay trees, *Laurus nobilis*, are the plants most commonly used, and a number of pleasing shapes can be contrived with a little care and some patience.

Training box

This is easier to train than bay, and it can be clipped into balls, cones, and spirals. The principle behind all topiary is to place a frame in position on or around the plant, and then clip away all shoots as they poke out of the confines of the frame. The simplest shape, much used for box, is the cone that is easily constructed from three stakes placed in a tripod around the plant. Trim to shape and a cone soon forms. For more complex shapes it is best to buy ready-made frames, balls, spirals, and pyramids, though you can construct your own frame using chicken wire. Tie in some branches to the frame to help the plant make a shape.

Clipping

Once the topiary form has become established the plant needs to be clipped regularly throughout the summer to maintain the required shape. Stop clipping as fall advances, for young shoots produced in late fall might not survive a hard winter.

Other suitable plants

While box and bay are the most common, good topiary shapes can also be made from privet, *Ligustrum ovalifolium*, although being semievergreen it is not so satisfactory. Ivy, *Hedera*, can be trained to grow into various shapes, and makes useful evergreen topiary in a small space. If you want to use ivy, first design the shape you require using chicken wire, and then sandwich some moss between another layer of wire. When the shape is satisfactory put it over a container filled with soil mix, and then set ivy plants around the edge and train them up the shape as they grow. Once they have reached the top they can be pruned back to keep them in shape.

TRAINING BAY TREES

One of the simplest plants to train into a ball or a mophead shape is bay, *Laurus nobilis*.

Once the plant has reached the height you require, you can stop it and cut off all the side-shoots that you do not want, leaving the trunk bare. Then cut the head of the tree into shape. It is probably easiest to clip bay trees by eye and it is surprising how good an effect can be achieved, even on large trees that have been allowed to grow wild in a garden. It is even possible to cut the head right off and new shoots will sprout that can

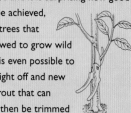

then be trimmed into the shape you want. Do not worry if the shape is uneven to start with. When the new growth starts you can let it grow out to cover any imperfections while keeping the remainder in trim.

training ivy into a cone shape

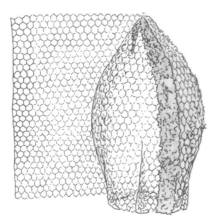

1 Make the basic shape from chicken wire and then cover it with a good layer of sphagnum moss, sandwiching it in place with a second layer of wire.

2 Put the wire shape on the container and then surround the rim with small plants, like ivy. These can be tied in to start with until they cling by themselves.

3 Cut away any shoots that grow too long or in the wrong direction. Ivy will soon cover the surface but keep turning the container to even the growth.

▲ *Clipping box into shape. Some topiary can be clipped by eye but complicated shapes may require guides to keep the training even.*

▶ *With patience, strange effects can be contrived, like the double balls of cypress shown here. This takes a number of years.*

Plants for containers—planting schemes

The smaller the garden, the more important the choice of plants. Plants will be seen close up, and the colors and form need to be considered carefully so that they complement the house and patio. Each container is a small and impermanent painting, decorating the space it inhabits.

creating a color scheme

Most garden color schemes work reasonably well. The green leaves help to give an overall balance and white and pale flowers link the stronger shades. But rather than leaving everything to chance, it is better to plan definite color schemes. This is especially important in a small container garden.

The color wheel

Color theory is based on the color wheel. An understanding of how this works explains the relationship between colors, and helps the gardener to achieve balanced plantings.

Primary colors The three primary colors are red, yellow, and blue. They cannot be obtained, in a painter's palette, by mixing other colors together. Mixtures of the primary colors,

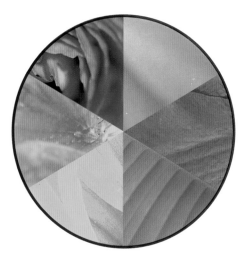

▲ *A color wheel composed of plants, showing the primary and secondary colors. Check to see which color combination you prefer.*

together with black and white, produce virtually all the other colors available. In gardening terms the primary colors fit together quite nicely. For example you could plant a spring container with forget-me-not, *Myosotis*, primrose, *Primula vulgaris* and a few early tulips, such as 'Brilliant Star', scarlet-vermilion, or 'Mme. Le Fefeber', fire-red. They would all flower together in early to mid-spring, and the effect would be bright and cheerful. If you wanted a quieter scheme you could leave out the tulips and just have the blue and yellow of the forget-me-nots and primroses. The forget-me-nots are important because they provide the groundcover necessary for this type of planting.

Later in the year beds or containers based on the primary colors might contain red and yellow celosias with blue cornflower, *Centaurea cyanus*—the variety 'Dwarf Blue' only reaches 30cm/12in and is suitable for containers. You might find these colors too strong in midsummer because the shades are deeper than the spring planting, and

colors appear brighter in the summer months than they do earlier in the year. when the sun is lower in the sky. The effect would be vivid rather than restful.

Secondary and complementary colors

If you mix any two primary colors in varying quantities you will obtain a secondary color. Red and blue make purple, red and yellow make orange, and blue and yellow make green.

Complementary colors are those that lie opposite one another on the color wheel, and in theory if you mix two of them you should obtain a pale gray, although if you try this with paint the pigments are seldom pure enough for this to happen. If you add white to a colour this produces a tint, and if you add black this produces a shade.

Adding combinations of both black and white produces a number of tonal values. These tonal values are most important for the gardener and the planning of planting schemes, and the best combination of plants is where there is a tonal harmony in the planting.

◄ *A red, yellow, and orange scheme for the fall can be created with a variety of dahlias and daylilies with low-growing scarlet begonias in front and taller red crocosmia plants at the rear. This produces a good blend of strong but not overvibrant colors.*

❶ *Crocosmia 'Lucifer'*

❷ *Dahlia 'Bishop of Llandaff'*

❸ *Begonia 'Barcos'*

❹ *Dahlia Unwins Dwarf Group*

❺ *Hemerocallis 'Bertie Ferris'*

❻ *Hemerocallis 'Lusty Lealand'*

❼ *Dahlia 'Preston Park'*

❽ *Dahlia Unwins Dwarf Group*

❾ *Dahlia 'Jeanette Carter'*

The effect of various plantings

Plantings based on the hot colors, red, yellow, and orange, are vivid and striking while the cooler colors are more restful. The same goes for the various shades. Pale colors blend softly together and are easy to live with.

All plant groupings in a small container garden need to be planned so that they fit in with the house and its surroundings. The walls of the house and garden may well be built of brick in various colors. New red bricks may not make the best background for plants. One solution might be to paint the inside of the garden walls white, but a longer term plan might be to grow ivy in a container to cover it. Green foliage is often the best foil for flowers.

▶ *Plantings of primary colors, such as red and yellow, certainly catch the eye, but the general effect can be a bit hot and restless.*

hot planting schemes

Brightly colored plants from the hot section of the color wheel achieve instant effect whether in a border or a container. Hot schemes need to be planned with care because the effect can be unsettling unless the color is controlled. Such plantings can be softened with white or pale flowers.

Hot schemes with red and yellow bulbs

The most important red and yellow bulbs are tulips and daffodils, *Narcissus*. They do not really flower at the same time with the daffodils coming first. If you want to try to achieve simultaneous flowering, you need to read the catalogs carefully and choose tulips from Division 1—Single Early Group, Division 12—Kaufmanniana Group or Division 14—the Greigii Group. These groups all flower relatively early in spring. Tulips have a complicated classification and there are 15 divisions in all. Daffodils are almost equally complicated and have 11 divisions. Those that flower latest are varieties from Division 5—Triandrus, Division 7—Jonquilla and Division 9—Poeticus. In general gardening terms most people refer to flowers from all these groups as *Narcissus*. In fact dwarf narcissus are very suitable for containers and there are

▲ *An attractive spring container of red, blue, and yellow flowers. Choose small tulips from the Kaufmanniana or Greigii groups.*

many good varieties. *N.* 'February Gold', *N.* 'Jumblie', and *N.* 'Hawera' are all clear yellow, while *N.* 'Shining Light' is a typical narcissus, with yellow petals and a strong orange-colored cup.

There are many red, yellow, and orange tulips. Among the best for the container gardener are the smaller varieties, such as *Tulipa praestans* 'Fusilier', 'Red Riding Hood', and 'Unicum', all red; *T. linifolia* Batalinii Group 'Bright Gem' and 'Yellow Gem', yellow; and *T.* 'Orange Monarch' and 'Shakespeare', orange. If you want to combine two hot colors in one flower, *T. clusiana* var. *chrysantha* is red and yellow, and 'Keizerskroon' is red with yellow on the petal margins.

◀ *A brilliant hot arrangement of annuals. The whole effect is softened by the white petunias that emphasize the startling reds and purples.*

You can plan a most effective hot planting scheme using different varieties of tulips, each in its own container. Choose tulips from the same division to insure, as far as possible, that they flower at the same time to make the most impact. And if you do not want just red and yellow then you can choose any number of color combinations.

Hot-colored bulbs and tubers for summer schemes

Other red bulbs or corms you might consider for the container garden include *Crocosmia* 'Lucifer', red, and *C.* 'Golden Fleece', yellow, although crocosmia reach 1–1.2m/3–4ft in height and will probably need staking. Daylilies, *Hemerocallis*, are more suitable for they are smaller. The varieties 'Red Joy', 'Red Rum', and 'Stafford' are red; 'Golden Chimes', 'Little Rainbow', and 'Nova' are yellow; and 'Francis Joiner' and *H. fulva* 'Flore Pleno' are orange. Daylilies flower in midsummer; some varieties are evergreen and continue to add interest during the months of winter.

A hot scheme of dahlias

The other excellent tuber for the dedicated container gardener is the dahlia. Dahlias should be lifted when the first frosts arrive in the fall, and be stored in a frost-free environment over winter. They are ideal plants to alternate with tulips if you want to produce a hot color scheme in late spring, and again in late summer in the same container. Lift the tulips when flowering is over and keep

them in a spare container until the foliage has died down, then store and replant the bulbs in the fall. Plant out the dahlia tubers in late spring or early summer after the tulips are over. Hot-colored dahlias include 'Bishop of Llandaff', 'Christopher Taylor', and 'Rothesay Superb', all red; 'Sunny Yellow', 'Lady Sunshine', and 'Ruskin Diane', all yellow; and 'Gateshead Festival' and 'Wiggles', both orange, but there are many thousands of varieties to choose from. Some of those mentioned will reach 1–1.2m/3–4ft high and require staking. Dwarf bedding dahlias are usually grown as annuals.

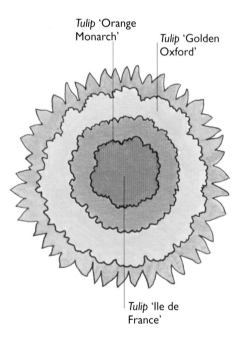

Tulip 'Orange Monarch'

Tulip 'Golden Oxford'

Tulip 'Ile de France'

▲ *A hot color wheel of tulips looks spectacular but it has to be planned and planted with care. The trouble with tulips is that there are a number of divisions, many with different shaped flower-heads, different heights, and all flowering at different times.*

◀ *'Paul's Lemon Pillar' is a popular climbing rose that is often trained up pergolas. The flowers are double, white, with a lemon scent.*

Red and yellow clematis

If you want to grow a climber but do not want to plant a rose try a clematis. There are not that many with red and yellow flowers because most are white or varying shades of blue and violet, but of the larger-flowered varieties there are 'Guernsey Cream', creamy yellow, and 'Rouge Cardinal', 'Niobe', 'Mme. Edouard André', 'Ville de Lyon', and 'Vino', differing shades of red. These all flower from midsummer onward. Of the smaller-flowered varieties there are *C. alpina* 'Constance', red; *C. macropetala* 'Rosy O'Grady', deep pink; and *C. viticella* 'Mme. Julia Correvon', wine-red. The best yellow clematis are

Hot schemes for midsummer containers—climbers and perennials

Red and orange flowers in containers in the summer must inevitably revolve around annuals and bedding plants. Red geraniums would be a popular first choice, closely followed by busy lizzie, *Impatiens*. However, larger containers can support larger plants, and when planning a planting scheme in a container garden it is a good idea to use some of these as visually stunning highlights.

Climbers for the container garden

The favourite climber is the rose—if you can, plant a climbing rose and train it against a wall. Most will flourish perfectly well in containers provided they are fed properly. There are two things to look out for but first check how much sun it will receive, and then how much room have you got. Do not choose a rose such as an old-fashioned rambler, because it will rapidly outgrow the confines of the container garden, and you need to have room to walk around it. Also only the pink rose 'Zéphirine Drouhin' is completely thornless. Climbing roses for a hot color scheme include 'Climbing Ena Harkness', scarlet; 'Paul's Scarlet Climber' and 'Parkdirektor Riggers', deep crimson; 'Golden Showers', golden-yellow and suitable for a north wall; 'Maigold', yellow-orange and suitable for a north wall; 'Gloire de Dijon', buff yellow; and 'Paul's Lemon Pillar', paler yellow.

busy lizzies

geraniums

▲ *Red geraniums can be surrounded by busy lizzies but schemes of this type can be softened by including white and pink varieties.*

C. *orientalis* and *C. tangutica*. The last two flower from late summer into the fall.

Two yellow wall shrubs

If you have large enough containers and want a background for a hot color scheme, there are two rather unusual yellow wall shrubs that you might consider: *Fremontodendron* 'Californian Glory' and pineapple broom, *Cytisus battandieri*. Both need a south or southwest wall and a good deal of sun. Otherwise, to vary the color schemes during the seasons, a firethorn, *Pyracantha*, could be planted in a raised bed and trained against a wall. It is prickly and evergreen, and a good guard against intruders. It has white flowers in late spring but the chief glory is the clusters of bright red, or red and orange berries that follow in the fall. They last the whole winter untouched by the birds.

Japonica, *Chaenomeles speciosa*, and its varieties also have thorny stems: they carry red flowers on bare branches in early spring, while *Abutilon megapotamicum* is evergreen and bears drooping red and yellow flowers through the summer.

Once you have decided on the climber or wall shrub that you want, you can consider the rest of the planting scheme. It would be a mistake to plant the hot-colored red-hot poker, *Kniphofia*, in a container. It takes up too much room and spreads endlessly. Also avoid the brilliant red poppies for they last such a short time in flower, but *Rudbeckia laciniata* 'Goldquelle' is reasonably compact with clear yellow

Rose 'Golden Showers'

Rose 'Ena Harkness'

▼ *The clematis 'Mme. Julia Correvon' flowers from midsummer to late fall. The wine-red flowers are single with yellow stamens.*

▲ *If you have room plant two climbing roses together. 'Golden Showers' is a free-flowering yellow rose, 'Climbing Ena Harkness' is red.*

cool planting schemes

Blue and white are the colors for cool planting schemes, and they can be complemented by adding gray and silver-leaved plants. They help to make any garden a calm and restful place in summer. Pale color schemes can be used to link stronger schemes and look best against a dark background.

Using blue and white plants

Blue plants can be used in a number of ways. In a traditional garden border, blue flowers, such as anchusas or dark blue delphiniums, can be used to contrast with the vivid red poppies, *Papaver*. In late spring red tulips might be planted amongst a bed of grape hyacinths, *Muscari*. These contrasting primary colors are very effective, but a garden full of such color contrasts would not be a restful place. In the confines of a container garden space is at a premium so avoid such luxuries.

In the early months of the year blue and white schemes are easy to create using bulbs. For example, a container planted with alternate blue and white hyacinths, *Hyacinthus*, looks and smells wonderful, but they will probably need some form of staking to keep them upright. Or include some other plants.

Winter-flowering heathers, *Erica carnea* and *E. x darleyensis*, have a number of white forms, and white *Erica* can be planted in containers with blue and purple crocuses, such as *Crocus chrysanthus* 'Blue Pearl', *C. c.* 'Ladykiller', *C. tommasinianus,* and *C. vernus* 'Pickwick'—all flower at the time when winter seems never-ending and are doubly welcome. If you do not want to go to the trouble of filling a container with ericaceous mix, necessary if *Erica* is to flower at its best, then other blue and white bulb combinations could include glory-of-the-snow, *Chionodoxa luciliae* Gigantea Group—*C. gigantea* is blue with white stripes, and *C. g. alba* is white.

If you have a larger container and would like to expand the range of plants to cover a larger canvas, then you can add some small conifers, such as *Chamaecyparis lawsoniana* 'Barry's Silver', green with silvery-white tips on the new

Erica x darleyensis 'White Perfection'

Crocus 'Blue Pearl'

Crocus 'Pickwick'

Viola x wittrockiana 'True Blue'

Viola 'Joker Light Blue'

Iris 'Joyce'

Erica x darleyensis 'White Glow'

◀ A charming mixture of spring-flowering plants. For interest and variety try V. 'Freckles' or the black 'Molly Sanderson'.

shoots in summer; *Picea glauca* 'Alberta Blue', smoky gray-blue; or *Juniperus communis* 'Compressa', green and found in many a rock garden. They all provide permanent color and form. Miniature daffodils, *Narcissus*, such as 'Jumblie', which is a yellow variety, add a touch of sunlight and can be planted in small groups with similar narcissus with contrasting colors that will flower at the same time. 'Jack Snipe' has white petals and bright yellow trumpets, while 'Jenny' is almost pure white.

Blue-flowering bulbs that flower at roughly the same time include glory-of-the-snow, *Chionodoxa*, and *Scilla sibirica*. Grape hyacinths, *Muscari*, flower slightly later. Alternatively plant some of the bulbous *Reticulata* irises that flower in late winter and early spring—'Harmony' and 'Joyce' have striking blue flowers with a splash of yellow.

Clumps of *Alyssum spinosum* and *Iberis saxatilis* continue the white theme into early summer, and can be intermingled with the brilliant blue of aubretia, *Aubrieta*, planted so that it falls over the front of the container. The only problem with such an arrangement is the straggly foliage when the flowering is over. Since bulbs absorb their strength from the foliage as it dies down you either have to live with this or, more extravagantly, dig up the bulbs and replant with new ones in the fall.

▶ *A deep purple, pale yellow, cream, white, green, and silver grouping of annuals frames an old chimney in a small garden.*

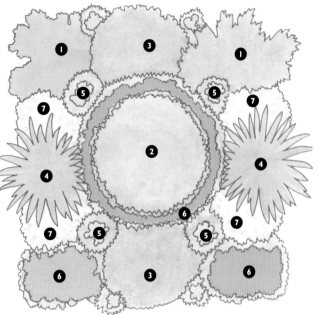

◀ *Conifers are the basis of this green, blue, and yellow arrangement that looks good all year.*

1 *Cedrus deodora* 'Feelin' Blue'

2 *Chamaecyparis lawsoniana*

3 *Picea pungens* 'Globosa'

4 *Thuja orientalis* 'Raffles'

5 *Narcissus* 'Jumblie'

6 *Muscari armeniacum*

7 *Iberis saxatilis*

blue and white schemes

Blue and white planting schemes, often mixed with yellow, are most successful in the spring before the annuals come into flower. All container gardeners should try one. Similar herbaceous border schemes later in the year include blue delphiniums or hardy geraniums grown against a background of the honey-scented, billowing white of the 2.1m/7ft high *Crambe cordifolia*, blue and white irises that complement each other and, as summer comes to an end, blue, purple, and white Michaelmas daisies, *Aster novi-belgii*, to provide a restraining influence on the golden colours of the fall. The container gardener, however, will have difficulty growing such plants effectively because they either take up too much room or have too large roots, and in almost all cases such attempts are doomed to failure.

Using African lilies

There are, nevertheless, a number of ideas that are worth considering. If you have a sunny garden or patio and a mild climate, consider planting a container with *Agapanthus*, African blue lily. They are ideal container plants, although they require staking. The best and hardiest are the Headbourne Hybrids that are widely available. 'Bressingham Blue,' another popular hybrid, is a deep violet color. Surround the agapanthus with two matching containers, lower in height, and plant one of the lovely white rock roses, *Cistus*, in each. *Cistus* x *cyprius* is justifiably popular, each petal marked with a maroon blotch in the center, while *Cistus* x *corbariensis* has clear white petals and yellow stamens. Rock roses will flower before agapanthus, through early to late summer.

◄ *Mauve petunias, verbena, and salvias are emphasized by white daisies. Take care when placing flowers against a dark background.*

▶ *Agapanthus make good container plants. Headbourne Hybrids are popular blue forms, 'Bressingham White' is white.*

Consider hardy geraniums

Another colourful scheme would be to take a selection of the smaller hardy geraniums and group them together. Cranesbills, *Geranium*, are a large genus and some are quite unsuitable for the container gardener because they grow too tall and are too vigorous, but some of the smaller ones are among the most charming and rewarding plants in any garden, flowering for months on end. The main difficulty is trying to group those that flower at the same time because they have rather different time clocks. *Geranium wallichianum* 'Buxton's Variety' is deservedly popular, its petals sky-blue on the outside and white veined within. However it can be difficult to find in ordinary nurseries, and it flowers rather late in the year from late summer into early fall. *Geranium clarkei* 'Kashmir Blue' has soft pale-blue flowers and *G. c.* 'Kashmir White' is white with

thin pink veins on the petals. Neither is too vigorous and they flower early in the summer months.

Other suitable white geraniums for containers include *G. sanguineum* 'Album,' white flowers throughout the summer; *G. renardii*, white to pale-lavender flowers with strong violet veins on the petals in early summer; and *G. pratense* 'Striatum', somewhat larger, with white flowers streaked with blue in midsummer. These white varieties can all be mixed with any of the lovely violet-blue forms, such as *G.* 'Johnson's Blue', the most popular geranium of all. The whole design can be further warmed by the addition of one of the wonderful pink varieties, such as *G. c.* 'Kashmir Pink'.

A blue and white scheme in summer can be mixed with climbers. White climbing roses suitable for a small space include the slow-growing 'White Cockade', delicately scented with small, perfect tea-shaped flowers, or 'Mme Plantier', a vigorous white noisette-flowered climbing rose.

Large-flowered white clematis that flower from midsummer onward include *C.* 'Henryi', 'Gillian Blades', and 'John Huxtable', and attractive blue forms include 'General Sikorski', 'H.F. Young', and the ever-popular 'Jackmanii Superba', although there are many other kinds available. They can create a cool space in a summer garden and make it both restful and pleasurable.

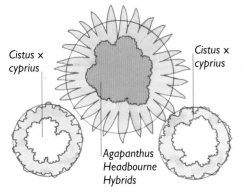

Cistus x cyprius

Cistus x cyprius

Agapanthus Headbourne Hybrids

▲ *An easy way to group colors is to grow one variety of plant in each container. Move them around until you have the right color balance.*

pale pink and red schemes

Hot and cool schemes may look well in isolation and garden designers can achieve spectacular effects with them, but a mixture of shades is still the most popular plan for ordinary gardeners. The secret is to combine plants to provide constant color and a changing emphasis throughout the year.

▲ *A pink and red spring mixture of pansies, heather, and ranunculus. The clipped box provides a pleasing green background.*

The effect of white flowers

There are two points to bear in mind. The first is the blending effect that white plants have on other colors. Red, blue, and yellow plants all work well together if there are white plants in between, and the use of white also strengthens the other colors and makes them more effective. The other main point is to try and include one plant with a stronger color impact, for instance a group of pale pink flowers might look slightly anaemic, a dark red rose in the middle gives the whole design more purpose.

Various color combinations work particularly well especially those from the same quarter of the color wheel— blue, pink, and white are one good combination and you can add some yellow plants for contrast provided that the yellow is not too strong and it matches the tones of the blues. Cream and pale orange flowers are equally effective. Another good color combination includes various shades of red through to pink, and another green,

white, and yellow. The main points are to match the general tone of each plant.

Certain color combinations are easier to achieve at different times of the year. Blue and yellow flowers are easy to find during the early months of the year but there are very few pink and red flowers in bloom. In the summer, pink, mauve, red, and white flowers often predominate and are easy to group together. The container gardener is also limited by the suitability of the various plants and this has to be born in mind.

A pink, white, and red scheme for the spring garden

One of the best small trees to grow in a container is a camellia, and one of the pink, white, or red varieties can be the starting point for a pink-based spring planting scheme. Camellias prefer a shady site, and their shiny dark green leaves remain attractive when the flowers have faded and fallen. Although some varieties will tolerate lime in the soil, the majority need acid soil, and therefore if you would like to grow a camellia and you have alkaline soil, a container filled with ericaceous mix is the only way you will achieve success. Ideally you should also try to collect and use rainwater because tap water may well contain lime. Alternatively sprinkle the soil with sulfur powder or add sulfur chips to keep the mix at the right pH level.

There are large numbers of suitable camellias and they come from two main groups, the *japonica* hybrids and the x *williamsii* hybrids. Eventually plants from both groups will grow too large for a container, but they are slow-growing shrubs and can be pruned back quite hard when they threaten to outgrow their surrounds. Pink camellias include 'Akashigata' ('Lady Clare'), 'Brigadoon,' 'Helen's Ballerina', 'Ave Maria', 'Lady Loch', 'Lasca Beauty', and 'Spring Festival'. White varieties include 'Lovelight', 'Janet Waterhouse', 'White Nun', and 'Charlie Bettes'. The red ones include 'Adolphe Audusson', 'R. L. Wheeler', 'Coquetii', and 'Royal Velvet'. A pleasant scheme for the early spring might include three camellias in separate containers underplanted with white *Anemone blanda* 'White Splendour', or the pink form *A. b.* 'Charmer'. Other low-growing plants include varieties of *Primula allionii*. They vary in color from white to pink to reddish-purple; *P. vulgaris* 'Cottage White' is white, and the long-flowering *P.* 'Wanda' is a wonderful deep red.

▶ *A most imaginative arrangement of white and mauve busy lizzies against a background of white astilbes growing in a raised bed.*

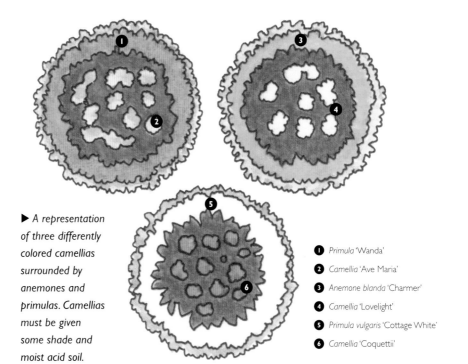

▶ *A representation of three differently colored camellias surrounded by anemones and primulas. Camellias must be given some shade and moist acid soil.*

❶ *Primula* 'Wanda'

❷ *Camellia* 'Ave Maria'

❸ *Anemone blanda* 'Charmer'

❹ *Camellia* 'Lovelight'

❺ *Primula vulgaris* 'Cottage White'

❻ *Camellia* 'Coquettii'

a scheme for a large container

If your garden gets a good amount of sun then you can create the equivalent of a summer border with a variety of colors. The only thing to watch out for is size but, with care, you can contrive many excellent effects. Any number of plants can be grouped together.

One idea would be to grow sweet peas, *Lathyrus odoratus*, up a trellis or wigwam of poles at the back of the container. Make sure that you can cut the flowers because regular snipping produces more buds. The fairly low-growing pink geranium *G. macrorrhizum*, can be placed in the middle, backed by

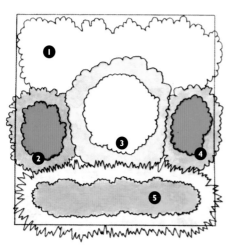

❶ Stachys byzantina
❷ Lathyrus odoratus
❸ Geranium macrorrhizum
❹ Penstemon 'Andenken an Friedrich Hahn'
❺ Dianthus

▲ A good pink, red, and white scheme for a container in summer. The pinks and sweet peas smell delicious, which adds to the attraction.

the silver-leaved lamb's ears, *Stachys byzantina*, with some pinks, *Dianthus*, planted in the front. For this scheme use scented pinks, such as 'Mrs Sinkins', an old cottage-garden favorite, white with feathery petals and an unrivaled scent. 'Doris' and 'Little Jock' are two good modern pinks, both scented, pale pink on the outside, with darker markings in the center. If the container is large enough then you can plant two penstemons to add a darker shade of red and give the scheme more emphasis. The best choice would be *P.* 'Andenken an Friedrich Hahn' that used to be called 'Garnet', with deep red flowers through summer into fall, unless winter happens to arrive very early.

A varied container of pink, red, and white miniature roses

One of the easiest containers to design is composed of small roses that are available in a number of colors, red, white, and pink. Small roses come in three groups, patio roses that grow to 45–60cm/1½–2ft, dwarf polyantha roses that are about the same size, and miniature roses that are generally slightly smaller.

To design an effective display start by planting one of the smaller cluster-flowered bush or floribunda roses to act as a centerpiece. The bright red 'Evelyn Fison' would be a good choice but, if

▲ Patio roses such as the white 'Bianco' carry a mass of small shapely flowers in summer. They repeat flower throughout the year.

you want a quieter display, 'English Miss,' pink, or 'Margaret Merril,' white with pink buds, are both lovely roses and exceptionally fragrant. All these floribundas will grow to 75–90cm/2½–3ft or slightly more. Then surround

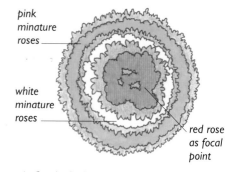

pink miniature roses

white miniature roses

red rose as focal point

▲ Circular beds or containers planted with roses always catch the eye in summer. Include scented roses if possible, and feed them too.

the center rose with red, pink, or white miniature roses. The two schemes that you could choose are pink roses on the inside surrounded by white on the outside, and white surrounded by pink, both of which look most attractive; a container of each on a patio would look marvelously fresh.

Since most patio roses have a spread of 45cm/1½ft you need to allow this distance between each plant. If you use miniature roses you halve that distance. 'Bianco' and 'White Pet' are both white patio roses, 'Innocence' is a white miniature rose and 'Katharina Zeimet' and 'Yvonne Rabier' are both attractive dwarf white polyanthas. Suitable pink roses include the patio roses 'Bedazzled', 'Queen Mother', and 'Hugs 'n Kisses'; 'Queen Margrethe' and 'Gracie Allen' are both white with pink hearts.

All these roses need to be fed. The ideal feed is well-rotted manure or compost but this may not be possible if you are growing roses in a container. Feed with bonemeal (unless your garden is frequented by urban foxes) in the fall and then add a balanced fertilizer in the spring. The roses should be pruned hard when they are dormant in late winter or early spring to keep them within bounds, and to encourage new growth. Cut them back to a half or a quarter of the original height, removing any dead or damaged wood completely. Thin them as appropriate.

▶ *A wigwam planted with sweet peas and nasturtiums makes an unusual focal point in a small garden in summer.*

foliage plants

Very often container gardens are small and shady places where the sun seldom reaches. Such gardens are often unsuitable for colorful plants, and the answer is to use a variety of foliage plants. There are several attractive combinations that can create wonderful effects in containers.

The importance of background

The first thing to think about in a small shady garden is the background, and a background of ivy, *Hedera*, that remains green throughout the year is suitable and easy. Common ivy, *Hedera helix,* will grow almost anywhere and is still a good choice. However there are many varieties, both green and variegated, that are more interesting. Try *H. h.* 'Dragon Claw' that has a medium-sized soft green leaf, if you have a shady garden, or the variegated form *H. h.* 'Goldheart' with its gold-splashed leaves to give a touch of color. Like all variegated ivies, this prefers some sun and shelter.

A container of ferns

Ferns are wonderful: soft, green, tolerant of deep shade, requiring little attention. A container of ferns is easy to plan and plant and if it is to be really successful it needs a story and focal point. The best fern to use for this is Wallich's wood fern, *Dryopteris wallichiana.* This is a striking plant. It is deciduous and carries erect strong, dark green fronds that are almost yellow when they first emerge in spring. The fronds are covered with dark brown or black scales. It can reach 1.8.m/6 ft in height, although it is unlikely to grow quite so tall in a container. This can be surrounded by the evergreen Japanese holly fern, *Cyrtomium falcatum*, and the smaller evergreen Hart's tongue fern, *Asplenium scolopendrium,*— the variety 'Crispum' with its wavy mid-green fronds is more attractive than the species plant which is rather plain.

There are two choices to plant at the edge of the container. The small rusty-back fern, *Asplenium ceterach*, evergreen, with attractive fronds, only grows to 20cm/8in in height. This is a most useful plant for growing in walls or in cracks in paving. The other choice for a small fern is the common polypody, *Polypodium vulgare*, that reaches 30cm/12in and is also evergreen. This container gives differing heights, leaf shapes, and colors throughout the year, and in the spring the grandest fern will rise up from the underworld and unfurl its leaves.

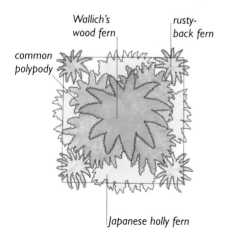

common polypody

Wallich's wood fern

rusty-back fern

Japanese holly fern

▲ *A container of ferns of different colors and leaf shapes can bring a cool shady garden to life in summer. There are a number to choose from.*

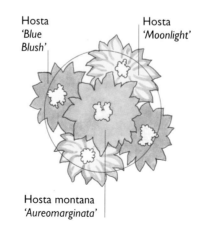

Hosta 'Blue Blush'

Hosta 'Moonlight'

Hosta montana 'Aureomarginata'

▲ *A container of hostas always looks attractive in a shady garden. Choose the varieties carefully to achieve the right balance of height and color.*

◄ *A polypody fern is the center of a green courtyard, including fatsia and a Japanese maple. The water feature is a soothing addition.*

▼ *Hostas grow well in containers for they prefer some shade and are less prone to slugs. Varieties of* H. undulata *have centrally marked leaves.*

A container of hostas

Many gardeners will not attempt to grow hostas because they are loved by slugs and snails who cheerfully demolish plants wherever they are grown. They flourish much better in containers where the approach of the slug can be more readily repelled and, because they prefer shade to sun, they make ideal plants for a shady patio garden. The beauty of hostas is the enormous variety of leaf color although they do carry spires of white to violet-blue flowers in summer. If you choose some of the smaller varieties, you can grow three or four hostas in a circular container 90cm/3ft in diameter. Good varieties to choose include: 'Moonlight' that reaches 50cm/20in high, light green leaves that merge into yellow during the summer, with thin white margins around the edge; *H. montana* 'Aureomarginata', dark green leaves with splashed yellow margins; 'Blue Blush' and 'Hadspen Blue', both with a height and spread of 25cm/10in x 60cm/24in, blue-gray leaves, while those of 'Hadspen Blue' are larger; 'Blue Moon' is another, smaller, blue-gray hosta; and *H. fortunei* 'Albomarginata', a bit larger, dull-green leaves with irregular cream margins.

evergreens for lasting interest

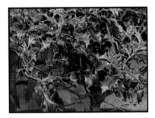

Evergreens should be present in every garden. They add interest, color, and shape, especially during the dull months of winter and many, particularly conifers, change in color in spring and summer. This provides varying color tones at different times of the year.

Evergreen trees and shrubs for permanent containers

There are more evergreen trees suitable for growing in containers than might, at first, be apparent. The main container-grown small tree is the sweet bay tree, *Laurus nobilis*, found clipped into shape at the front of many town houses. These can be bought ready-shaped from nurseries, or they can be raised from semiripe cuttings taken in late summer. They grow fairly slowly and take time to develop. They have the added advantage that the leaves are useful for flavoring food.

Another excellent small tree for the container garden is the camellia. There are many varieties and they need shade, moisture, and acid soil mix to flourish, but they have unrivaled flowers in early spring, mainly in white, pink, or red although there are a few yellow varieties, and some, such as 'Tricolor', have white, pink, and red variegated petals.

◄ *A gravel forecourt can be used to arrange the plants symmetrically. The use of evergreen emphasizes the formal nature of the planting.*

▶ *The red berries of a standard holly tree brighten the fall, complemented by the vivid Virginia creeper trained along the fence.*

The other tree or small shrub that shares similar requirements with camellias is the rhododendron, another excellent container plant. There are more varieties of rhododendron than any other garden plant so any choice is particularly invidious. They have a laxer habit than camellias, and it is not so easy to underplant them with early spring bulbs, but the flowers are lovely and come in many different colors, some are scented, and there are many evergreen varieties that keep their interest when the flowering period is over.

Grow rhododendrons and camellias in suitably large individual containers, unless you have a large raised bed that has room for more than one. Suitable rhododendrons that are evergreen and do not usually reach more than 1.5m/5ft in height and spread include 'Azuma-kagami', pink; 'Blue Diamond', violet-blue; 'Doc', rose-pink with deeper colored margins and spots; 'Fabia', orange-red; 'Hatsugiri', crimson-purple; 'Hello Dolly', apricot-orange; 'Hydon Dawn', pale pink to white; 'Kirin', deep pink; 'Mrs Furnival', light rose-pink; 'Percy Wiseman', peach-cream; 'President Roosevelt', red with variegated leaves; 'Ptarmigan', white; 'Purple Gem', light purple; 'Rose Bud', rose-pink; 'Scarlet Wonder', bright red; 'Kure-no-yuki' ('Snowflake'), semi-dwarf white; and *R. russatum*, red to purple.

Holly trees may not seem an ideal choice for the container garden. Common English holly, *Ilex aquifolium*, and its varieties have prickly leaves—not ideal in a confined space, male and female plants are needed to produce berries, and most grow too large for containers. Nevertheless they are worth considering growing in a larger, formal, garden, for they can be trimmed hard to make neat low-growing hedges and none of them grows very quickly. The varieties *I. a.* 'Argentea Marginata' and 'Silver Queen' have gold and white-edged leaves respectively that provide an added touch of color. The other evergreen holly for the smaller garden is the Japanese holly, *I. crenata*, and its varieties.

GRAY-LEAVED EVERGREENS

There are two other small trees that can be grown in containers, and both provide gray foliage throughout the winter. The first is the Australian cider gum tree, *Eucalyptus gunnii*. This is an excellent tree for a container because it can be treated as a shrub and cut back hard to the ground each spring. It will then throw up a number of young shoots throughout the summer with pale gray leaves that remain on the branches throughout the winter. The other small evergreen tree being grown more in containers, especially as the winters are generally rather milder, is the olive tree, *Olea europaea*. Olives are very slow growing and will not outgrow their situation too quickly, and eventually develop a rounded head with gray-green leaves with silvery gray undersides that flicker in the breeze.

conifers and grasses

Conifers are popular in all gardens but they have a special part to play in container gardens. They can be used in two ways: planted in individual containers to act as accent points, drawing the eye to that part of the garden, or they can be used more subtly to create an illusion of space.

Conifers on a roof garden— an illusion of space

Roof gardens are best planned as a series of rooms. Sometimes, however, such a plan is not possible and in this case the containers or Versailles tubs will march down each side of the roof space. Conifers graded in height with the tallest in the nearest container and the smallest in the farthest will extend the length of

the garden, even though this is an optical illusion. It is the same principle as changing a square or rectangular lawn in a small town garden into an irregularly curved oval, with the far end considerably narrower than the end nearest the house. The garden instantly appears longer and more spacious.

Winter color with various varieties

Conifers have the added bonus that they provide interest throughout the winter and, when teamed with the evergreen hedging box, *Buxus sempervirens*, the effect is doubled. This may be difficult to achieve in an informal patio garden with many different containers of varying shapes, but it is possible to design and plant such a scheme in a low-level raised bed on a formal patio. Plant box hedging around the edge of the bed to make a frame and, if there is room, it can be divided into a variety of geometric patterns with the conifers planted as accent points within this formal scheme. The effect, especially when there is snow or frost on the ground, can be

spectacular. Choose conifers in contrasting colors with an upright habit that will not grow too fast. Among those worth considering are *Chamaecyparis lawsoniana* 'Barry's Silver', green with silvery white tips in summer; *C. thyoides* 'Rubicon', bronze-green in summer turning purple-red in winter; *Juniperus communis* 'Compressa', green; *J.* 'Gold Coast', yellow; *J. c.* 'Hibernica', gray-green, very upright; *Picea glauca* 'Alberta Blue', blue-gray; and *Thuja orientalis* 'Aurea Nana', gold and green.

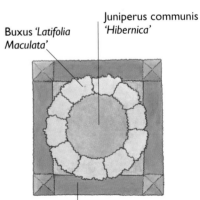

Buxus 'Latifolia Maculata'

Juniperus communis 'Hibernica'

Buxus sempervirens

▲ *Conifers can be positioned in a square container surrounded by an evergreen box hedge, with a contrasting leaved box inside.*

▲ *Picea glauca var. albertiana 'Conica', a variety of the white spruce, has blue-green leaves and a neat shape. It may grown 2–4m/6–12ft high.*

Ornamental grasses and rushes

One way of making a container patio garden unusual is to plant some grasses or rushes in individual pots and then move them around, changing their position throughout the year. This alters the perspective and decoration of the garden and insures that it has continuing interest. In a small space it is best to choose grasses that will not grow too tall, and there are a number to choose from with attractive foliage. Zebra grass, *Miscanthus sinensis* 'Zebrinus', is one. It grows to about 1.2m/4ft and the upright leaves have creamy white bands. It is a perennial and dies back in the winter months. Pheasant-tail grass, *Stipa arundinacea*, is evergreen and turns orange-brown in winter. Since it is not totally hardy and has a tendency to flop down, a raised container is best. For the small garden *Hakonechloa macra* 'Aureola' would be a good choice. It grows to 40cm/16in and the leaves are green, striped with yellow in the summer turning reddish-brown in winter.

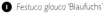

① *Festuca glauca* 'Blaufuchs'
② *Stipa arundinacea*
③ *Miscanthus sinensis* 'Zebrinus'
④ *Hakonechloa macra* 'Aureola'

▼ *Grasses are excellent for displaying in container gardens where their individual colors and forms can be appreciated.*

TALL PLANTS

The principle of planting one fairly tall-growing plant in an individual container can be extended to include flowering plants such as lupins, delphiniums, foxgloves, or hollyhocks, although these perennials will only provide form and color over a relatively short period.

▶ Elymus magellanicus, *wild rye, has intense blue leaves and comes from South America. It is one of the most striking of the grasses.*

bedding plants

Bedding plants are the stand-by of the container garden. Many are annuals, some biennials, and others can be planted out as garden perennials once their flowering season is over. As their name implies, annuals grow, flower, and die within one year. The majority are plants of the summer.

Bedding schemes for the winter and early spring

The stand-by bedding plants for all spring and winter containers are the colored primulas, daisies, and violas that have been bred to produce their brightly colored flowers during the months of winter and early spring. They are best planted in separate containers rather than being grouped together for the varying habits and foliage do not mix very well. They are available in many colors.

Primulas

Winter and early spring-flowering primulas belong to the primula-polyanthus group. Those called polyanthus have longer flower stalks than primulas, and are grown as biennials. The

seed is sown in the summer and the young plants come into flower in late winter and early spring the following year. Unless you are a real enthusiast, and want to raise your own plants from seed, it is best to buy plants from the local nursery when they become available in winter and then plant them out. Many are very brightly colored and the gardener can use them to experiment with schemes of primary colors, in red, yellow, and blue, either planting the colors in sequence or in small blocks. As a general rule these bright colors look best if they are planted singly, one color block succeeding another.

Daisies

When you look at the red, pink, and white balls held aloft on 5cm/2in stalks rather like miniature dahlias, it is difficult to believe that the common daisy found on so many imperfect lawns is the ancestor of such highly developed plants. Those daisies sold as bedding plants have all been bred from the *Bellis perennis* of gardens, and the most common ones are from the Pomponette, Roggli, and Tasso series. They are all reared as biennials, in the same way as the brightly colored primulas, with the seed sown in the summer and the plants flowering early the following spring in full sun or partial shade. As the color range is limited a pleasant design can be created in any

◀ *Heathers, polyanthus, pansies, and the red buttercup make a good arrangement in colors varying from deep red to pale pink.*

▶ *The brilliant yellow-orange flowers of* Primula forrestii *surround the golden-yellow foliage of a small cypress tree.*

circular container with red plants in the center, surrounded by rings of pink and then white flowers. Another very pleasant combination is to fill three similar small containers with each color and place them together.

Violas

Without any shadow of doubt, cultivated varieties (cultivars) of *Viola* x *wittrockiana* are the most valuable plants for any garden with containers, and they surpass all others for winter and early spring bedding schemes. Many kinds of viola have been developed over the years, each with different characteristics, but they all flower for a long period and provide a real winter treat. Winter-flowering violas, bought and planted in mid-fall, will still be flowering in spring and early summer the following year, over six or even nine

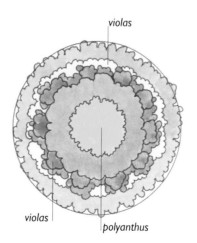

violas

violas

polyanthus

▲ *A diagram of a blue and yellow winter/early spring bedding scheme that can be designed using winter pansies or varieties of polyanthus.*

months later. As with primulas and daisies, violas are usually grown as biennials. They are either single-colored, or have the traditional pansy-type markings in two colors with a darker "face" in the center of the bloom. How they are planted must be a matter of personal choice, but groups of single-colored varieties, either in separate containers or planted together in a large container, are extremely effective. This follows one of the first rules of gardening—plant in blocks of color for the maximum impact. White flowers planted with those of a clear blue enliven the winter months, and this is a simple and most effective planting scheme. It is best to confine violas to containers because in garden beds their bright colors only draw attention to the bare drab stalks of the other plants in winter.

◄ *Petunias and marigolds go well together. Note the green foliage prevents this planting from becoming too garish.*

Pelargoniums, are a must, the trailing forms that hang down over the edge of the container are most useful for hiding a wall, and the scheme should include lobelias, busy lizzies, many pelargoniums, schizanthus, and fuchsias. This gives a bright glorious mixture.

If such a bright scheme is too strong and you prefer quieter colors, you can follow the same idea but concentrate on paler flowers. Mixed sweet pea, *Lathyrus odoratus*, can be grown in containers against a wall, and the wall pots above it can be filled with petunias from one of the softer mixed series, such as Milleflora Fantasy Mixed or Daddy Mixed. Even here a number of white plants, such as the petunia Supercascade White, will help the scheme to work and some of the soft-colored fuchsias can be added.

There are so many summer annuals that a gardener might spend months each winter devising different plantings and color schemes. Annuals are best used in three ways: as fringe plants to frame a border in summer, to fill any gaps, or to fill in a specific area and make a color statement. The best example of the latter is the park bedding schemes that can be seen in many towns and cities in the summer months.

In a container garden they can be used in all ways. If you have a large raised bed, then you can add white or red pelargoniums in summer. White is a good color because it links all the other colors together in the bed.

Red, white, and blue

Individual containers can be used for individual plants and color schemes, and the effect you achieve depends entirely on your choice of plants. Very often you can be too bold. The red, white, and blue effect using violet-blue lobelias, the scarlet *Salvia splendens*, and white pelargoniums can be a bit glaring, especially in a confined space. Leave out the blue or red and the two colors work better together. There are a number of white and red annuals that you can plant, such as reddish-orange mimulus, red and pink busy lizzie, *Impatiens*, red *Amaranthus caudatus*, red and white forms of *Begonia semperflorens*, and white petunias.

Color against a wall

Annuals are ideal for planting in wall pots. Here you should aim for a mass of mixed colors, mainly red and pink, but blue, purple, even orange, shades will not look out of place provided there are sufficient white plants to bind the scheme together. Geraniums,

SUMMER ANNUALS FOR A RIOT OF COLOR

────────

There was once a gardening program on television that featured an elderly couple who planted out over 30,000 annuals each year around their trailer. In high summer they deadheaded and watered them twice every day. The effect was quite wonderful and underlines both the possibilities of annuals, and the importance of removing the dead flowers to encourage the plants to flower again and again. Once a flower has set seed, it thinks its job is done and stops flowering.

◀ *A brilliant display of annuals in high summer, planted to cover a wall. The containers are matched on either side to make a mirror display.*

❶ *Fuchsia* 'Gartenmeister Bonstedt'

❷ *Petunia* 'Lemon Plume'

❸ *Petunia* 'Carpet Mixed'

❹ *Schizanthus* 'Gay Pansies'

❺ *Million Bells* 'Terracotta'

❻ *Impatiens* 'Coral Bells'

❼ *Lobelia* 'Sapphire'

❽ *Tagetes* 'Safari Tangerine'

❾ *Pelargonium* 'Gillian'

Orange annuals for the fall

Orange can be a difficult color to blend with other plants but an individual container of orange, yellow, and lemon marigold, *Tagetes* Marvel Mixed, planted with some nasturtium, *Tropaeolum*, gives a lift to fall days. The leaves of the nasturtium will hang down over the container's edge, and the marigolds can stand in the center.

You can substitute pot marigold, *Calendula officinalis*, for the African marigold, *Tagetes,* and achieve almost the same effect, although the flowers are smaller and less opulent. Add the leaves of both to late summer salads, and the petals of the pot marigold can be used for food coloring.

▶ *Nasturtiums, red geraniums, and the red lily 'Fire King' make a brilliant red and orange corner on a patio in high summer.*

creating an alpine garden

The small size of alpines makes them most suitable for growing in a container as they are neat attractive plants. Their only disadvantage is that so many flower in late spring and early summer, and if you want the bed to be colorful for the remainder of the year you have to choose with care.

Soil and site

The majority of alpines need a sunny open site, preferably facing south or south-west. If you want to create an alpine bed and cannot offer such a position in your garden, you can concentrate on those alpines that come from woodland areas and like moist soil and dappled shade. There are a number of these, and they are best grown in a peat bed. Many gardeners make special raised beds for alpines, and this is most

effective when the bed is constructed from natural stone, with cracks and crevices, in which many alpine plants flourish. If you are building a raised bed from bricks or stone and are using mortar to bind the material together, leave some gaps between the courses that can be filled with soil. Many alpines flourish in these situations.

It is essential that any growing medium should be free draining. The best mix to use is a mixture of two parts good quality loam topsoil (if available), mixed with one part of coarse grit and

one part peat or peat substitute. Add some slow-release fertilizer if you use topsoil. Make sure that there is a good layer of hardcore in the bottom of the container, that there are plenty of drainage holes if you are planning to plant alpines in a trough or window box, and finally, when planted, cover the surface with a 1cm/½in layer of stone chippings or gravel. The chippings not

▼ *Low stone troughs or old sinks are ideal containers for a bed of alpines. These must have free drainage. Check the requirements of the ones you choose: most alpines prefer a sunny open site.*

1. Aubrieta 'Greencourt Purple
2. Saxifraga Moss Varieties Mixed
3. Fritillaria meleagris
4. Geranium dalmaticum
5. Gentiana aucalis
6. Armeria maritima
7. Pulsatilla rubra
8. Campanula carpatica 'Bressingham White'
9. Gypsophila repens 'Dorothy Teacher'

planting an alpine garden

1 Prepare the mix of 2 parts loam to 1 part coarse grit and peat substitute, or buy specialized mix. Space the plants out on the surface of your container.

2 Firm all the plants in position, allow more room than you think between them, and then put as many decorative rocks on the container as you wish.

3 Cover the surface of the container with a mulch of stone chippings. These help to retain the moisture in the soil mix and suppress weeds.

only mulch the plants, retaining moisture during dry periods in the summer, but also help to smother weeds. Even though they are small do not plant alpines too close together. It is surprising how quickly a number of them spread.

Some popular alpines

Stone cress, *Aethionema*—evergreen or semievergreen subshrubs with clumps

of pink flowers from late spring onward. The most common are *A. armenum*, *A. grandiflorum* and *A.* 'Warley Rose'.

Alyssum **and** *Aurinia*—two closely related groups of clump-forming plants with evergreen leaves and yellow or white fragrant flowers. *Alyssum spinosum* has white flowers, and *Aurinia saxatile* yellow.

Rock jasmine, *Androsace*—these plants make dense cushions with single or clustered flowers. *A. lanuginosa* has soft pink flowers, *A. pyrenaica*, white flowers.

Rock cress, *Arabis*—mat- or cushion-forming plants suitable for growing in crevices. *A. caucasica* has white and pale pink flowers. *A. c.* 'Flore Pleno' has pure white double flowers.

Sea thrift, *Armeria maritima*—cushion-forming plants whose pink flowers are familiar to everybody who visits the

seaside. There are a number of species and cultivars in deeper colors.

Aubrieta—this is the favorite plant for all cottage garden walls with evergreen gray-green leaves and violet and purple flowers that hang down in long tresses, which cover the plant throughout the early summer months.

Bellflower, *Campanula*—there are a number of small alpine bellflowers. They include: fairy's thimble, *C. cochleariifolia* with white to lavender flowers; *C. carpatica*, white and blue flowers that spread quickly; and Dalmatian bellflower, *C. portenschlagiana*, that has deep purple flowers in late summer.

New Zealand daisy, *Celmisia*—evergreen with white daisy-like heads with a pronounced yellow center. *C. spectabilis* is particularly striking.

Sowbread, *Cyclamen*—most attractive tuberous-rooted plants, generally with pink or white flowers. Varieties of *C. coum* flower in late winter and early spring. *C. hederifolium*, better known as *C. neapolitanum*, flowers in the fall.

Fleabane or wall daisy, *Erigeron karvinskianus*—small evergreen perennial, often grown down and in walls, with daisy-like flowers that open white and then turn from pink to red.

Fairy foxglove, *Erinus alpinus*—a tufted perennial, evergreen in mild winters, that has a mass of white, pink, or purple flowers. The plants usually self-seed.

Fritillaria—some of the small fritillaries look lovely in an alpine garden when they flower in late spring. The lovely snake's head fritillary, *F. meleagris*, only reaches 30cm/12in in height, while the yellow fritillary, *F. pontica*, is only half this size.

Gentians, *Gentiana*—one of the most popular alpine plants, gentians are grown for their vivid blue, trumpet-shaped flowers. *G. alpina* and *G. aucalis* flower in late spring to early summer, and *G. sino-ornata* flowers in the fall.

Cranesbills, *Geranium*—only the smallest cranesbills qualify as suitable alpine plants. They include the evergreen *G. cinereum* with white or pale pink flowers, *G. c.* ssp. *subcaulescens* with vivid magenta flowers and black centers, and *G. dalmaticum*, usually evergreen, with bright pink flowers.

Alpine gypsophila, *Gypsophila repens*—a spreading, mat-forming plant with white through to rose-pink flowers. The best variety is 'Dorothy Teacher', which has delicate pale pink flowers.

Rock rose, *Helianthemum nummularium*—a dwarf evergreen shrub with bright yellow flowers in summer.

Flax, *Linum*—*Linum arboreum* is a dwarf evergreen shrub with yellow flowers in late spring, and *L. suffruticosum* ssp. *salsoloides* is a cushion-forming perennial with white flowers, with pink or violet veins in summer.

Lithodora diffusa—small evergreen shrub with striking blue flowers in late spring.

Penstemons—*Penstemon* are better known as herbaceous perennials but there are some small mat-forming species that come from alpine regions. They include *P. newberryi* with deep pink flowers in early summer, and rock penstemon, *P. rupicola*, with pale flowers in late spring.

Phlox—there are many small alpine phloxes. They include moss phlox, *P. subulata*, with purple to white flowers in late spring, creeping phlox, *P. stolonifera*,

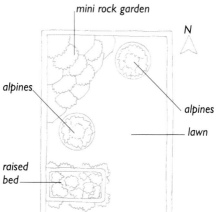

▲ *A complete area of the garden can be devoted to alpines in containers and this can be complemented by a mini rock garden in the sun.*

◄ *The saxifrage is a must for any alpine container gardener. These form springy mats of flowers in white, pink, purple, and yellow.*

▶ Alpines look at their best in a raised trough. The white clouds of Iberis sempervirens contrast with the deep pink of the sea thrift.

with purple flowers in early summer, *P. adsurgens* with pink flowers and *P. douglasii* with mauve to crimson flowers.

Milkwort, *Polygala calcarea*—mat-forming evergreen perennial with trailing stems of bright blue flowers in early summer.

Primrose, *Primula*—ideal plants for a shaded alpine garden because they will not flourish in full sun. There are many colored varieties available.

Pasque flowers, *Pulsatilla*—popular clump-forming flowers whose foliage is among the finest in the alpine garden. The most popular are varieties of *P. vulgaris*, with purple flowers, f. *alba* has pure white flowers with deep yellow centers and *P. rubra* has red-violet flowers.

Rock soapwort, *Saponaria ocymoides*—the epitome of an alpine plant, it carries pale pink flowers from late spring through the summer. The variety 'Alba' has white flowers.

Saxifrage, *Saxifraga*—an important group for the alpine gardener. The majority form compact cushions with flowers ranging from white through to pink, purple, and yellow. Among the most popular are *S. burseriana*, with white flowers, *S. exarata*, with yellow flowers throughout the summer and *S. x irvingii* 'Jenkinsiae', which is dark-centered with pale pink flowers in early spring.

Stonecrop, *Sedum*—small sedums are good succulent plants for the alpine

garden. Golden carpet, *S. acre*, has yellow flowers throughout the summer, *S. sieboldii* has colored leaves and pink flowers, and the variety *S. s.* 'Mediovariegatum' has amazing yellow, blue, and red leaves, and pink flowers.

Houseleek, *Sempervivum*—large group of succulent plants notable for their extraordinary rosettes of leaves topped with pink flowers in summer. The most

spectacular are cobweb houseleek, *S. arachnoidum*, and common houseleek, *S. tectorum*, hens and chicks, with red leaves.

Prostrate speedwell, *Veronica prostrata*—mat-forming perennial with blue flowers and a number of good varieties.

▼ A diagrammatic plan of an alpine garden with a color scheme that could be achieved by several different plants.

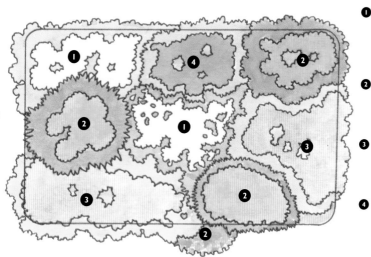

❶ White
Alyssum spinosum
Androsace pyrenaica
Campanula carpatica
'Bressingham White'

❷ Pink
Aethionema 'Warley Rose'
Geranium dalmaticum
Saponaria ocymoides

❸ Lavender/Purple
Aubrieta
Phlox stolonifera
Pulsatilla vulgaris

❹ Blue
Campanula
cochleariifolia
Lithodora diffusa

water gardens and features

Water is one of the most attractive features in any garden, and running water can create a great sense of peace. In fact there are more opportunities to make a water container garden than you might think, and with some imagination wonderful effects can be contrived.

◄ *A miniature water garden in a container adds interest in any garden. Choose plants carefully and check the depth of water they prefer.*

The complete water garden

A patio garden can be transformed into a cool oasis if you build a central bed in the middle of the garden but, instead of filling it with hardcore and soil, add a liner and then turn it into a raised pond. The best design has troughs running around the edges of the pond under water that can be filled with earth and then planted with marginal aquatic plants, or shelves for planting on. Always let the water settle for several days after filling the pool because this will give any sediment time to sink to the bottom.

To make such a pond you must excavate the area. Line it with thick plastic sheeting then lay concrete over wire mesh for the floor, and do the same for the walls putting shuttering in place to hold the wet concrete in position. If you do not feel that you have the necessary expertise to construct such a pond this can always be done by a

creating a water garden

1 Fill up any drainage holes in the container and insure it is watertight. Silicon plugs are available that can be held in place with waterproof cement.

2 Choose the plants you wish from a specialist supplier and check the depth they prefer. Put bricks in the bottom to raise the level of each plant.

3 Fill the container with water and make sure there is a good gravel mulch around each plant. This stops soil leaking and sinks the plant.

professional. If you match the materials used for the patio floor with the surrounds of the pool then the whole design looks infinitely more harmonious. Do allow ample wall space around the pond, which can be used for seating, and in the summer guests can sit and gaze at the water and the plants.

Introducing fish If there is sufficient water you can even include a goldfish or two, assuming you are not troubled by herons. And if you plan to have some fish in your pond make sure that the pond is well established, that there are plenty of oxygenating plants, and that the fish are introduced gradually. If you have bought them in a plastic bag filled with water and oxygen, float this on the surface of the pool until the temperatures are even

and then introduce some of the pond water little by little. Never put fish directly into pond water and never renew the water all at one time. Leave any pump switched on overnight to help to oxygenate the water.

Water features

Fountains in a small container garden might be too much to ask for but water spouts can be included in almost all small gardens and miniature fountains can be contrived by small pumps placed in the center of any garden pond. These can be set at various heights. In any garden with a wall a water spout can be inserted in the wall and then connected up to a pump. Get a professional to connect the electrics for you unless you know exactly what you are doing. The water will

tumble down into a trough from which it is then recirculated. Such a feature can be flanked by matching containers of foliage plants such as hostas, or one of the delicate grasses, such as Bowles' golden sedge, *Carex elata* 'Aurea'.

Even if you cannot install a waterspout you can make the smallest water garden by filling a waterproof tub or tin bath with water and planting it with some floating aquatics or miniature waterlilies. Paint the inside of any container of this type with a suitable sealant, because the metal may be harmful to the plants.

All waterlilies need some depth of water in order to grow properly. Check the depth of water in your pond to make sure it is suitable and the requirements of each plant before buying and planting.

plants for a water garden

Plants for a pond can be divided into four main groups—marginal plants, plants that will grow in shallow water, deep-water plants such as waterlilies, which require a considerable depth of water if they are to flourish, oxygenating plants, and floating aquatics that exist floating on the surface.

Deep-water plants

The pride of all aquatic plants is the waterlily. Small waterlilies require a water depth of 30–45cm/12–18in, large ones, 45–60cm/18–24in. Young plants should be planted in containers using special aquatic soil or garden soil provided it does not contain any fertilizer. Plant the new root in a planting basket or an ordinary container, with the tip of the rhizome at surface level. Cover the soil with washed pea gravel and then sink the container in the pool. The container should start off in shallower water and gradually be lowered into deeper water as the plant becomes established. Anyone wanting to grow waterlilies should visit a specialist nursery and choose one of the many hybrids available in a number of colors, white, yellow, red, and pink. Another possible deep-water plant is Cape pondweed, *Aponogeton distachyos*, but it is not as spectacular as the waterlily either in leaf or flower.

Oxygenating plants Oxygenating plants are essential to any pool, particularly if you are planning to keep fish. They compete with algae for the dissolved nutrients in the water and eventually starve the algae to death. The best known are water thyme, *Lagarosiphon crispa*, still known as *Elodea crispa*, which looks rather like a lot of curled snakes; milfoil, *Myriophyllum aquaticum*; and curled pondweed, *Potamogeton crispus*, the best oxygenator for polluted water.

◀ *An old zinc bath makes a good water feature surrounded by ferns. A number of water plants only flourish in standing water.*

► *A water feature surrounded by giant cowslips, hostas, and knautia. The sleeping nymph lies unawakened beneath a cover of lichen.*

Floating aquatics They also help to reduce algae in a pool but they do so by cutting down the amount of light that penetrates the water surface. Most of them spread fairly rapidly and need to be controlled. They include fairy moss, *Azolla filiculoides*; frogbit, *Hydrocharis morsus-ranae*, which has attractive white flowers; and water chestnut, *Trapa natans*, which has very pretty leaves and white flowers during the summer.

Marginal plants

This is the largest group of plants suitable for a pond or water garden, and the number and type you grow depends on the size of your pond and the depth of the marginal shelf around the edge. Some marginals grow in fairly shallow water, up to 15cm/6in deep, while others require twice this depth of water to flourish. Be warned, a number of the best known are extremely vigorous and need to be carefully controlled if they are not to take over the pond completely.

Shallow marginal plants include kingcup or marsh marigold, *Caltha palustris* var. *alba*, with white flowers, while 'Flore Pleno' has double yellow flowers and is less vigorous than the species; *Houttuynia cordata*, with attractive blotched leaves with red margins; *Iris laevigata*, blue flowers in summer (many varieties to choose from); water mint, *Mentha aquatica*, with lilac flowers in

summer; water forget-me-not, *Myosotis scorpioides*, with bright blue flowers in early summer; and the small bulrush, *Typha minima*, but do not plant the common bulrush *T. latifolia* in a small space.

Deep-water marginals include the water plantain, *Alisma plantago-aquatica*, with attractive foliage and very small white flowers; water violet, *Hottonia palustris*, with violet, lilac, or white flowers in spring; pickerel weed, *Pontederia cordata*, with blue flowers in late summer; and possibly the spectacular arum lily, *Zantedeschia aethiopica*.

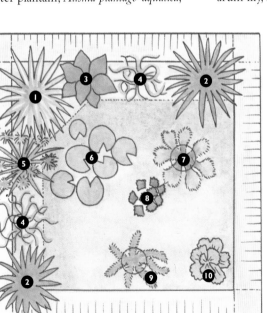

◄ *A grouping of aquatic plants around a garden pool, with a ledge running round the side for marginal plants.*

1 *Typha minima*
2 *Iris laevigata*
3 *Caltha palustris* 'Flore Pleno'
4 *Lagarosiphon crispa*
5 *Houttuynia cordata*
6 *Nymphaea* 'Indiana'
7 *Hydrocharis morsus-ranae*
8 *Azolla filiculoides*
9 *Myriophyllum aquatica*
10 *Trapa natans*

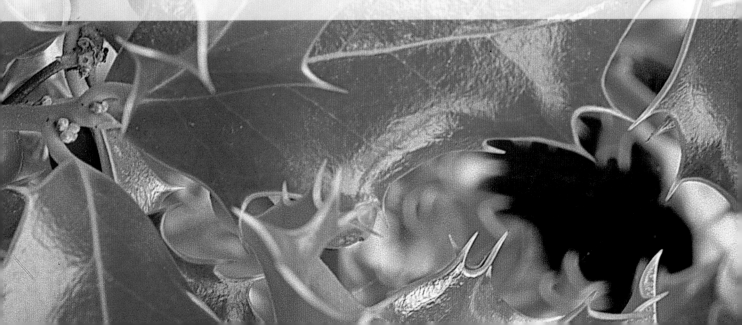

Seasonal ideas

The best gardens provide interest for twelve months of the year. In the summer, gardens are full of color with bedding plants, roses in bloom, and many perennials in flower. The colors of the fall are gold and orange, while the spring provides the bright yellow and blue of daffodils and bluebells. Winter, too, has its attractions, and with a little planning any container garden can provide color and variety, even in the bleakest months of the year.

a container garden in winter

Many plants are suitable for a container garden in winter: evergreens, shrubs with berries, winter-flowering shrubs, early spring bulbs, and most importantly, winter-flowering annuals or biennials. It is best to confine them to one or two containers, leaving room for the plants of spring and summer.

Evergreens for the winter garden—conifers

The most popular, and most suitable, evergreen trees for containers are conifers. They offer a choice of colors,

▲ *Conifers are among the best plants for the winter. There are yellow, blue, and green varieties, and many change color throughout the year.*

blue-gray, green, and yellow-green, and many are dwarf, only reaching a height of 1.8m/6ft or less over a period of years. However, if you are particularly fond of the coloring of other conifers, it is worth checking on their growth rate with a reputable conifer nursery. While many are scheduled to reach a height of 12–15m/40–50ft in optimum conditions in open gardens, they can grow very slowly and will only reach 3m/10ft after 10 years. If they grow too large too fast, then they can always be removed. This applies to the lovely blue conifers *Picea pungens* 'Koster' and *Chamaecyparis lawsoniana* 'Pembury Blue', both popular choices in a number of gardens. Playing safe, the following dwarf conifers are worth considering: Upright conical trees—*Juniperus communis* 'Compressa', green; *J. c.* 'Gold Cone', and 'Golden Showers', golden yellow; and *J. c.* 'Hibernica', gray-green. Low-growing spreading trees—*J. x media* 'Golden Saucer', yellow; *J. x m.* 'Pfitzeriana', green; and *J. horizontalis* 'Douglasii', blue-gray.

Rounded conical trees—*Chamaecyparis lawsoniana* 'Barry's Silver', silver-gray; *C. l.* 'Minima', green; *Taxus baccata* 'Aurea', and *Thuja occidentalis* 'Rheingold', both golden yellow.

Evergreen and winter-flowering shrubs

There are a number of these, including: *Camellia japonica* and *C.* x *williamsii* hybrids. Attractive evergreen small trees or shrubs, camellias have glossy evergreen leaves and gorgeous multipetaled flowers, generally red, pink, or white. They are slow growing, and can be pruned back quite hard when they threaten to outgrow their space (you do lose some flowers). They need at least semishade and acid soil to flourish. Pink camellias include 'Akashigata' ('Lady Clare'), 'Brigadoon', 'Helen's Ballerina', 'Ave Maria', 'Lady Loch', 'Lasca Beauty', and 'Spring Festival'. White varieties include 'Lovelight', 'Janet Waterhouse', 'White Nun', and 'Charlie Bettes'. And red ones include 'Adolphe Audusson' and 'R. L. Wheeler'.

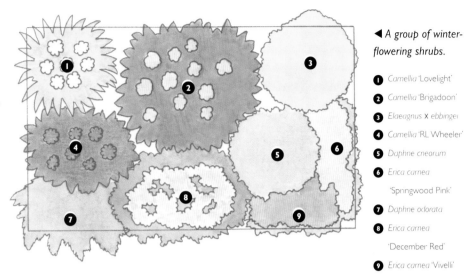

◀ *A group of winter-flowering shrubs.*

1. *Camellia* 'Lovelight'
2. *Camellia* 'Brigadoon'
3. *Elaeagnus* x *ebbingei*
4. *Camellia* 'RL Wheeler'
5. *Daphne cneorum*
6. *Erica carnea* 'Springwood Pink'
7. *Daphne odorata*
8. *Erica carnea* 'December Red'
9. *Erica carnea* 'Vivelli'

Daphne: this is a group of deciduous and evergreen shrubs that are noted for their heavily scented flowers. The following are worth considering—*Daphne cneorum*, evergreen with rose-pink flowers in late spring; *D. mezereum*, deciduous, with heavily scented pink to purple flowers in late winter and early spring; and *D. odora*, evergreen, with very fragrant flowers in winter and early spring but it is not fully hardy.

Elaeagnus x *ebbingei* and its cultivars are evergreen and grown for their yellow and green-splashed leaves. They have small white, rather insignificant flowers in the fall. Eventually they will grow too large for a container garden and have to be replaced, although this will take some time.

Erica carnea and *E.* x *darleyensis*. The winter-flowering heathers are great stand-bys for the winter container gardener. They prefer acid soil, although there are some varieties that tolerate alkaline soil provided it is not too limy. The colors range from white through pink to a deep purple-pink. The varieties *E. c.* 'Springwood Pink' and 'Springwood White' both trail and are suitable for covering the fronts of window boxes.

Firethorns, *Pyracantha*, make excellent evergreen wall shrubs whose only disadvantage is the long spikes that grow on the branches. Their chief glory is the berries, red, orange, and yellow,

▶ *Some dwarf conifers are very small indeed and grow remarkably slowly. They are suitable for small containers.*

according to the variety grown, that stay on the plants throughout the winter. In the spring they carry white flowers.

Skimmia japonica is another evergreen shrub, and the variety 'Bowles' Dwarf' is

small and compact (male and female plants are needed to produce flowers and fruit). 'Rubella' is a compact male clone. Skimmias have bright red berries that last throughout the winter.

◄ Helleborus lividus *has beautiful green flowers early in the year. All hellebores are poisonous and should be handled with care.*

Clematis cirrhosa is an evergreen climber with green leaves, bronze underneath. Small cup-shaped cream flowers appear in late winter and early spring. The variety *balearica* has fragrant cream flowers with red speckles inside, and 'Freckles' has creamy pink flowers that are similarly heavily speckled.

Ivy, *Hedera*, creates a permanent background in a container garden, and the best ivies to grow are varieties of Canary Island ivy, *H. canariensis*, although they may suffer in hard winters, or common ivy, *H. helix*; *H. c.* 'Gloire de Marengo' has gold-splashed leaves, *H. h.* 'Anne Marie' has leaves with white margins, and *H. h.* 'Atropurpurea' has bronzy leaves. Many other varieties are available in varying shades of green.

Winter jasmine, *Jasminum nudiflorum*, is an excellent wall shrub that does not climb, cling, or twine and therefore needs to be tied in. It is grown for the long pendent green shoots and the bright yellow flowers that appear before the leaves in late winter and early spring. Cut out dead wood, and shorten flowering shoots by a third after flowering.

Winter flowering plants

The Christmas rose, *Helleborus niger*, and the Lenten rose, *H. orientalis*, are both slightly misnamed because they seldom appear exactly when the name suggests. Putting that quibble aside, they are wonderful winter plants with bold clumps of flowers, white, pink, creamy yellow, or green, according to the kind

being grown, and the flowers are often marked with spots and veins on the inside. They like a degree of shade and some, such as stinking hellebore, *H. foetidus*, will flourish in deep shade.

Iris unguicularis is the winter-flowering rhizomatous iris that produces blue-purple flowers on short stalks early in the year. The sedge-like leaves are evergreen. It is a good plant for a single container because otherwise it spreads too freely. After 3–5 years split and replant the rhizomes, discarding the portions from the center.

Early bulbs

Early snowdrop, *Galanthus* spp., will flower at the beginning of the New Year, with the main flowering period being the following month. (In the northern hemisphere their common name used to be Fair Maids of February.) Lovely as

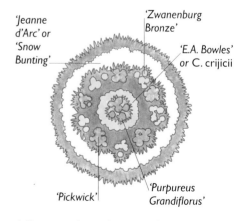

'Jeanne d'Arc' or 'Snow Bunting'

'Zwanenburg Bronze'

'E.A. Bowles' or C. crijicii

'Pickwick'

'Purpureus Grandiflorus'

▲ *You can make a color wheel of crocuses, varying the colors according to your taste. Plant them thickly for maximum impact.*

▶ *A grouping of climbers and containers that will give flowers in the early part of the year. Winter jasmine flowers on bare branches and needs to be pruned after flowering.*

❶ *Clematis cirrhosa* 'Freckles'

❷ *Jasminum nudiflorum*

❸ *Hellebore argutifolius*

❹ *Crocus* 'Queen of the Blues'

❺ *Iris unguicularis*

❻ *Hedera helix* 'Anne Marie'

❼ *Crocus vernus*

they are it is doubtful whether they are really suitable for a container garden because they should have been planted when they were in leaf the previous year, and then left through the summer for the leaves to die down until they spring to life again in the middle of winter. If you want to grow snowdrops, plant them quite deeply in a container with small groups of crocus bulbs.

Crocuses are much easier than snowdrops, and can be planted early in the fall to flower the following spring. Some of the best are varieties of Dutch crocus, *C. vernus*. Look out for 'Pickwick', lilac-striped; 'Jeanne d'Arc', white and purple; 'Vanguard', pale lilac; and *C. chrysanthus* hybrids such as 'E.A. Bowles', gold and bronze; 'Snow

Bunting', white; and 'Gipsy Girl', yellow and purple. There are many available.

Winter aconite, *Eranthis hyemalis*, is a tuberous perennial that will make large clumps in alkaline soil, so do not grow it in any container with acid soil mix. The yellow flowers open just after the first snowdrops, and when they flower together they make a lovely picture, signifying the approach of spring.

Finally, there are the winter annuals. The best flowers are provided by a number of the winter-flowering primulas that appear in so many bright colors, and the winter-flowering pansy, *Viola* x *wittrockiana*. Every garden should have some containers planted with them because they flower from early fall right through the winter into the spring.

▼ *A number of the smaller irises make excellent plants in a container in early spring. This vigorous variety is I. histrioides 'Major' with beautiful deep-blue flowers.*

spring

Spring is one of the loveliest times of the year in the garden but the container gardener needs to plan carefully. Space is often limited and containers that will be filled with summer annuals or vegetables need to be empty and prepared to receive the summer plants.

Spring-flowering bulbs

Most people associate spring with bulbs. Daffodils and narcissus are everybody's favorite but there are many other bulbs that are suitable for the container garden. They include tulips, scillas, grape hyacinth, *Muscari*, hyacinth, *Hyacinthus*, glory-of-the-snow, *Chionodoxa*, and dog-toothed violet, *Erythronium*. With a little trouble you can create a considerable display of spring bulbs in a small container by taking advantage of the differing sizes of the bulbs. The container needs to have been planted early in the fall the previous year, and planned with care. Plant the largest bulbs, the daffodils, at the bottom, and then plant other bulbs in layers with the smallest at the top. All bulbs should be covered at least two and a half times their height with soil. The large bulbs will grow between the smaller ones, and the container will

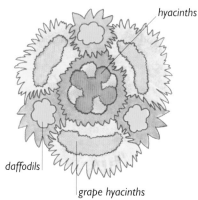

hyacinths

daffodils

grape hyacinths

▲ *An arrangement of primary colors for late spring. This type of selection can be brightened by adding white and orange narcissi.*

◀ *The deep, deep purple of these 'Black Swan' tulips recalls the tulipomania of the 18th century. 'Queen of the Night' is also deep purple.*

◀ Narcissus 'Tête-à-Tête' is a popular bulb for containers and makes a good display indoors. Plant in the fall for early spring flowering.

although not all are suitable for growing in containers, a number are. Plan carefully because much depends on how much room is available, and what you intend growing in the summer.

Some of the best flowering shrubs are those that flower early in the year, notably camellias and pieris. They both require acid soil with camellias needing partial shade, and pieris full sun or partial shade. The attraction of pieris is the new red leaves and bunches of white flowers. The most commonly grown are varieties of *Pieris japonica*. Both pieris and camellias grow slowly enough to be included in a container garden.

Another lovely spring-flowering shrub that does not grow too quickly is the pearl bush, *Exochorda* x *macrantha* 'The Bride'. It prefers neutral or slightly acid soil, and has waterfalls of white flowers that hang from the branches.

produce a succession of flowers. It may be difficult to plan for them all to flower together. There are many varieties of daffodils and tulips, all with different flowering periods. Broadly speaking the daffodils flower before the tulips, the scillas and chionodoxa flower at roughly the same time, just after the crocuses and before the daffodils, while grape hyacinths, hyacinths, and dog-toothed violets flower a few weeks later.

Spring-flowering shrubs

When confronted with the question "What should I plant to flower in spring?," many a gardener finds it difficult to come up with anything beyond spring bulbs and forsythia. However, there are many shrubs that flower in spring and

❶ *Scilla siberica*

❷ *Muscari armeniaca*

❸ *Chionodoxa luciliae*

❹ *Narcissus*

❺ *Hyacinthus* 'Pink Pearl', 'Innocence'

❻ *Tulip kaufmanniana*

❼ *Erythronium* 'Pagoda'

❽ *Erythronium revolutum*

▶ Containers of spring bulbs that will come into flower one after another. They can include tulips, grape hyacinths, and daffodils.

◄ Clematis macropetala 'Jan Lindmark' has more purple flowers than the species plant. The single flowers appear early in the year.

There are many rhododendrons (some scented) that can be grown in containers that flower in late spring and early summer. Again, they need acid soil. Suitable small varieties include 'Blue Diamond', violet-blue; *R. calostratum*, rose-pink; 'Cilpinense', pale pink; 'Doc', rose-pink; 'Greeting', orange-red; *R. kiusianum*, pink to purple; 'Moerheim', violet-blue; 'Patty Bee', lemon-yellow; 'Kure-no-yuki', pure white; and 'Vida Brown', rose-pink.

Other good shrubs for the spring include *Spiraea japonica* 'Goldflame', bronze-red young leaves, and some of the viburnums. Eventually most viburnums grow too large for a normal container garden, but the lovely *V. plicatum* 'Mariesii' does not gallop away, and *V. p.* 'Roseumi' is a reasonably compact example with leaves that turn dark red before the fall.

Early-flowering clematis

The most popular spring-flowering climber is the clematis. *C. armandii* is evergreen with heavily scented white flowers in early spring, but it is not totally hardy and is extremely vigorous. You do need plenty of room to grow it. A better choice for the container gardener would be one of the *alpina* and *macropetala* varieties that flower from mid-spring into early summer. They are totally hardy, although they will not tolerate wet soil. They are quite small, usually only reaching 3m/10ft in height and are exactly right for growing in containers. They should be pruned lightly when flowering is over in midsummer, and only cut back hard if they have outgrown their allotted space. Alpinas have single bell-shaped flowers and include 'Frances Rivis', lantern-like mid-blue flowers; 'Pink Flamingo', pale

pink; 'Ruby', red with white stamens; and 'White Columbine', white. *Macropetala* varieties are very similar to *alpina*s but look as if they have double flowers because they have inner stamens shaped like petals. The best known include 'Blue Bird', 'Markham's Pink', 'Rosy O'Grady', and 'White Swan'.

The fruit blossom of spring

In Japan they have a festival of spring, devoted to the blossom of the cherry tree. There are few container gardens with the room to grow individual ornamental cherry trees, and even the upright *Prunus* 'Amanogawa' will eventually grow too tall and large, but fruit trees trained against a wall or fence are possible. The blossom they carry in

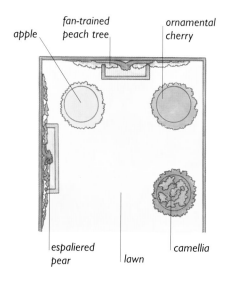

▲ A small garden can take fruit trees in containers, as shown in this plan. Make sure there is plenty of room for growth.

▶ *Small fruit trees can produce surprisingly good crops when grown in containers. They should be fan-trained, espaliered, or minarette.*

spring is one of the real bonuses. The earliest fruit trees to flower are the peach and apricots, followed by pears, then apples. Peach and apricot flower on bare branches early in spring before the leaves appear. The flowers are single, pink or red, and it is essential to protect them whenever any late frost threatens. Pears have clusters of white flowers just as the trees are starting to come into leaf. The blossom arrives earlier than on the apple trees and covers the trees with white flowers. Plums have white blossom about the same time as the pear trees, that also emerges just as the trees are starting to come into leaf. It is not so spectacular as pear blossom.

Apples have probably the loveliest blossom of all, and it is something that no keen gardener should be without. The pink-tinged white flowers open from pink buds later in the spring. Some of the crabapple varieties have blossom in many colors, which range from pure white to deep rose-pink.

Spring-flowering perennials

There are not all that many perennials that flower in spring, and the container gardener with only a small amount of space is, perhaps, better to concentrate

▶ *Apple blossom is probably the loveliest of all with its pink-edged petals. You need at least two varieties of apple trees for pollination.*

on spring bulbs, which are reliable and always lovely to look at. If you have got room though, probably the best spring perennial is lungwort, *Pulmonaria*. There are different kinds (many with spotted leaves), which look a bit like the inside of the lung, hence their name. They are one of the sights of spring and have erect sprays of pink, white, red, blue, and purple flowers that last for several weeks. They prefer shade and will spread quite freely, providing good cover.

summer

Summertime is when gardens look at their best. The trees are in new leaf and many plants are in flower. The favorite garden flowers for containers in summer are the summer annuals. But for any gardener who wants to be different there is a multitude of choices, some unusual, some well known.

Summer-flowering bulbs

When people think of bulbs they inevitably think of spring bulbs but there are many that flower in summer. They should not be ignored because they are quite easy to grow, and many are ideal in containers. They include Peruvian lilies, *Alstroemeria* Ligtu Hybrids, in a multitude of pastel shades in late summer; *Galtonia candicans* and *G. viridiflora*, with white lily-like flowers that need some protection in hard winters; *Gladiolus*, extremely popular corms, available in

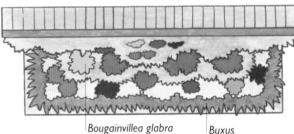

Bougainvillea glabra 'Variegata' *Buxus sempervirens*

◄ *Climbers and shrubs in shades of red, pink, and purple can be grouped in a sunny sheltered position. Add some white flowers to highlight the colors.*

many sizes and colors; Jacobean lily, *Sprekelia formosissima*, with beautiful red flowers in early summer, but needing a warm south wall and winter protection; and the peacock flower, *Tigridia pavonia*, a most exotic looking flower rather like an orchid with an inner spotted face—the flowers range in color from yellow through orange to red.

Lilies

Lilies are a huge genus with over 100 species and countless hybrids. There are six divisions. They need to be staked in advance so that the stems of the plants

◄ *Lilium 'Sun Ray' is quite a small lily with bright yellow flowers, lightly dotted with brown. Although a good container plant, it is not scented.*

are held upright as they grow. Otherwise they will flop over. Grown in a container the bulbs should be planted in deep pots in fertile soil mix made up with equal parts of loam, peat substitute, and leaf mold, and the addition of some well-rotted manure or slow-release fertilizer. Cover the bulbs with at least 7.5cm/3in of soil. Among the best are the Asiatic Mixed hybrids, smaller than the trumpet lilies, but very suitable for a large container, and the showy trumpet lilies. The latter includes *L. speciosum* var. *rubrum* with pink flowers and red spots, regal lily, *L. regale*, with wonderfully scented white inner flowers, striped purple-violet on the outside, and *L. r.* var. *album* with almost pure white flowers. There are also yellow or orange ones.

planting summer bulbs

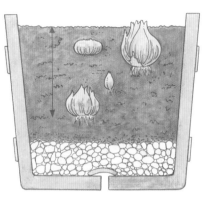

1 It is easiest to plant the bulbs and fill the container at the same time. As a general rule, plant bulbs deeply, at least 2½ times the height of the bulb.

2 In a raised bed or open ground a bulb planter is a helpful tool. Most have various depths marked on the sides and are hinged so you can remove the soil.

3 Some bulbs have to be planted just below or on the surface. These include amaryllis and hyacinths grown in containers for flowering indoors.

Summer-flowering shrubs and climbers

The temptation to rely on annuals entirely in the summer garden should be resisted. All gardens look better for varied planting, with shrubs and climbers adding color at different height levels.

Climbers that flower in summer include the coral plant, *Berberidopsis corallina*, that needs shade, acid soil, and protection in hard winters. It is evergreen and carries dark red ball-like flowers on long stalks that hang down the length of the branches. *Bougainvillea glabra* is a strong-growing evergreen climber that can be grown in containers, provided

that it is pruned hard to keep it within bounds. It is suitable for gardens free of winter frost. The flowers are normally brilliant shades of purple and red.

Summer is also a good time for the large-flowered clematis. They can be

trained along a trellis and up a wall. The most attractive are 'Comtesse de Bouchaud', pink; 'Jackmanii Superba', violet; 'Henryi', creamy white; 'Marie Boisselot', white; 'Lasurstern', lavender-blue; and 'Nelly Moser', pinkish-mauve.

▶ *Bougainvillea grows quite happily in containers provided it is kept free from frost and placed in a warm sunny position.*

◄ Summer jasmine is an attractive climber, semievergreen in mild climates, with scented white flowers in summer. It needs controlling.

Like the climbing hydrangea which it resembles, *Schizophragma hydrangeoides* clings by aerial roots. It has fragrant, tiny white flowers in summer that are surrounded by creamy white bracts. The effect is quite striking and it looks good against a colored plain background. It needs a bit of space and in a container garden is most suited to a permanent bed against a wall. Plant 60cm/2ft away from the bricks, and tie the plant to a support until it becomes established.

The Confederate jasmine, *Trachelospermum jasminoides*, is another evergreen climber that grows in partial shade, and does best in neutral to slightly acid soil. The leaves turn bronze-red in winter. It is not fully hardy and does not tolerate strong winds. The flowers appear in mid to late summer and are pure white with five flat petals, rather like a miniature catherine wheel.

Flame creeper, *Tropaeolum speciosum*, is another unusual climber but it can be maddeningly difficult to get established, and may need shelter in hard winters. It requires a deep container, neutral to acid soil, and the roots need to be cool at all times but with the flowers in the sun. Once established it will scramble up other plants or a trellis and has trails of brilliant, bright red flowers from midsummer onward. It looks at its best when it is allowed to peep out prettily through a wall shrub.

Flowering shrubs for the summer garden

There are a number that can be considered. Flowering maple, *Abutilon*, is frequently trained against a south-facing wall because it needs sun and warmth. 'Boule de Neige' is evergreen with bell-shaped white flowers from spring through the summer, *A.* x *suntense* is deciduous with violet-blue flowers, 'Gorer's White' has white flowers, and *A. vitifolium* 'Veronica Tennant' has pink to mauve flowers.

Pineapple broom, *Cytisus battandieri*, is another shrub usually grown against a south-facing wall because it needs sun and warmth. In late summer it carries large clusters of fragrant bright yellow flowers that look a bit like miniature pineapples and have a pineapple scent. *Deutzia* is one of the more unusual shrubs that carries fragrant white to pink flowers in clusters from the middle of spring through to midsummer. Two of the best kinds are *D.* x *elegantissima* 'Rosealind' with pink flowers and the pink *D.* 'Mont Rose' with violet-streaked petals. Both can be accommodated in a medium-sized container.

The flannel bush, *Fremontodendron* 'California Glory', is another evergreen wall shrub that should be trained against a south-facing wall. It will usually tolerate occasional low temperatures. It has beautiful large yellow flowers throughout the summer from late spring onwards. *Hebe* is a large genus of evergreen shrubs, many of which have spikes of blue, white, pink, and lilac

▶ *Hostas come in a wide variety of leaf colors, yellow to smoky blue, with pale white to violet flowers held on spikes in summer.*

flowers, although there is a great variety of flower color and form. Some make large shrubs, and other species, such as *H. cupressoides* 'Boughton Dome', are suitable for growing in alpine gardens. Two smallish popular shrubs suitable for containers are *H.* 'Bowles Hybrid' that has lavender-blue flowers and *H. pinguifolia* 'Pagei', pure white.

Summer perennials There is a great tendency to ignore perennials in a summer container garden. This should be resisted as they can be very attractive and are good for filling bare spaces. They are best used in two ways. If you have the room you can make a careful plan to create a small herbaceous border using specially bred miniature varieties of common herbaceous flowering plants, such as lupins, hollyhocks, and delphiniums; some of the smaller varieties of hardy geraniums, phlox, penstemons, pinks, or scabious are also suitable for such a plan.

The second approach that can be extremely effective, and is better where room is constricted, is to choose some of your favourite perennials and plant them in individual containers where they can be grouped with other plants. Hostas are ideal, as are some of the lower-growing plants, such as the pincushion flower, *Scabiosa caucasica*, or the blue balloon flower, *Platycodon grandiflorus* 'Mariesii'.

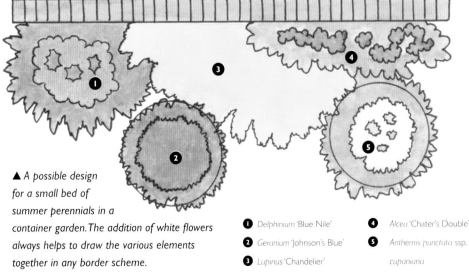

▲ *A possible design for a small bed of summer perennials in a container garden. The addition of white flowers always helps to draw the various elements together in any border scheme.*

❶ *Delphinium* 'Blue Nile'
❷ *Geranium* 'Johnson's Blue'
❸ *Lupinus* 'Chandelier'
❹ *Alcea* 'Chater's Double'
❺ *Anthemis punctata* ssp. *cupaniana*

fall

For many people, fall is the loveliest time of the year. The season is over, the crops have ripened, the leaves on the trees turn yellow and gold and then fall to the ground, slowly at first but with increasing speed as the first frosts or equinoctial gales shorten their lives.

The importance of fall color

Fall color does not last for ever and depends very much on the weather, rain or sun, frost or warm wet winds, but it is something to be treasured and every garden, however big or small, should contain some plants that look their best at this time of year. Among the most popular are the Japanese maples, varieties of *Acer palmatum*, that are generally slow growing, making mounded shrubs, although eventually they become too big for the average container. They have mid-green leaves in the summer, but in the fall these change to varied shades of orange, yellow, red, and gold.

The varieties 'Burgundy Lace', 'Butterfly', 'Garnet,' and 'Red Pygmy' are all good and widely available. They prefer sun or partial shade and slightly acid soil.

Another shrub that does not grow too quickly and that provides sensational fall color is *Fothergilla major*. It prefers neutral to acid soil and has small, white, bottlebrush flowers in late spring and early summer. In the fall the leaves turn from yellow through orange to red, blue, and black before falling. They stand out like the brightest flower in the garden in high summer.

Fall berries

Many of the best berries are much appreciated by birds and squirrels, and do not remain long on the trees. Rowan berries, for example, hardly last any time at all. Small crabapples are not so popular and can be grown for their bright red and yellow fruit, as well as the

◀ *The brilliant red berries and bronze leaves of cotoneaster 'Cornubia' are spectacular in the fall. It is a large shrub and needs space.*

lovely apple blossom in spring. They are good for a container garden, provided there is room to grow them as pyramids —*Malus* 'John Downie' has red fruit, and 'Golden Dream' bright yellow. Both have the advantage of being self-fertile, and if they are grafted on to a dwarfing rootstock they will not grow too large.

Snowberry, *Symphoricarpos* x *doorenbosii*, is another possibility. Grow it on its own in a container because it has a suckering habit and spreads too freely if unconfined. The fall berries are slightly poisonous to humans and are not appreciated by birds so they may remain on the bushes for many months during the winter. The best-known varieties are 'White Hedge' with clusters of white berries, and 'Mother of Pearl', which has pinkish colored berries.

Firethorn, *Pyracantha*, is well-known for its clusters of berries, as is hawthorn,

Crataegus. Hawthorns are too large for a container garden, but smaller shrubs include shallon, *Gaultheria shallon*, and varieties of *G. mucronata*. Like the

snowberry, they are suckering shrubs and need to be confined in a single container. They were formerly known as *pernettya* and must be grown in acid soil. They have prominent round berries in colors ranging from white to magenta, depending on the variety grown.

The other excellent shrub for fall and winter color is *Skimmia japonica*. The many forms have bright red berries and small varieties fit well into window boxes where they brighten the winter months. The only drawback if you wish to grow them as permanent shrubs in a container garden, is that both male and female plants are necessary if they are to flower and bear fruit.

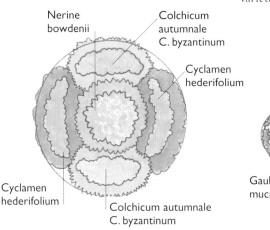

Nerine bowdenii
Colchicum autumnale C. byzantinum
Cyclamen hederifolium
Cyclamen hederifolium
Colchicum autumnale C. byzantinum

▲ Fall bulbs are at their best either growing in drifts in grassland or, in the case of nerines, given the shelter of a warm wall.

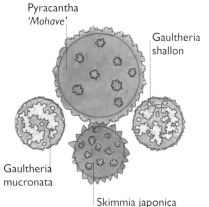

Pyracantha 'Mohave'
Gaultheria shallon
Gaultheria mucronata
Skimmia japonica

▲ Always consider whether any shrub in the garden has colored berries in fall. This is a bonus for birds as well as gardeners.

The most spectacular climber of the fall is Virginia creeper. The best one to grow is Boston ivy, *Parthenocissus tricuspidata* and its varieties. The true Virginia creeper is *P. quinquefolia*, that used to be known by the charming Latin name of *Vitis inconstans*; this provides a brief show of fall glory before the leaves drop. A number of the oriental vines also provide brilliant color, *Vitis coignetiae* and *V. vinifera* 'Purpurea' are the two most commonly grown. Golden hop, *Humulus lupulus* 'Aureus', is another climber whose leaves turn golden yellow in the fall. One climber that gives fall flowers and color is the small-flowered *Clematis tangutica* and its varieties that have nodding yellow flowers, followed by attractive silver seedheads.

Fall bulbs

Fall bulbs are dominated by the fall crocus, *Colchicum*, that flowers from late summer through the fall into winter, depending on the species grown. The most common is meadow saffron, *C. autumnale*, which has pink flowers. It has a number of varieties, 'Alboplenum' is white and 'Pleniflorum' has rounded pink flowers. Other popular species are *C. byzantinum*, with pinkish-lilac flowers, and *C. speciosum* with flowers of a deeper pink. The variety *C. s.* 'Album' has pure white flowers shaped like wine goblets. The flowers of autumn crocuses emerge before the leaves giving them their other common name, naked ladies. A number will naturalize in the wild but all can be grown in containers. Plant them in a deep container in well-drained soil in late summer.

There are two other notable autumn-flowering bulbs or corms that grow well in containers. Guernsey lily, *Nerine bowdenii*, is one. It prefers to be pot-bound and needs a warm sunny position. It produces sprays of pink flowers that last for several weeks. The second is the autumn cyclamen, varieties of *C. hederifolium*, that you may still find sold under its former name of *C.*

◄ The leaves of the ornamental vine, Vitis vinifera 'Purpurea', turn deep purple in the fall. The grapes it produces are not really edible.

▶ *Smaller dahlias can be grown in small spaces in containers. Some of the dwarf mixtures available, which grow to 60cm/2ft, are ideal.*

neapolitanum. They have charming little flowers in shades of pink to white held aloft on stalks. They are also suitable plants for an alpine garden.

Dahlias

Dahlias are *the* fall flower. No other plant is so easy to cultivate or provides such spectacular blooms, and you have a choice of over 20,000 varieties. Dahlias are divided into 11 groups depending on the shape of their flowerheads. These vary from single through pompom to orchid and peony. Some are enormous with flowerheads over 25cm/10in in diameter, but many are much neater with flowerheads under 10cm/4in across. The colors range from pink, red, yellow through orange, and white. Anyone who wants to cultivate dahlias should consult a specialist catalog to choose specimens of the type, size, and color that will suit

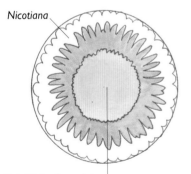

Nicotiana

Pink Michaelmas daises

▲ *Plant a container with* Aster novae-belgii *'Apple Blossom' and surround it with tobacco plants, such as* Nicotiana *'Domino White'.*

their garden. Plant the tubers in mid to late spring when all danger of frost has passed. The plants need to be staked, and this is best done at planting to avoid damaging the tubers. Plant them at least 10cm/4in deep in fertile soil mix, and add a phosphate-based fertilizer (bonemeal is the easiest). Protect the young shoots from slugs.

Fall-flowering perennials

The most popular fall-flowering perennials are Michaelmas daisies, *Aster novi-belgii*, and their twin the New England aster, *A. novae-angliae*; both come into bloom when almost all other

flowers have finished flowering. They carry clumps of daisy-like flowers in varying colors from blue and lilac, to pink and white, and a number have the typical yellow centers of the daisy family. They are quite tall plants and generally reach about 1.2m/4ft and do require staking at this height. They are not particularly suitable for a small container garden. *A. n-b.* 'Apple Blossom' is pure pink and 'Marie Ballard' a delicate light blue. Another good fall perennial is *Ceratostigma willmottianum.* This has leaves that turn red in the fall, and attractive pale blue flowers shaped like those of the periwinkle.

The productive
container garden

It is surprising how much fruit and vegetables can be grown in a small container garden. You will never be able to keep the household in onions or potatoes for a year, but you can plan a succession of vegetables that will taste a great deal better than anything you can buy in the local supermarket.

planning and planting

Growing vegetables and fruit in a small space means careful planning. Decide how much space you have available and how it can best be used. Fruit trees can be grown against a wall, and give blossom in the spring and fruit in the fall, and "mini" vegetables can be grown in window boxes.

The essence is careful planning. There is little point in sowing a whole packet of lettuce seeds at the same time for this just produces a hundred or so plants at once and most of them will be wasted.

The first thing therefore is to decide how much space you can devote to vegetables and fruit. Do you have room for just one container of vegetables, or can you spread them around the garden?

Which direction does your patio wall face and can you train a fruit tree against it? How many growing bags do you want in the garden or on the patio? Do you just want to grow tomatoes, or some peppers or cucumbers? Is there room for pots of peas or pole beans trained up a small trellis or a wigwam of poles, or a special container of herbs?

Once these questions have been answered you then have to decide exactly what you want to eat and grow. Many gardeners like to grow containers of herbs or create separate strawberry planters. Containers of vegetables need to be planned to see which kinds can be grown together at the same time, or whether the planting can be staggered throughout the year.

The key to planning successful vegetable growing in a container garden is the amount of time that every vegetable takes to mature. Parsnips, for

◄ *A really ambitious container vegetable garden with perpetual strawberries, tomatoes, and fennel all growing in galvanized containers.*

◀ Vegetables and herbs can make a colorful display on a patio in summer, although they will not all flower at the same time.

1 Pole beans
2 Globe artichoke
3 French beans
4 Thyme
5 Tomato 'Tumbler'
6 Purple pod beans
7 Mint
8 Parsley
9 Sugar Snap peas
10 Basil
11 'Oregon' snow peas
12 Nasturtiums
13 Marigolds
14 Lollo Rosso

example, really need to be sown very early in the year and are seldom harvested before late fall. Although their foliage is an attractive green in summer, they may well be in the ground for 10 or 11 months, occupying valuable space. This is fine in the traditional kitchen garden or allotment where there is plenty of room, but you cannot afford

artichokes

▲ Jerusalem artichokes grow well in containers. They require staking but their upright foliage adds height to the garden in summer.

this luxury in a container garden where every plant has to earn its keep, both in looks and on the table.

Also remember to plant any vegetables closer together than is recommended and to concentrate on quick-maturing crops, such as lettuces, to make the best use of the available space. Check the dimensions of each plant and feed them more than you would normally since they will be hungrier than usual for nutrients.

Lastly, think about the appearance of the containers. Plan the vegetables to display contrasting colors of foliage and form. Consider how they look as they mature—onions look straggly and floppy as they ripen, and a worn-out broccoli plant is not a thing of any great beauty. These are the kind of vegetables best avoided where space is limited.

The vertical dimension

A number of vegetables can be grown to add height to a container garden. Among them are Jerusalem artichokes, which can be planted in a container by themselves. They remain in the ground until the fall when they are harvested, but they are tall and stately and if confined in one place cannot spread all over the garden as they do in open ground; they make delicious soup. Peas and pole beans are two other favorite vegetables that add height. Peas can be trained up sticks or a small trellis, and take well to containers. The snap pea varieties, such as Sugar Snap, are particularly delicious, but the variety grown is a matter of personal taste. Pole beans make another excellent container crop, and their red, or red and white, flowers are most attractive when they are grown in a container.

herbs

A study of herbs is one of the most interesting aspects of gardening. Most people think of herbs as plants used in the kitchen, but herbs are the original medicines of humans and lists of them have been found on Sumerian tablets written 5,000 years ago at the dawn of civilization.

Many gardeners use containers to grow herbs, whether they have a large garden or not. This has many advantages: the containers can be positioned on the patio or terrace outside the kitchen door, so that they are easily available to the cook; many herbs, such as mint, are invasive in the ground and are better confined within a pot; a number of herbs are tender and the containers can be brought indoors in the winter, or they can be sheltered by the walls of the house or covered with protective fabric.

Herbs are fascinating plants, for if you have room, you can pick out different aspects of herb gardening and grow scented, medicinal, or culinary herbs from different parts of the world. A container of flowering medicinal herbs could include calamint, *Calamintha*, California poppies, *Eschscholzia*, cornflowers, *Centaurea*, arnica, *Arnica*, and sweet woodruff, *Galium*, grown as a ground-cover plant. A container of

▶ *Thyme is a decorative herb and many garden varieties are grown as rock plants. It grows wild on mountainsides in the Mediterranean.*

scented herbs might include heliotrope, *Heliotropium*, sweet rocket, *Hesperis*, hyssop, *Hyssopus*, bergamot, *Monarda*, sweet cicely, *Myrrhis*, and the scented geranium, *Pelargonium*, with sweet violets, *Viola odorata*, planted in the front.

Containers of kitchen herbs can be devoted to one herb, such as mint, or herbs from one part of the world, perhaps the Mediterranean. This is particularly suitable if you have a sunny open patio and can grow the herbs that love the heat, such as thyme, oregano, marjoram, sage, and rosemary. Sages, in particular, come in many varieties with attractive leaves in contrasting colors of green and purple.

Common kitchen herbs

Chives—can be grown as decorative edging in containers, and both the flowers and leaves are used in the kitchen as a strong and tasty flavoring. Surplus leaves can be frozen for use in the winter when the foliage has completely died down. Sow in seed trays indoors in spring, and then plant out in groups of three or four seedlings. Established groups can be divided every three or four years in the spring or fall. They look particularly attractive in pots.

◀ *Differing leaf colors of the common sage look good in a herb garden. The varieties are* Salvia officinalis *'Pupurascens' and 'Icterina'.*

Mint—the most common mints grown for the kitchen are spearmint and peppermint. Spearmint is considered by many as the best for making mint sauce and for flavoring mint drinks in summer.

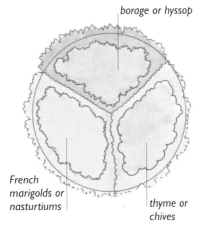

borage or hyssop

French marigolds or nasturtiums

thyme or chives

▲ *There are many different colored herbs, both medicinal and culinary. With careful planning you could make a color wheel in a round bed.*

Other favored mints are apple mint, there is a variegated kind with attractive white and green leaves, and Bowles' mint, a popular mint and the best for flavoring new potatoes.

Buy mint from a reputable nursery and never attempt to grow mint from seed because the varieties are unlikely to breed true. Propagate by division. Also note that mints have hairy leaves which can cause skin irritations and rashes. Handle with care. Similarly mint tea should not be drunk continuously over a long period of time.

Oregano—a favourite Mediterranean herb used to flavor stews and pasta dishes, oregano is a bushy rhizomatous perennial with flowers on upright stalks. They attract bees and insects, and emerge

◀ Origanum vulgare 'Aureum' is a cultivated form of oregano, often called wild marjoram. Sweet marjoram, O. majorana, tastes different.

directly in the kitchen garden. The densely ruffled leaves can be used to flavor soups, stews, and other dishes.

Rosemary—can be grown easily in any container herb garden given a sheltered position, for although it comes from the Mediterranean it will tolerate some frost and cold weather. It flowers early in the year at the end of winter. In the kitchen it is the traditional accompaniment for roast lamb and has many other uses. It is a slightly untidy plant but it will not regenerate from old wood so care must be taken not to go overboard when trimming it back. To propagate take semiripe cuttings in summer.

Common sage—*Salvia officinalis* has been a culinary herb for centuries. The leaves are often dried and stored for use. Sage and onion stuffing is the traditional accompaniment for roast poultry. Sow seeds in a cold frame in spring, take semiripe cuttings in summer. There are a number of colored-leaved varieties that are welcome in a container herb garden.

Common thyme—a number of thymes can be used in the kitchen including caraway-scented thyme, which was traditionally used to flavor a baron of beef. Sow seeds in spring in a cold frame, and take semiripe cuttings in summer.

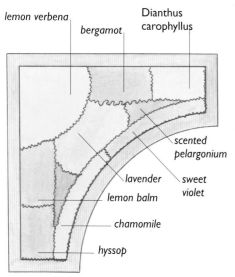

lemon verbena

bergamot

Dianthus carophyllus

scented pelargonium

lavender

sweet violet

lemon balm

chamomile

hyssop

▲ A small raised bed in a sunny corner is an ideal place to grow a number of culinary herbs. Many have the added bonus of scented foliage.

pinkish-white from deep red bracts although there are several color variations. Varieties that have been bred for the herb garden include 'Aureum' (gold leaves), 'Aureum Crispum' (curly gold leaves) and 'Compactum' (smaller in habit). 'Heiderose' is more upright with pink flowers. Oregano self-seeds and can be divided in the spring.

Parsley—a biennial that is best grown as an annual. It is difficult to germinate and requires a high temperature. Some people delay sowing until the summer, but it is a help to soak the seed in hot water overnight and pour boiling water on the soil if parsley is to be sown

▶ Low-growing rosemary plants can sometimes be trimmed into hedges along the front of containers. It prefers a sheltered site.

GOOD HERBS FOR CONTAINERS

Scented herbs

Anise hyssop, *Agastache foeniculum*
Lemon verbena, *Aloysia triphylla*
Garden calamint, *Calamintha grandiflora*
Lawn chamomile, *Chamaemelum nobile*
Clove pink, *Dianthus caryophyllus*
Sweet woodruff, *Galium odoratum*
Heliotrope, *Heliotropium arborescens*
Sweet rocket, *Hesperis matronalis*
Hyssop, *Hyssopus officinalis*
Jasmine, *Jasminum officinale*
Lavender, *Lavandula*
Lemon balm, *Melissa officinalis*
Bergamot, *Monarda didyma*
Scented geranium, *Pelargonium*
Hedgehog rose, *Rosa rugosa*
Sweet violet, *Viola odorata*

Extra herbs for the kitchen

Anise hyssop, *Agastache foeniculum*
Dill, *Anethum graveolens*
Chervil, *Anthriscus cerefolium*
French tarragon, *Artemesia dracunculus*
Borage, *Borago officinalis*
Caraway, *Carum carvi*
Coriander, *Coriandrum sativum*
Bay, *Laurus nobilis*
Sweet basil, *Ocimum basilicum*
Sweet marjoram, *Origanum majorana*
Nasturtium, *Tropaeolum majus*

Medicinal herbs

Arnica, *Arnica montana*
Borage, *Borago officinalis*
English marigold, *Calendula officinalis*
Lady's smock, *Cardamine pratensis*
Purple coneflower, *Echinacea purpurea*
Viper's bugloss, *Echium vulgare*
Meadowsweet, *Filipendula ulmaria*
Herb robert, *Geranium robertianum*
Hyssop, *Hyssopus officinalis*
Ox-eye daisy, *Leucanthemum vulgare*
Pennyroyal, *Mentha pulegium*
Sweet cicely, *Myrrhis odorata*
Parsley, *Petroselinum crispum*
Common sage, *Salvia officinalis*
Feverfew, *Tanacetum parthenium*
Tansy, *Tanacetum vulgare*

Good flowering herbs

Yarrow, *Achillea millefolium*
Thrift, *Armeria maritima*
Daisy, *Bellis perennis*
Borage, bugloss, *Borago officinalis*
English marigold, *Calendula officinalis*
Cornflower, *Centaurea cyanus*
Clove pink, *Dianthus caryophyllus*
Jasmine, *Jasminum officinale*
Bee balm, bergamot, *Monarda didyma*
Scented geranium, *Pelargonium*
French marigold, *Tagetes patula*
Sweet violet, *Viola odorata*

fruit

Fruit grown in containers needs to be trained against a wall. The only exceptions are fruit trees on a roof garden that can be grown as free-standing pyramids, or strawberries grown in individual pots or strawberry planters. The possibilities vary according to the size of your garden.

Note that if you want to grow fruit in a window box your choice is limited to some alpine strawberries grown among other herbs and vegetables. On a balcony or a patio, any fruit you grow will really be decided by the aspect and amount of space you have. Roof gardens may attract the sun all day, but they may lack the warm walls necessary for tender fruits.

Limited options

If you cannot offer a warm wall and your patio faces east or north, then the options are limited. Morello cherries like a north wall. Some of the hardier apples that resist late frosts may well fruit on walls with an easterly aspect, although they are unlikely to yield as much as in a sunnier position. Pears flower earlier than apples and are less resistant to late frosts, and at the least will need a southeasterly wall. A number of plums, though, particularly the favorite 'Victoria', will yield good fruit without too much sun if they can be sheltered in early spring from late frosts.

In colder areas some of the hybrid berries or currant bushes that can be trained against a wall are more likely to succeed than stoned fruit. But if you do try to grow fruit on a very shady patio, do not persist if the tree or bush fails to flower and produce within three years. It is better to start again with an alternative.

Growing tender fruit outdoors

Container fruit trees need not just be confined to fruit that remains outside all year. Many a patio is brightened by small

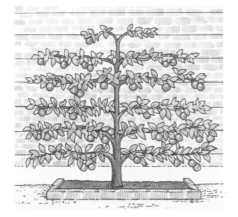

▲ *An apple tree in a small bed trained as an espalier against a wall. The steps for training these are shown on pages 114–15.*

▲ *When potting on a small fruit tree choose a pot slightly bigger than the original. Fill in the sides; insure the soil level stays the same.*

▲ *A small bush fruit tree such as lemon or orange can be taken indoors in winter and then placed outside for the summer.*

pruning a bush fruit tree

1 To make a bush, cut back a maiden in the first winter to the required height. The aim is to create 4 strong branches. Fruit will take 4–5 years.

2 Remove the leader and select 4 good branches growing at angles. Cut away any others and then reduce the main branches by half to two-thirds.

3 By the end of the second year, secondary branches will have formed. Select 8 of these and cut as above. Cut back inner branches to four buds.

trees of citrus fruits, and oranges and lemons can be put outside in the summer and brought inside in winter where they can be treated as house plants. The most suitable varieties are the x *Citrofortunella* varieties of small oranges and lemons, or some of the small lemon trees. They need a minimum winter temperature of 10°C/50°F, and can be put outside in the summer after a period of acclimatisation.

Hints and tips for growing fruit trees

The four keys to success begin with space and training. Cordon-trained trees occupy the least space, about 1.8m/6ft by 1.2m/4ft while fan-trained trees might require three times this amount depending on the rootstock used. Measure how much wall space you have

and plan accordingly. Second, consider minarette trees. If you want a free-standing tree, try planting one or more of the modern minarette fruit trees in a large container and use them as standard accent points in the container garden. Minarette trees grow upright on a single stem and will eventually reach a height of 1.8–2.4m/6–8ft. They can be planted as closely as 60cm/2ft apart, and therefore two or three trees can be grown together in a big container. Third, check the rootstock on which the fruit tree has been grafted. You need to be sure that your tree is grafted on to a dwarfing or semidwarfing rootstock, otherwise it

▶ *A vine grown in a container and trained over a pergola to make an arch. This transforms this small garden into a series of rooms.*

will grow too big for the container. And, finally, check the pollination requirements. Many fruit trees are not self-fertile, and you need to grow at least two varieties if you want fruit.

unusual fruit in containers

Don't be put off growing fruit just because the space in your garden is limited. Even if there is insufficient room for apples or pears many container gardens can support currants, or one of the unusual berries. These take up little space and are seldom found in the shops.

There are a number of excellent fruits that the container gardener can consider. *Fig*—a good tree to grow in a container because if planted unchecked in the garden the roots spread with abandon and the tree grows bigger and bigger, seldom fruiting. The common fig can be grown out of doors in any reasonably warm situation. It will ripen best in areas that do not suffer from severe winter frosts, and in cooler areas will do better grown in a greenhouse. Figs need to be pruned properly if they are to provide fruit. Consult a pruning manual for detailed instructions. The embryo fruits need protection over the winter.

Plums and damsons—plums are a good choice to grow on a sheltered patio because they flower early in the year, although plum blossom often needs protection against the unwelcome frosts of late spring. Choose varieties grafted on to Pixy (dwarfing) rootstocks. In some years the trees may bear an overload of fruit. If so, the fruit should be thinned because otherwise the branches may break under the weight of the crop. If you only have room for one tree, choose one of the luscious dessert plums and train it as a fan against a warm wall.

Sweet and acid cherries—the development of the Giessen rootstock means that a fan-trained cherry can be planted in a container and only require a wall space of 1.8m/6ft high by 3.6m/12ft wide. A number of self-fertile varieties have also been developed. The

◀ *Fig trees will fruit on warm walls. Confine their roots when planting and study the pruning requirements in a specialist manual.*

pruning and training a hybrid berry

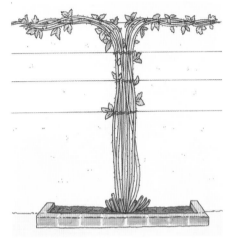 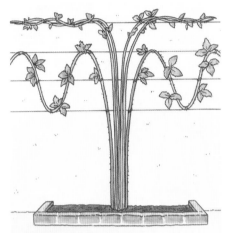 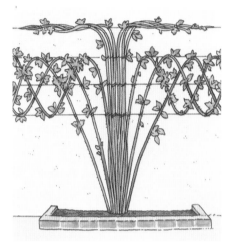

1 Pruning and training hybrid berries is simple. Each plant develops new canes each year. Tie these in vertically. Cut fruited canes to the ground.

2 Choose 6 good canes and weave them along a wire frame. The finished result will look like the bottom half of illustration 3.

3 The fruit as it looks at the end of the year when the berries have ripened. New canes are tied vertically and the old canes cut away completely as stage 1.

favourite acid cherry 'Morello', which can be grown on a north wall, needs about the same size space. Grown against a wall, a net can be placed over the ripening fruit of any cherry to protect it from hungry birds. If you don't do this they may well take the whole crop.
Peach—peaches can quite easily be grown outdoors in temperate zones, but there is no point in pretending that the cultivation of peach trees is a simple matter. Anyone who wants to grow a peach tree on a patio is advised to study their requirements carefully before starting. If you plan to grow a fan-trained peach on a patio four things are essential: you need a wall, 1.8m/6ft x 3.6m/12ft; you need a firm framework of wires on which you can tie canes to secure the branches; you need the time and

patience to establish the fan properly; and you have to remember that peaches produce fruit on wood of the previous year, and then study the pruning requirements to achieve this. Finally you must remember to spray in winter to protect against the damaging diseases that often affect them.

Soft fruit

Currants—they grow well in cool temperate climates and make a good alternative for the patio gardener who lives in a colder climate. Black, red, and white currants can all be grown in containers against a wall, and can be trained as cordons or espaliers.
Hybrid berries—some of the hybrid berries, thornless blackberries, tayberries, and loganberries can be grown in a

container against a wall. They do need a framework of wire but they are easy to train, and are a satisfactory substitute for raspberries, which are unsuitable for growing in containers because they are too spreading and vigorous.
Strawberry—the favorite fruit for the patio gardener. Strawberries are especially attractive grown in special planters or tubs, with white flowers in late spring and delicious red fruits ripening in summer. They can also be grown in growing bags, planted in late summer to bear fruit the following year. It is possible to retain strawberry plants in growing bags for two years but it is probably best if they are replaced annually. Since they are a greedy crop make sure you add slow-release fertilizer when you plant them.

vegetables

In the limited space of a container garden it is best to concentrate on your favorite vegetables: they will taste far better than anything you can buy in the shops. Grow quick-maturing crops, the "mini" vegetables that have been developed for containers, and special vegetables for special occasions.

There are many reasons for growing vegetables in containers: they can be picked fresh and eaten immediately; they taste considerably better than any vegetable you can buy; you know exactly how they have been grown and the fertilizers that have been used; and you have the satisfaction of personal achievement, of producing your own food for your own family.

Containers devoted to vegetables need very careful planning. Space is extremely limited and there will only be room to raise a few plants of each vegetable. Check on the amount or room that each variety requires, and try to get seed of the smaller varieties or grow the special "mini" vegetables designed for container gardens. Also grow those that will give you the greatest yield in the smallest space.

Beets—a delicious vegetable, and when eaten fresh with butter and garlic it is a culinary delight. The leaves are most decorative and beets grown in a container look attractive on a patio garden. Sow outdoors from mid-spring onward when the soil has warmed up. Soak the seed overnight before sowing and it will germinate in 10–14 days.

Cabbage—a cabbage might not be everyone's choice for growing in the limited space available in a container garden, but it is considerably more compact than most brassicas, and a number of the red and savoy cabbages are attractive plants. Most cabbages are grown to mature in the fall, but spring cabbages are also a possibility for the keen gardener and provide fresh vegetables early in the year. Sow summer, fall, and winter cabbages thinly in succession between early spring and early summer; you will only have room for a few. Sow spring cabbages in late summer.

Carrot—if you are growing vegetables in containers you need to concentrate on those carrot varieties that are short and dumpy, rather than the larger winter carrots that take longer to mature. Also give the carrots as much depth as possible because they will not grow very well in a shallow growing bag. The attractive green foliage makes a pleasing contrast to other vegetables when they

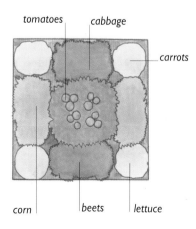

▲ *A variety of vegetables that could be grown in a container. Choose some of the "mini" vegetables now available, which taste as good.*

tomatoes · cabbage · carrots · corn · beets · lettuce

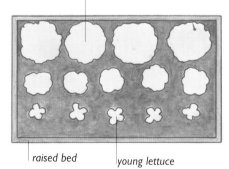

mature lettuce · raised bed · young lettuce

▲ *Grow lettuces in succession to insure a fresh supply in summer. There are a number of varieties such as 'Salad Bowl' and 'Lollo Rosso'.*

are grouped in a trough or planter, and of all vegetables, except possibly peas, a fresh carrot tastes far better than anything you can buy. Seed should be sown very thinly *in situ*. If you like you can sow seed in modules and then plant them out in position. If you have room sow them at two-weekly intervals to produce a succession of crops.

Cucumber—outdoor or ridge cucumbers used to be practically unheard of, and when they were grown, they only produced small, rather bitter, misshapen fruits. Modern varieties, however, have changed all this as plant breeders have developed long, smooth cucumbers suitable for growing out of doors, that are tolerant of lower temperatures. Put the seeds on their edge in pots, or better still directly into the soil outside or sow in degradable pots: cucumbers do not like being transplanted. Seeds germinate at 20°C/68°F.

Eggplant—the eggplant is a vegetable that needs warmth and protection to grow well, but there is no reason why it should not flourish outside, provided that you can give it a warm sheltered position in full sun. It is a useful vegetable to start off in a container indoors and then move outside as summer advances. Ideally it

▶ *Swiss chard or rhubarb chard is grown for its brightly colored leaves that can be cooked and eaten as spinach.*

should have a minimum day and night temperature of 16–18°C/60–64°F for growth to continue unchecked. Eggplants have deep roots and should be grown in large containers in fertile soil. They should be allowed to develop without forcing, and require regular watering during the growing period. Sow seed indoors in spring at a temperature of 21–30°C/70–86°F.

Lettuce—a good stand-by for the container gardener. Lettuces mature quickly, take little room and can be grown easily in between other vegetables, and can be planted to take the place of crops that have already been harvested. The container gardener is unlikely to fall into the common trap of growing too many lettuces at one time. Sowings should be planned carefully to insure that you have as long a supply as possible. Rather than sow directly into the ground the container gardener should sow two seeds in a small degradable pot, using as many small pots as necessary. If both germinate discard the weakest seedling. Harden the plants off by putting them outside before planting out in position. There are four types of lettuce, butterhead, crisphead: looseleaf, and romaine.

Salad greens—dark green, extra tender leaves add a piquant flavor to sandwiches and salads. Just a few leaves of argula, mache/corn salad, or upland cress will lend a tasty, distinctive, peppery sharpness. Sow from mid-spring onward for a continuous harvest.

For even more variety, mesclun is a mixture of young salad leaves. The seed comes already mixed to be sown at two-weekly intervals for a continuous supply of tender leaves. Growth is rapid with the first harvest beginning in about three weeks from sowing.

Peas—peas are one of the commonest and most loved garden vegetables, but they can be maddeningly difficult to grow because they are popular with birds and mice. They can also be difficult to germinate because they do not relish cold soils, and conversely they are a cool-weather crop and dislike open hot positions. They can be grown successfully in containers, and should be grown as a feature plant in pots up a decorative trellis. If you plan to do this check the height of the variety you choose before planting, this can vary from 45cm–1.5m/1½–5ft. If your patio or roof

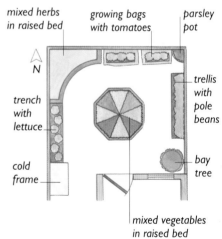

mixed herbs in raised bed

growing bags with tomatoes

parsley pot

N

trench with lettuce

cold frame

trellis with pole beans

bay tree

mixed vegetables in raised bed

▲ A patio garden laid out to grow vegetables in the summer. In winter the central bed could be filled with winter-flowering pansies for color.

◀ 'Salad Bowl' lettuce makes a brave splash of color. It is advisable to grow just a few lettuces at any one time as they will be wasted.

staking and tying tomatoes in pots

1 Standard tomatoes growing in pots trained up 1.2m/4ft stakes. If possible, run a wire along the wall behind and tie the stakes to this for security.

2 As the tomato plants grow, tie in the leading growth and pinch out the sideshoots that emerge at the joint of the branches and main stem. Water well.

3 When the tomato has set 4 trusses of fruit, or reached the top of its stake, nip out the growing point two leaves above the top truss. Feed well.

garden is exposed they may require shelter, both from the wind and birds. When ripe, peas should be cooked immediately after picking as the sugar starts to turn to starch once the pod has been picked. If you have room for more than one container, sow seed in succession from spring to early summer. *Bell pepper*—new varieties of this tropical fruit have been developed that flourish in more temperate climates; they are good plants to grow outside on a warm patio. They are popular as a vegetable in salads, and when roasted or served stuffed. They are similar in habit to tomatoes and are grown in the same

▶ *Eggplants are rather unusual plants that can be grown in containers on a sunny patio. They should be treated like bell peppers.*

◀ 'Lollo rosso' lettuce can be picked a leaf at a time. They add color and interest to any vegetable container.

▼ New varieties of cucumber produce sweet-tasting fruit and can be grown outside.

POLE OR STICK BEANS

Pole beans are relatively simple to grow, and the plants can be trained up canes against a wall to form a colorful backdrop with their bright red, or red and white flowers, and succulent pods. Dwarf forms are available that grow about 45cm/18in high and are suitable for troughs and window boxes. For best results pole beans need to be grown on very fertile soil, and they must be picked continually when the pods start to form. For container-grown plants, plant two seeds in a 7.5cm/3in pot of seed and cutting mix, and discard one if both germinate. Plant out when all danger of frost has passed.

way either inside, in a greenhouse, or outside. Sow them in mid-spring under cover at 21°C/70°F. The seeds will germinate in 14–21 days.

Radish—one of the easiest of all vegetables to grow, radishes are the best way to introduce children to the delights of gardening. They germinate easily, and mature quickly, in about a month. Gardeners with large vegetable gardens often use them as a marker crop between rows of vegetables that take longer to germinate, and for the adventurous there are several winter-maturing radishes and the giant Japanese mooli radishes.

For the container gardener, the ordinary globe-shaped summer radish is a good companion plant to grow in pots with lettuces or chard, or it can be used as a useful filler among brassicas.

Tomato—outdoor tomatoes are quite easy to grow and are among the best vegetables for the container gardener. They are attractive plants in flower and fruit, but they do best in a relatively warm climate and are difficult to grow outside unless they can be offered the protection of a south-facing wall and a sheltered position.

Tomatoes can be divided into two types: bush and cordon. The cordon varieties are the most common, and to be successful they need to be trained up a stake or tied in to wires. Tie the plants in at regular intervals using a loose knot and garden string or raffia. And pinch out all the sideshoots where the leaf stalks join the stem. This leaves you with one straight stem and a number of trusses of fruit. When the fourth truss has small tomatoes the growing tip should be pinched out, or "stopped" at two leaves above the truss. This allows the tomatoes to develop properly and ripen well.

If by any chance the summer ends rather earlier than it should, and you are left with a large number of green tomatoes, they can be picked and brought inside the house to ripen. Alternatively use them to make green tomato chutney, a delicious relish prized above many others.

Bush tomatoes are simpler. They grow either as small bushes, as the name implies, or trailing along the ground. They do not require training or stopping, but you do have to cover the ground to keep the fruit off the soil. Dwarf tomatoes, plants that grow little more than 20cm/8in high, are very suitable for growing in window boxes and small pots, but the yield is not large. Sow two seeds in a small pot and discard the weaker if both germinate.

Zucchini—another member of the cucumber family, zucchini are widely grown and are a favorite summer vegetable. The yellow-skin variety are also very visually pleasing.

The ones grown in the garden are far better to eat than any bought in a store. The best zucchini to grow are the compact bush varieties and, provided the fruits are harvested regularly, they will continue to produce fruit over a long period. Sow in the same way as cucumbers and the seeds will germinate at 15°C/59°F. Generally zucchini are raised in pots first, and then planted out when the soil has warmed up and all danger of frost is past.

Plants grown in pots should be hardened off by putting them outside during the day before they are finally planted in position in the container. They generally do best if they are grown in a rich soil mix.

▶ *A splendid frame used for tomatoes that have been immaculately grown and cared for. All tomatoes need plenty of sunshine.*

Plant directory

All the plants included in this directory are suitable for growing in containers. The lists are by no means comprehensive but provide ideas for a wide range of interesting plants. So much depends on the site of each garden, the aspect, and climate. Choose carefully and, if necessary, consult a comprehensive encyclopedia that gives greater details about growing requirements.

Trees

FRUIT TREES
Malus domestica
Apple

Height 1.8m/6ft

Spread 1.8m/6ft

These are grown most successfully in containers as cordons or espaliers trained against a wall, and are a popular choice on roof gardens, where they can be used to divide up the space. Grafted on an M9 dwarfing rootstock, they occupy 1.8m/6ft and 3m/10ft of wall space respectively, both 1.8m/6ft high, so make sure this amount of space is available. Columnar trees, single standards, can be grown as freestanding trees in containers and reach 1.8–2.4m/6–8ft. Most apples need a pollinator, so two varieties need to be grown, unless a neighboring garden has apple trees. Check with the nursery before buying as some varieties will not pollinate others. Suggested dessert varieties include: 'Gravenstein', 'Fiesta', 'North Pole', 'Golden Sentinel', and 'William's Pride'.

Pyrus communis
Pear

Height 1.8m/6ft

Spread 1.8m/6ft

Pears are grown in the same way as apples but they are trickier for the blossom flowers earlier in the year and is thus more liable to damage by late frosts. However, the beauty of the blossom makes this worthwhile. They prefer a south- or southwest-facing wall. In a container garden they should be grafted on a semi-dwarf rootstock. As with apples you need to grow two compatible varieties at the same time for they are not reliably self-fertile. Check with the nursery when buying the trees. Favorite pears include: 'Highland', 'Conference', 'Comice', 'Warren', and 'Harrow Delight'.

Prunus domestica
Plum

Height 1.8.m/6ft

Spread 3.7m/12ft fan-trained

In a container garden plums should be grafted on to Pixy rootstock and trained as a fan. Fan-training is more difficult than training an espalier, and a good pruning manual will provide instructions. Columnar trees are also available. It is best in limited space to grow one of the self-fertile varieties, such as, 'Italian Prune', 'Golden Transparent Gage', 'Cambridge Gage', 'Santa Rosa', or the old favorite 'Victoria'. This last one will grow quite well in a certain amount of shade.

ORNAMENTAL TREES
Acer palmatum var. *dissectum*
Japanese maple

Height 1.8m/6ft

Spread 3m/10ft (after some years)

Japanese maples are ideal container plants. They create an Oriental feel in a small garden. They hug the ground and the long, feathery, deeply divided leaves hang down most attractively. Their chief glory is the wonderful shades of red, yellow, and purple that the leaves turn in the fall. If you cannot find *A. p.* var. *dissectum*, choose one of the slow-growing varieties, such as, *A. p.* Dissectum Atropurpureum Group.

Pyrus communis 'Conference'

Prunus domestica

Acer palmatum var. *dissectum*

Ilex aquifolium

green leaves and white scented flowers in spring followed by orange or yellow fruit. Lemon trees have pale green leaves and exceptionally fragrant flowers followed by lemons. The variety 'Meyer' is the one most usually grown for it has a more compact habit than the species. Both of these small trees make an excellent focal point in a container garden in the summer, especially if planted in a grand terracotta urn.

Ilex aquifolium
Holly

Height 3m/10ft

Spread 2m/6ft

Hollies should be grown in containers more often than they are for they grow very slowly and have good evergreen foliage and lovely red berries in the winter that can be cut for Christmas decoration. They can also be clipped and trained as low-growing hedges. The male variety 'Silver Queen' has white-edged leaves and the female 'J. C. van Tol' has dark green leaves. Both male and female plants are needed to produce berries.

Camellia 'Donation'
Camellia

Height 5m/16ft

Spread 2.5m/8ft

Camellias can either be classified as a small tree or shrub. Eventually, growing in the wild under favorable conditions, they reach considerable proportions. But they are slow-growing and tolerant of pruning, so can be confined satisfactorily in containers for many years. They make ideal formal small trees with their neat pointed evergreen leaves and perfect flowers in early spring. They need both shade and acid soil to flourish. There are many varieties. Most camellias are pink, white, or red. *C.* 'Donation' is widely grown in container gardens and has pink semidouble blooms. It prefers deep shade.

× *Citrofortunella microcarpa/*
Citrus limon
Calamondin, Panama
orange/lemon tree, citrus tree

Height and spread 45–60cm/18–24in

Citrus trees grown indoors as pot plants in temperate climates are good small decorative trees to put out on patios in the summer, provided these are sheltered and sunny. The calamondin orange has dark

Camellia 'Leonard Messel'

Laurus nobilis
Bay tree, sweet bay
Height 12m/40ft
Spread 9m/30ft

Growing in the wild in good conditions the evergreen bay tree can become quite large. However it is justifiably one of the most popular trees for all container gardeners for it does not resent being confined in a pot, it grows pretty slowly, and it can be clipped to shape to make balls, mopheads, and cones. Grown and trained as a standard it is a dignified tree that is welcome in many small gardens and on patios and balconies. The leaves are dark green and pointed and are used to flavor marinades and sauces in the kitchen. Bay trees have small white, insignificant flowers in spring, followed by tiny black fruits.

Olea europaea
Olive
Height and spread: 6m/20ft or more.

The slow-growing olive from the Mediterranean is increasingly grown in containers in temperate climates. Winters are getting milder and small trees can always be given some shelter in very hard weather. Olives are evergreen with pointed leaves, gray-green above and silvery-gray beneath. The trees form a rounded head. They need a good fertile compost and feeding with liquid fertilizer every month in the growing season. The small white flowers are fragrant and the fruit starts green, turning black as it ripens.

Conifers

Conifers are one of the mainstays of the container and alpine garden. The varieties described are all slow growing and have different-colored foliage. Grouped together they provide contrast of shape and color.

Cedrus deodara 'Feelin' Blue'
Deodar cedar
Height 30cm/12in
Spread 90cm/3ft

Most cedars are large trees that require a good deal of room but a number of new varieties have been developed as dwarf forms that can be grown in container gardens and in alpine beds where space is limited. This deodar cedar has a weeping habit with attractive blue-green leaves and branches that hang down. Like all cedars it prefers well-drained moist soil and full sun. Other small cedars include *C. deodara* 'Golden Horizon', slightly larger, the leaves will be darker and bluer if grown in shade; and *C. d.* 'Aurea', golden foliage.

Chamaecyparis lawsoniana 'Barry's Silver'
False cypress
Height 1.5m/5ft
Spread 75cm/30in

There are a number of false cypresses with varying foliage colors. 'Barry's Silver' is a comparatively recent introduction that originated in New Zealand. It is quite slow growing and in the summer the tips of the new leaves appear silvery white, changing to green. It has an upright habit. It is best planted in a sheltered position in full sun where the soil does not dry out. Other varieties include 'Little Spire', blue-green, and 'Stardust', yellow.

Laurus nobilis

Juniperus communis 'Compressa'

Buxus sempervirens

Juniperus communis 'Compressa'
Common juniper

Height 30cm/12in

Spread 9cm/4in

Probably the most popular conifer for the small garden, *J. c.* 'Compressa' makes a slender compact column, bright green with silver-backed foliage. It is extremely slow growing and is most unlikely to outgrow its allotted station in the garden. It is suitable for planting in window boxes if needs be to add some vertical interest, and looks well in an alpine garden. *J. c.* 'Depressa Aurea' is another good small juniper with golden yellow leaves in summer, turning bronze-green in winter. It will eventually reach 30cm–1. 5m/2–5ft.

Picea glauca 'Alberta Blue'
White spruce

Height and spread: 45–60cm/18–24in

A lovely conical dwarf conifer with intense silvery-blue new shoots in early summer that gradually darken as summer progresses. This is another dwarf conifer that looks ideal in alpine gardens and all forms of container. It prefers sun or light shade and well-drained soil. *P. abies* 'Ohlendorffii' is another slow-growing spruce suitable for the container garden that has dark green foliage, and is definitely ball-shaped. It might eventually reach 3m/10ft in height.

Thuja orientalis 'Raffles'
Red cedar

Height 30–45cm/12–18in

Spread 30cm/12in

One of the bonuses in growing red cedars is the changing colors of the foliage throughout the year. The variety 'Raffles' has yellowish-green leaves in spring but these turn to reddish-bronze as the cold winds of fall come at the end of the year. It is small and slow-growing with a conical habit and very suitable for a container of conifers. The plant is poisonous and the leaves are harmful if eaten.

Shrubs

Buxus sempervirens
Common box

Height (grown as a tree): 5m/16ft

Spread 5m/16ft

Box is actually a tree, but it is virtually always grown as a small shrub, used for formal edging and topiary in many gardens throughout the world. Box is an essential ingredient in all knot gardens and a neat, clipped low-growing box hedge conveys an instant impression of professional competence. In containers box is very often found trained into various topiary shapes, for the small leaves lend themselves to clipping to shape. A number of good

Fatsia japonica

varieties have been developed: 'Aureovariegata' has variegated gold-splashed leaves; 'Elegantissima' is very dense; and 'Suffruticosa' is compact and slow growing.

Exochorda macrantha 'The Bride'
Pearlbush

Height 1.2m/4ft

Spread 1.5m/5ft

This is a slow-growing shrub very suitable for any container or small garden. It flowers in late spring or early summer and flourishes in sun or partial shade. In flower it is one of the most beautiful shrubs in the garden with cascades of pure white flowers hanging down the pendent branches. It deserves to be better known. The flowers are born on the previous year's growth and it is better if left unpruned. Exochordas flourish in most garden soils but do best in neutral soil. Some species dislike lime.

Fatsia japonica
Japanese aralia

Height and spread: 1.5m/5ft

This is an architectural shrub grown entirely for its shape and large sculptural evergreen leaves. It does have small clumps of white flowers in late summer that appear on long stalks, which look a bit like a space station from a sci-fi movie, but they are very insignificant, as are the black berries that follow them. The plants are not fully hardy but they tolerate shade and pollution and make excellent container plants in a town garden for their large leaves are very striking. There are a number of varieties.

× *Halimiocistus wintonensis*

Height 60cm/2ft

Spread 90cm/3ft

Another small shrub that deserves to be a great deal better known than it is, and it is a good addition to any container garden. The genus is a cross between *Cistus* and *Halimium*, the rock roses, and has many of the qualities of the parents. All are excellent shrubs to include in an open sunny position and look well with other rock roses in an alpine garden. The shrubs are evergreen with gray-green leaves and the flowers are a beautiful white saucer shape with yellow stamens in the center surrounded by a dark maroon band.

Hebe 'Rosie'
Hebe

Height 30cm/1ft

Spread 60cm/2ft

Hebes are a large genus with over 100 species of evergreen shrubs of varying sizes, ranging from 2.5m/8ft to dwarf species suitable for rock and scree gardens. They vary in hardiness. They are grown for their conical spikes of flowers, often blue, white, or purple, that emerge in midsummer and last for a long time. 'Rosie' is a comparatively new, dwarf variety, very suitable for containers and alpine gardens that has lovely darkish-pink flowers that last for several months. It is very hardy.

Hydrangea macrophylla
Common hydrangea

Height 1.2m/5ft

Spread 1.8m/6ft

Hydrangeas make good container plants and create an instant and colorful effect in any garden. They should be planted on their own. The most striking is the hortensia division of *H. macrophylla*. These shrubs carry large heads of flowers, pink, white, blue, and lilac, depending on the variety grown and the acidity of the soil. 'Générale Vicomtesse de Vibraye' is one of the best to grow. It makes a good container plant and can also be raised as an indoor plant when young. The flowers are either pale blue, if grown in acid soil, or varying shades of pink.

Kolkwitzia amabilis 'Pink Cloud'
Beautybush

Height 3m/10ft

Spread 4m/13ft

This is another shrub that is seldom grown and deserves to be better known and used in all gardens, not just the container garden. In fact, it should be confined to its own container for it has a suckering habit. It is fairly slow growing and takes a long time to reach its full size. It needs fertile soil and prefers sun or partial shade. The glory of the shrub is the cascades of pink flowers that appear in late spring and hang down on the branches. The variety is preferred to the species plant as the flowers are a deeper pink. It is deciduous and the young leaves may become damaged by late frosts, so it may need some protection.

Lavandula angustifolia 'Hidcote'
Lavender

Height and spread 45cm–90cm/18in–3ft

Lavender is one of the very best shrubs to grow in a container garden, provided that it has a warm and sunny position, for it originally comes from the Mediterranean and like all shrubs from that region prefers sun and warmth. The leaves and flowers are both wonderfully fragrant, and it is good used as a dried flower to stuff scented pillows. The variety 'Hidcote' has dark purple flowers and is commonly grown. 'Munstead' has deep blue-purple flowers and 'Loddon Pink' has pink flowers. The other main lavenders grown are *L.* × *intermedia*, English lavender, and *L. stoechas*, French lavender. Prune all lavenders hard in the spring to keep them in shape.

Hydrangea macrophylla

Pieris formosa

Pieris formosa var. *forrestii*
Pieris

Height 4m/13ft

Spread 3.5m/11ft

Don't be put off growing a pieris by the eventual size that it might attain. They grow quite slowly and only achieve their maximum dimensions in optimum conditions. They are lovely shrubs for a spring container garden, as the young leaves appear bright red, changing to light green as summer progresses, and the white flowers emerge from dark pink buds. They must be grown in acid soil and partial shade and dislike cold winds in spring. Varieties of *P. formosa* are fairly upright, 'Wakehurst' is very popular, those of *P. japonica* are more rounded in form.

Spiraea japonica 'Goldflame'
Spiraea

Height 1.8m/6ft

Spread 1.5m/5ft

Spiraeas are deciduous shrubs and a number are very suitable for containers and small gardens, for they hug the ground

Lavandula angustifolia 'Hidcote'

Spiraea japonica 'Goldflame'

forming low clumps. *S. j.* 'Goldflame' is one of the commonest and is largely grown for its golden, bronze to red, young leaves that emerge in spring, turning green as the year progresses, and again to gold with the onset of fall. It also has spires of deep pink flowers from midsummer onward. It prefers full sun and most fertile soils.

Small roses

Small roses belong to one of three groups: miniature roses, the smallest, that usually only reach 30cm/12in in height; patio roses that reach 45cm/18in; and dwarf polyantha roses that may reach 60–90cm/2–3ft.

'Pretty Polly'
Miniature rose

Height 25cm/10in

Spread 45cm/18in

An excellent miniature rose with masses of small rose-pink, fully double flowers. As with all miniature roses this is a good flowering plant for a very small patio garden or even a window box: some gardeners grow them as flowering hedges around beds or containers. In interesting contrast, 'Black Jade' has deep red, almost black, flowers from spring to fall. 'Little White Pet' blooms for the same long period. Red buds open to sprays of white.

'Stars 'n' Stripes'
Miniature rose

Height 30cm/12in

Spread 60cm/24in

Miniature roses are attractive bushy plants
with tiny flowers. They are extremely
useful in a container garden where there is
little room, and can even be grown in
window boxes. In large gardens they can be
grown as a small hedge. 'Stars 'n' Stripes'
was developed on the west coast of
America and has white flowers, blotched
and striped with red, like a miniature of the
old rose *R. gallica* 'Versicolor'. Other
miniature roses include; 'The Fairy', pale
pink moss-like flowers, and 'Innocence',
creamy white flowers.

'Singin' in the the Rain'
Patio rose

Height and spread 60cm/2ft

This is one of the best patio roses for it has
a mass of dark green foliage and the flowers
are an apricot-peach color held upright
like many-petaled cups. It is slightly
fragrant. Patio roses are just a bit larger than
miniature roses and they repeat flower well.
'George Burns' has yellow, red, pink, and
cream striped flowers while 'Gracie Allen'
has white flowers with a pink heart. If you
prefer stronger colors, 'Europeana' is
velvety dark red, 'Sun Flare', yellow, and
'Judy Garland', chrome yellow blushing to
hot orange and scarlet.

'Katharina Zeimet'
Dwarf polyantha

Height and spread 30–90cm/1–3ft

There are two types of dwarf polyantha
roses: those whose flowers resemble
rambler roses, which are close-packed and
held in large sprays, and the roses whose
flowers are shaped like small miniature
hybrid tea roses. Both are appealing.
'Katharina Zeimet' is one of the best of the
rambler types with white, fragrant flowers;
pink-flowered roses of this type include
'Coral Cluster' and 'Nathalie Nypels'.
'Cécile Brünner', the 'Sweetheart Rose', is
the best known of the hybrid tea forms.
The flowers are blush pink; 'Perle d'Or' is
similar with apricot flowers.

Climbing roses

Climbing roses need to be differentiated
from ramblers. Climbers have larger flowers
and most repeat flowerings. Most modern
climbers repeat throughout the summer.
Ramblers are often very vigorous—too
vigorous, in fact, for any container garden,
however wonderful they look growing
through an old tree.

'Blairii Number 2'
Bourbon

Height 4.5m/15ft

Spread 1.8m/6ft

A Bourbon rose, a class of rose that mostly
dates from the latter part of the 19th
century, 'Blairii Number 2' has retained its
popularity as a climber for 150 years. It has
beautiful, pink many-petaled, fragrant
flowers, darker in the center and pale
toward the edges. It really only flowers
once in summer, although there is a small
second flowering. The young leaves are
reddish green when they emerge, changing
to mid-green as the summer progresses. It
is sometimes prone to attacks of mildew.

'Compassion'
Modern climber

Height 3m/10ft

Spread 2.5m/8ft

One of the very best and most popular of
the modern climbers, 'Compassion' has
large tea-shaped flowers, paleish pink on
the outside and apricot-yellow on the
inside. They are substantial blooms and
deliciously fragrant, giving the lie to
anyone who says that modern roses have
no perfume. It repeat flowers throughout

Rosa 'Sweet Dream'

Rosa 'Compassion'

the summer and has a strong bushy growth with dark green leaves. It looks its best when grown as a focal point on a southfacing wall where the blooms make the most impact.

'Constance Spry'
English rose

Height 3.5m / 12ft
Spread 3.5m / 12ft

This is one of the first English roses bred by David Austin. It can be grown as a shrub but makes an excellent climber when the lax shoots are given support and tied in to a frame The flowers are huge, clear pink, with the most pronounced myrrh fragrance. It makes a definite statement in any garden. Its only disadvantage is that unlike so many of the English roses it only flowers once, but those who grow it think the advantages far outweigh this.

'Copenhagen'
Modern climber

Height 2.5m / 8ft
Spread 2.5m / 8ft

This is another modern climber with flowers of superb fragrance. They are medium-sized, hybrid tea-shaped and deep scarlet. The rose will repeat flower throughout the summer and looks exceptional if it is grown in company with a large-flowered white clematis, such as 'Gillian Blades'. Another modern climber with deep red flowers that can be grown as an alternative is 'Crimson Cascade'. This rose is similar in size but has larger flowers. It is extremely vigorous and disease resistant.

'Golden Showers'
Modern climber

Height 3m / 10ft
Spread 3m / 10ft

One of the very best and most amenable of all the climbing roses, 'Golden Showers' has double, clear yellow flowers that fade to a paler cream as they age. It repeat flowers throughout the summer and the flowers have a pleasing fragrance. Its main advantage is that it will flourish happily on a north wall, making it invaluable for any garden denied the benefit of walls with better aspects. 'Danse du Feu' is another climber that will grow against a north wall. This rose has orange-scarlet flowers.

'Climbing Iceberg'
Floribunda

Height 3m / 10ft
Spread 2.5m / 8ft

The climbing form of the ever-popular 'Iceberg' is an excellent rose to grow against a wall and forms an admirable background to all other plants. The foliage is light green and the white flowers,

sometimes tinged with pale pink, are held in delicate sprays. Its only disadvantage is that it has little or no scent. 'Iceberg' remains in flower longer than almost any other rose in the garden and it is not unusual to be able to gather sprays in midwinter, on Christmas Day.

'Maigold'
Climber

Height 3.5m / 12ft
Spread 3m / 10ft

Like 'Golden Showers', 'Maigold' has some supreme advantages over other climbing roses as it is one of the toughest roses around, and be grown almost anywhere. It has superb bronze-yellow, semidouble flowers, which are produced in abundance. The flowers are extremely fragrant. It has a mass of dark glossy leaves and is generally disease-free but, alas, it only flowers once during the summer. It is probably the best rose to grow in poor conditions against a north-facing wall and should be considered by anyone who wants to grow a climbing rose and can only offer these conditions.

Rosa 'Constance Spry'

Rosa 'Copenhagen'

'New Dawn'
Modern climber

Height 3m/10ft

Spread 2.5m/8ft

A deservedly popular climbing rose was one of the first modern climbers. It is very vigorous, has lovely, glossy, light- to mid-green leaves, and delicate silvery pink flowers with a slightly deeper color in the center. The flowers are born in clusters and repeat throughout the summer. They have a light delicate fragrance. 'New Dawn' is not prone to disease and tolerates a partially shaded site although it should not be planted against a north-facing wall.

'Paul's Lemon Pillar'
Hybrid tea

Height 6m/20ft

Spread 3m/10ft

The classic pillar rose that is found in many gardens growing up pergolas or old tree stumps. It can be grown in containers at the foot of an arch and trained over a pergola. The rose has large, creamy lemon, tea-shaped, fully double flowers with petals

Rosa 'New Dawn'

that curl back at the edges. The flowers are very fragrant. The leaves are dark green. It is a strong, hardy, vigorous rose that should be tied in to make a columnar shape.

'A Shropshire Lad'
English rose

Height 2.5m/8ft

Spread 1.8m/6ft

This is another English rose that makes an excellent climber planted against a warm wall. It is a rose well worth growing for the flowers are large, of the typical cupped-rosette form found on many English roses and deliciously fragrant. The color is a beautiful peachy pink, fading slightly as the flowers age. Although it will grow best as a climber against a south wall, it can be planted in any position in the garden.

Climbers and wall plants

Abutilon × *suntense* 'Violetta'
Flowering maple, Indian mallow

Height 5m/16ft

Spread 3m/10ft

Some abutilons are evergreen, some deciduous, and none are fully hardy, but varieties of the deciduous *A.* × *suntense* are among the easiest to grow if they can be provided with a sheltered south-facing wall. They make excellent plants for containers. Flowers of the species are large and saucer-shaped. The variety 'Violetta' has intense violet flowers that appear in late spring. Any frost-damaged shoots should be cut back to sound wood in spring.

Clematis alpina 'Frances Rivis'
Clematis

Height 4m/13ft

Spread 1.8m/6ft

The alpina varieties of clematis are very suitable for growing in containers for they are relatively small in size and far less vigorous than montanas. They flower in spring. The flowers are single, and bell-shaped, like narrow pixies' caps with pointed petals. 'Frances Rivis' is the largest of the alpinas and has lovely dark blue flowers followed by fluffy seedheads. The alpinas are very hardy and will survive planted in the most unpromising positions, but they will not tolerate water-logged soil.

Clematis tangutica
Clematis

Height 4.5m/15ft

Spread 1.8m/6ft

One of the latest flowering of the clematis that brightens the autumn, *C. tangutica* carries funny, solitary, bright yellow flowers, bell-shaped but whose ends often appear as if they are crimped together.

Rosa 'Paul's Lemon Pillar'

They have striking seedheads that remain on the plant over the winter. The variety 'Helios' is shorter in growth and particularly suitable for a small container garden and there are a number of other hybrids. It is fully hardy.

Fremontodendron 'California Glory'
Flannel bush

Height 3m/10ft

Spread 3m/10ft

Fremontodendrons must be grown against a wall. They need tying in and are not considered particularly hardy although they will survive surprisingly cold winters given adequate protection. They are evergreen with rather sparse dark green leaves, up to 7.5cm/3in long. They are grown for the large deep buttercup-yellow flowers that appear in late spring and continue throughout the summer. The flowers are a shallow saucer shape. They prefer deep soil, so plant in a large container and see that there is good drainage. Cut back any frost-damaged shoots to good wood in spring.

Hydrangea petiolaris syn. *H. anomala* ssp. *petiolaris*

Clematis tangutica

Hedera helix 'Glacier'
Common ivy, English ivy

Height 1.8m/6ft or more

Spread 1.8m/6ft

Hedera helix, the common English ivy, has given rise to a large number of varieties. These can be grown against a wall to provide evergreen cover throughout the year, used as groundcover, or grown indoors as a house plant. The variety 'Glacier' is excellent for all these purposes. It has dark gray-green leaves with variegated margins marked silver and cream. When grown outside, it needs a sunny position to show its best color.

Hydrangea petiolaris syn. *H. anomala ssp. petiolaris*
Climbing hydrangea

Height 10m/33ft

Spread 10m/33ft

This is one of the best shrubs to cover a wall for it is not fussy over situation or aspect, and grows well in extremely shaded town gardens. It is a vigorous shrub but it can be cut back hard each spring. It clings to the wall by aerial roots and the bright green leaves turn yellow in the fall before they drop. In the summer it is covered with clusters of white flowers surrounded by prominent sterile flowers.

Jasminum officinale
Common jasmine, summer jasmine

Height and spread 12m/40ft

This is another vigorous climber often found growing in containers that will quickly cover a wall or trellis with its long trailing dark green shoots. Jasmine needs a frame to wind itself around. The flowers are white and emerge in summer, lasting into the early fall. They are very fragrant. It is best to prune jasmine after flowering is over, when it will often need to be cut back quite hard to keep it within its allotted space. It does not grow well in cold exposed sites.

Lapageria rosea
Chilean bellflower

Height and spread: 5m/16ft

A twining climber that will need support and protection in cold winters and will only flourish with the aid of a warm shady wall, as it comes from the forests of Chile and does not like full sun. It also needs acid soil. However if you can provide suitable

conditions it is a most attractive plant, evergreen with long dark green leaves, and long flowers, pink or rose-pink in color, and shaped a bit like narrow trumpets. These first appear in midsummer and last until the fall.

Pyracantha 'Orange Glow'
Firethorn

Height and spread: 3m/10ft

These are tough evergreen shrubs that can easily be trained against a wall and will grow in any situation from full sun to full shade. The less sun the plants get the fewer flowers and fruit they will bear. When grown against a wall they should be cut back hard in spring and trained to wires and then again in summer to remove shoots growing outward and reveal the clusters of berries. They have white flowers in spring followed by orange, red, or yellow berries that last through the winter.

Solanum crispum 'Glasnevin'
Chilean potato vine

Height and spread: 6m/20ft

There are two members of the potato family that are popular climbers, *S. crispum* and *S. jasminoides*. Both are evergreen or semievergreen, and both are only partly hardy. The variety 'Glasnevin' is the one most popularly grown in temperate climates and has proved it can survive quite severe winters, given the protection of a warm wall. They are all scrambling climbers and the young shoots generally need to be tied in to a trellis or some other support. 'Glasnevin' has lovely purple-blue flowers that last from summer into the fall.

Perennials

Container gardeners concentrate more on annuals and climbers than they do on perennials. Nevertheless there are a number that should be considered as permanent features in the garden.

Agapanthus Headbourne hybrids
African blue lily

Height 90cm/3ft

Spread 45cm/18in

In spite of their common name agapanthus are herbaceous perennials that are popular plants for containers where they flourish. They are grown largely for their dramatic clusters of flowers that emerge in late summer and resemble huge balls of bluebells held aloft on a large thick stalk. They like a sunny position and have thick roots that store water in dry periods. *Agapanthus* are not fully hardy and may need some protection in hard winters, but the Headbourne Hybrids, and a number of the named varieties, such as 'Blue Giant' and 'Alice Gloucester' are generally hardier than the species.

Jasminum officinale

Pyracantha 'Orange Glow'

Aponogeton distachyos
Cape pondweed, water hawthorn
Spread 1.2m/4ft

A rhizomatous perennial, the water hawthorn comes from South Africa, and has large deep green oval leaves that float on the surface of the water, like those of a water lily. The plants carry small white hawthorn-scented flowers in spring, and again in the fall, that are held aloft on forked flowering branches about 5cm/2in above the water. It prefers full sun but will tolerate partial shade. The water hawthorn is a good plant to grow to restrict the spread of algae in a pond or water garden.

Aquilegia vulgaris
Granny's bonnets, columbine
Height 90cm/3ft

Spread 45cm/18in

A favorite cottage garden perennial that flowers in late spring and early summer and is suitable for growing in any container, either on its own, or in company with other flowers. Granny's bonnets have dark

blue-violet flowers, and a number of the varieties have flowers varying from white, through pale shades of blue, to pink and yellow. They are the most attractive flowers, rising on long stalks above pools of green leaves. They self-seed freely and when they are grown in a confined space need to be controlled ruthlessly.

Aster novi-belgii
Michaelmas daisies
Height 90–120cm/3–4ft

Spread 60–90cm/2–3ft

Michaelmas daisies are one of the most colorful plants to be found in the container garden, and they flower in the late summer and early fall. They are usually found in varying shades of pink, violet, purple, and white and most of them have the typical yellow center of the daisy family. Among the most attractive are 'Marie Ballard', pale blue; 'Jenny' and 'Royal Ruby', deep pink; 'Lassie', pale pink; and 'Kristina,' white. They like well-drained soil and will flourish in partial shade. They require staking when grown in containers.

Dicentra formosa
Bleeding heart
Height 45cm/18in

Spread 60cm/2ft

D. spectabilis, bleeding heart or Dutchman's trousers, is a favorite spring border perennial. However it is probably too large for the average container garden and a better choice for a confined space is *D. formosa*, that spreads quite freely and has charming small purple flowers held up rather like branches of purple heather above silvery gray leaves. The variety 'Stuart Boothman' is very similar, slightly larger, and f. *alba* has white flowers and is less vigorous. They all flower in late spring and early summer and prefer some shade and neutral soil. Propagate by division.

Euphorbia amygdaloides
Wood spurge, milkweed
Height 75cm/30in

Spread 30cm/12in

There are over 2,000 species of euphorbia and they range in size from trees to tiny succulents. Probably the best-known garden euphorbia is *E. characias* ssp. *wulfenii*, which is a huge spectacular border plant. This, however, is not suitable for the average container garden. The wood spurge, *E. amygdaloides*, is much more suited as it is a small ground-covering plant that flourishes in shade. It has dark green leaves and green-yellow flowers that are held aloft on stalks. The variety 'Purpurea' has reddish-purple leaves and yellow flowers, and var. *robbiae*, 'Mrs Robb's bonnet', has much broader leaves. This variety may become invasive, so keep an eye on it.

Solanum crispum 'Glasnevin'

Aster novi-belgii

Geranium farreri

Geranium farreri
Cranesbill, hardy geranium

Height 10–15cm/4–6in

Spread 15cm/6in

Few garden plants provide as much pleasure to the gardener as the cranesbills. They flower throughout the summer and range in size from the spectacular *G. psilostemon*, to the tiny *G. farreri*, beloved by alpine gardeners. This small plant has flowers in an enchanting pale pink with conspicuous black anthers. Other favored cranesbills that are suitable for a container garden include *G. wallichianum* 'Buxton's Variety', sky-blue with white veins and dark anthers in the center, and *G. clarkei* 'Kashmir White', which is white with deeper pink veins.

Helianthus × multiflorus
'Loddon Gold'
Perennial sunflower

Height 1.5m/5ft

Spread 90cm/3ft

Most sunflowers are grown as annuals and afford great amusement on the principle that "I can grow a bigger one than you can." The perennial sunflower, too, is quite a large plant but it can make a dynamic impact in a container garden if you have room to accommodate it. It has great bushy flowerheads of bright yellow and does not really require staking. There are a number of other varieties including, 'Capenoch Star', single yellow flowerheads, and 'Soleil d'Or', double yellow flowerheads. They need to grow in full sun.

Helleborus orientalis
Hellebore, Lenten rose

Height 45cm/18in

Spread 45cm/18in

Lenten roses flower early in the year shortly after the Christmas rose, *H. niger*. The flowers are saucer-shaped and hang down from their stems. There are a number of colors and shades of mauve, pink, white, and red are common. The flowers are attractively marked on the inside and remain on the plant for several weeks, at a time of the year when there is little else in flower. In mild climates the leaves are evergreen. There are many named varieties: Millet hybrids are popular. They need some shade and prefer to be sheltered from rain and wind if possible.

Helleborus orientalis

Hosta 'Blue Moon'
Plantain lily

Height 10cm/4in

Spread 30cm/12in

Hostas grow better in containers than they do in borders where, in damp conditions, slugs devour them with an unbelievable relish. Slugs are not so prone to climb the sides of containers and the area is easier to control. Hostas are grown chiefly for their wonderful foliage, blue-gray, green, yellow-green, and variegated white that, when grown together, can make such an impact in a shady garden where they flourish best. 'Blue Moon' is a small hosta with blue-gray foliage, 'Aureomarginata' has white-edged green leaves, and 'Gold Standard' has yellow leaves, edged with green.

Lobelia cardinalis
Cardinal flower

Height 90cm/3ft

Spread 30cm/1ft

The cardinal flower is a short-lived rhizomatous perennial with dark red stems and bright green, bronze-tinted leaves. It is grown for its brilliant scarlet flowers that emerge in late summer and early fall. Few garden plants have such vivid coloring. The flowers can form the basis for a hot color scheme in late summer. Cardinal flowers prefer deep, moist soil in full sun although they will tolerate partial shade. *L. erinus* varieties are low-growing trailing perennials usually grown as annuals.

Lupinus Gallery Hybrids
Lupins

Height 50cm/20in

Spread 20cm/8in

Many lupins, including the popular Russell Hybrids, are rather large for the average container garden, reaching 1.2m/4ft, but if you are seeking to create a cottage garden effect in a small space, then the smaller Gallery Hybrids, developed as a dwarf strain, are well worth considering. The colors are rather paler than the Russell Hybrids but there is a good choice of the traditional pale pink, yellow, blue, red, purple, and lavender available. The flowers are more compact than in the larger varieties. Like with all lupins they prefer a sunny position. Lulu Series and Dwarf Russell Mixed are two more small series.

Nymphaea 'Gonnère'
Waterlily

Spread 90–120cm/3–4ft

Waterlilies have to be chosen with care, and the ones that you can grow depend entirely on the depth of water and the size of your pool. 'Gonnère' is one of the most beautiful white waterlilies, with many-petaled flowers, fragrant, with a clear yellow center. It needs a pool about 90cm/3ft deep to flourish and its spread is less than many of the larger lilies. All waterlilies grow best in full sun and they will not grow in running water, although some will tolerate very gentle movement.

Penstemon 'Andenken an Friedrich Hahn'
Penstemon

Height 75cm/30in

Spread 60cm/24in

Penstemons are rather underrated as garden perennials, which is a pity. They make outstanding plants, evergreen or semievergreen, with long tubes of flowers from midsummer through into the fall. They are easy to raise from cuttings taken in summer, or division in spring. They make excellent plants in a container garden if you do not want to include too many annuals. There are many excellent named varieties; three of the best known are: 'Andenken an Friedrich Hahn', deep red; 'Apple Blossom', a charming pink; and 'Maurice Gibbs', red with white centers.

Lobelia cardinalis

Lupinus

Phlox paniculata
Perennial phlox

Height 1.2m/4ft

Spread 60–90cm/2–3ft

Another glorious summer-flowering perennial that lasts in flower for weeks from the middle of summer into the fall. There are many varieties in varying shades of pink, red, purple, lilac, blue, and white. The glory of phloxes is their mop-headed flowers that look a bit like a colorful cloche hat on the top of the flower stalk. Among the most popular varieties are: 'Amethyst', violet; 'Eva Cullum', deep pink; 'Fujiyama', white; 'Le Mahdi', blue-purple; 'Mother of Pearl', white tinged with pink; and 'Prince of Orange', orange-red.

Primula vulgaris
Primrose

Height 20cm/8in

Spread 30cm/12in

Primulas are a large genus with over 400 species and thousands of varieties. In spite of this the common primrose, *P. vulgaris*, has remained the firm favorite for many

Phlox paniculata

gardeners. The flowers are a delicate pale yellow, with a darker yellow center. They are fragrant, and they have a charming modesty, as if apologizing for rising above their green leaves. They are also extremely easy to grow and propagate through division when flowering is over. They prefer growing in some shade and will not flourish in hot, dry conditions.

Pulmonaria saccharata
Lungwort

Height 30cm/12in

Spread 60cm/24in

Pulmonarias are one of the loveliest sights in spring when the flowers emerge on stalks held above the blotched and spotted leaves that give the flower its common name. They are good plants to grow in a container, for they spread freely in open ground and if the container is raised the flowers can be inspected at eye level. Generally the flowers are blue or pink with some white varieties, and a number open pink and turn blue after some days. Blue and pink flowers are often present on the same flower stalk. There are a number of named varieties; Argentea Group has silvery leaves with red flowers turning violet, and 'Mrs Moon' has pink buds, opening to lilac-blue flowers.

Scabiosa caucasica 'Clive Greaves'
Scabious, pincushion flower

Height 60cm/2ft

Spread 60cm/2ft

Wild small scabious, *S. columbaria*, is a common and lovely wildflower, but the genus is quite large and there are over 80

species. The cultivated varieties retain much of the charm of the parent and many have the lovely blue and lilac coloring, although various shades are available ranging from purple to white. Scabious is a flower of the late summer when many others are over and should be planted to continue the flowering interest in the garden. 'Clive Greaves' has lavender-blue flowers, 'Perfecta Alba' has white, as does 'Mrs Willmott'.

Stachys byzantina
Lambs' ears

Height 45cm/18in

Spread 60cm/24in

Certainly one of the best-known gray foliage plants in the garden, Lambs' ears can be grown anywhere as a foil for the green foliage of so many garden plants. It makes a dense mat of silvery white, wooly, felted leaves topped in summer by purple lavender flowers held aloft on spikes. They prefer full sun and will tolerate most soils provided they are well drained. There are a number of varieties: 'Big Ears' has green

Primula vulgaris

leaves with a gray bloom, and 'Silver Carpet' has silver leaves. This variety is grown as groundcover, for it does flower.

Annuals and bedding plants

These are the mainstay of the container gardener and different displays and color schemes can be contrived from year to year, Some of the plants are perennials but they are normally grown as bedding plants.

Ageratum houstonianum
Floss flower

Height 15–30cm/6–12in
Spread 15–30cm/6–12in
Low-growing, half-hardy annuals that are native to Mexico. Blue, pink, or white varieties can all be found although the most common color is blue. The mounds of small flowers are held just above the foliage. There are a number of named varieties: those most commonly grown are the Hawaii Series; the dwarf 'Swing Pink', pink-red; 'Blue Danube', a soft powder blue. Sow seed in spring at 16°C/60°F.

Amaranthus caudatus
Love-lies-bleeding, tassel flower

Height 75cm/30in
Spread 45cm/18in
A hardy annual that has extraordinary crimson tassels that droop down. On some varieties the flower tassels are upright. It is rather larger than many annuals. Varieties of *A. tricolor* are bushy with vividly colored leaves. Sow seeds in spring at 20°C/68°F.

Antirrhinum majus
Snapdragons

Height 30–45cm/12–18in
Spread 30cm/12in
These are half-hardy perennials that are normally grown as half-hardy annuals. They are a favorite flower of children who love popping the flowerheads open, hence the common name. The flowers come in all shades of brilliant colors: red, yellow, orange, and white. There are a number of series: Rocket Series is the tallest, Sonnet Series flowers early and is intermediate in size, and both Tahiti Series and 'Floral Showers' are dwarfing.

Aubrieta   cultorum
Aubrieta

Height 5cm/2in
Spread 60cm/2ft
Aubrieta is a hardy perennial that can be propagated by seed sown indoors in early spring or outdoors in early summer. It forms trailing mats of blue flowers and is grown in cracks of walls. It needs to be clipped back after flowering. The flowers are nearly always purple-blue in color, 'Hartswood Purple' and 'Joy' are popular.

Begonia
Begonias

Height 25cm/10in
Spread 30cm/12in
There are many different types of begonias but the ones usually grown in the summer garden are varieties of *B. tuberosa*, the tuberous begonias that have colorful large flowers, or *B. semperflorens*, which carry a mass of small flowers often with bronze foliage. Both should be treated as half-hardy annuals. There are an enormous variety of flower shapes and colors. Cocktail Series is a good *semperflorens* variety, the tuberous 'Can-Can' has huge yellow flowers with red-picotee margins.

Bellis perennis
Daisy

Height 15–20cm/6–8in
Spread 15cm/6in
Ornamental daisies are another hardy perennial usually treated as an annual. The flowers are held aloft on large pompoms and are red, pink, or white in color. They can be overwintered but most gardeners

Pulmonaria saccharata

Antirrhinum majus

229

replant them each year. Sow seed indoors at 10°C/50°F in early spring. The best known are the Pomponette, Roggli, and Tasso Series, although there are many others that are available.

Brachyscome iberidifolia
Swan River daisy

Height 30cm/12in

Spread 30cm/12in

Popular small annuals that form clumps of flowers that appear as massed daisies, the colors are usually white, lilac-pink, or purple. The Splendour Series is the one most commonly grown. Dwarf Bravo Mixed is a bit smaller and Summer Skies has flowers in attractively varied shades of blue, pink, and white.

Calceolaria Herbeohybrida Group
Slipper flower, pouch flower, slipperwort

Height 25cm/10in

Spread 15cm/6in

These are half-hardy biennials normally grown as summer-flowering container

Calceolaria integrefolia

plants. They look like large bunches of small lozenges and are often a striking yellow or orange in color. Sometimes the yellow varieties also have attractive orange drops in the center. 'Bright Bikinis' has yellow, orange, and red flowers, Anytime Series is compact and comes into flower very quickly. Sow seeds at 18°C/64°F in late summer or early spring.

Calendula officinalis
English marigold, pot marigold

Height 30–45cm/12–18in

Spread 30cm/12in

Extremely popular annuals that have been cultivated for many centuries. They are yellow and orange in color and look rather like miniature chrysanthemums. They are hardy annuals so seed can be sown outside in spring or fall where they are to flower. The Pacific Beauty Series is the most popular. *C. officinalis*, the traditional pot marigold, has single flowers.

Callistephus chinensis
China aster

Height 20–45cm/8–18in

Spread 20–45cm/8–18in

Half-hardy annuals that quickly make good bushy plants with flowers that are like miniature chrysanthemums in a multitude of colors: pink, yellow, red, mauve, and white. Some of the more open varieties resemble Michaelmas daisies. There are many series. Among the best known are Ostrich Plume, Comet, Milady Mixed, and Thousand Wonder. Sow seed at 15°C/60°F in early spring or outside later where the plants are to flower.

Campanula carpatica
Bellflower

Height 30cm/12in

Spread 30–60cm/12–24in

There are many bellflowers, aptly named for their glorious bell-like flowers usually found in various shades of blue, purple, and white. *Carpatica* are clump-forming, hardy perennials that make excellent edging plants for beds or pathways. They are extremely vigorous and may need to be controlled. The most popular varieties are 'Jewel', deep purple; 'Blue Clips', blue; and 'Bressingham White'. In the spring, sow seed *in situ* or divide established plants.

Catananche caerulea
Cupid's dart, blue cupidone

Height 75cm/30in

Spread 30cm/12in

An attractive clump-forming, short-lived perennial with gray-green grass-like leaves in summer, that produces large numbers of single flowers on upright stalks, dark to pale blue, throughout the summer. It is sometimes grown as an annual. There are a

Calendula officinalis

number of named varieties. 'Bicolor' has white petals with a purple center, 'Major' has lilac flowers with a dark center, and 'Perry's White' has white flowers with a creamy center. The varieties need to be raised by division or root cuttings for they will not come true from seed.

Celosia argentea
Cockscomb

Height 20–50cm/8–20in

Spread 15–45cm/6–18in

There are two types of celosia: the Plumosa Group has open, feathery, pyramidal flowerheads, while the Cristata Group has crested, tightly clustered flowerheads. The Plumosa Group are those used in summer bedding schemes in many parks and gardens. They appear in very bright colors of yellow, pink, orange, and red and simply cannot be missed. Varieties from the Century Series are the most commonly grown, the Kimono Series is smaller and more suited to a container garden scheme. Sow seed at 18°C/64°F from early spring onward.

Campanula carpatica 'Blue Gem'

Chrysanthemum parthenium 'Aureum'

Centaurea cyanus
Cornflower, batchelor's buttons

Height 25–90cm/9–36in

Spread 15–25cm/6–10in

Cornflowers are hardy annuals available in blue, claret, red, or pink. However, the traditional color of the cornflower is deep blue and many gardeners prefer to grow this color and no other. There are a number of series, including the Boy Series, which includes the bright blue 'Blue Boy', but individual varieties are available, such as 'Jubilee Gem', 'Pinkie', and 'Florence Blue'. Sow seed *in situ* in spring or in the fall the previous year.

Chrysanthemum parthenium syn.
Tanacetum parthenium
Feverfew

Height 45–60cm/18–24in

Spread 30cm/12in

This short-lived perennial is another plant that has had its name changed and you may also find it listed under *Tanacetum parthenium*. The border varieties have yellow or white flowers and some have yellow leaves. The best are the double forms, such as 'Plenum' and 'Snowball', both white. Sow seed in late winter or early spring at 10°C/50°F; take softwood cuttings in spring.

Cineraria maritima
syn. *Senecio cineraria*

Height 20–30cm/8–12in

Spread 23–30cm/9–12in

The 'correct' name for this plant is now *Senecio cineraria* but you are far more likely to find it listed under its old name. It is the classic foliage bedding plant with silvery-white leaves that make an excellent foil to all colorful annuals. The best-known varieties are 'Silver Dust' and 'Cirrus'. Sow seed in spring at 20°C/68°F. If you can overwinter them you can take semiripe cuttings at the end of the summer.

Clarkia amoena
Satin flower

Height 75cm/30in

Spread 30cm/12in

Most attractive annuals with fluted flowers, sometimes with a marked center. They can also be found listed as *Godetia amoena* and *G. grandiflora*. The flowers are usually pink, white, or a deep lavender. The Satin Series is smaller. *C. unguiculata*, also sold as *C. elegans*, is larger with erect spikes of flowers,

Consolida ajacis

which in the Royal Bouquet Series look like small hollyhocks. Sow seed *in situ* in early spring, do not transplant. They make good dried flowers.

Consolida ajacis
Larkspur

Height 30–50cm/12–20in

Spread 15–25cm/6–10in

Attractive annuals grown for their erect spikes of flowers usually in soothing pastel colors of white, pale blue, and pink, although some are deep violet. The smaller varieties are the ones most usually grown; Dwarf Hyacinth Series and Dwarf Rocket Series are both popular. They are strong plants and withstand wind well. The Giant Imperial Series is much larger, reaching 90cm/3ft, and should be planted at the back of a container or border. Hardy annual seed should be sown outside *in situ* in spring or the previous fall. The plants are poisonous to humans.

Convolvulus tricolor
Bindweed

Height 30–40cm/12–16in

Spread 23–30cm/9–12in

Common bindweed is one of the most pernicious garden weeds but its cultivated relations are charming plants and range from shrubs to annuals. *C. tricolor* is grown as a hardy annual. The series Flagship Mixed appears in a variety of colours: red, deep blue, light blue, white, and pink. The trumpet-shaped flowers have strongly marked white and yellow centers. *C. sabatius* is a lovely blue hardy perennial normally grown in rock or scree gardens.

It may need some protection in hard winters. Sow seed *in situ* in mid-spring. Take cuttings of perennials.

Coreopsis tinctoria
Tickseed

Height 30cm/12in

Spread 15cm/6in

The smaller tickseeds are varieties of *C. tinctoria*. The ones most usually grown are Dwarf Mixed or the variety 'Mahogany Midget'. The latter has bronze-red flowers with a yellow center that are carried in profusion from midsummer until the autumn. *C. grandiflora* and its varieties are hardy perennials, sometimes grown as annuals, and usually have yellow flowers. 'Early Sunrise' and 'Tiger Flower' are two good varieties. Sow seed *in situ* in spring.

Dianthus chinensis
China pink, Indian pink

Height 15–25cm/6–10in

Spread 10–15cm/4–6in

Dianthus is a large genus with many different types of pinks and carnations that

Eschscholzia californica

are grown both indoors and out. The common border pinks are those grown as half-hardy annuals where the seed is sown in spring at 16°C/60°F and the plants flower in late summer of that year. A number of series have been cultivated, and there are a number of named varieties. The Baby Doll and Carpet Series both have single flowers that range from red to white, but are mainly pink. The striking 'Raspberry Tart' has pink flowers with deep red centers. 'Dad's Favorite' has white flowers with a red margin and purple center.

Erigeron karvinskianus
Midsummer daisy, Mexican daisy, fleabane

Height 15–30cm/6–12in

Spread to 90cm/3ft

This is an excellent plant to grow hanging down a wall, in a hanging basket or balcony container. Small daisy-like flowers emerge white in midsummer and then gradually turn through pink to red. If grown in a basket or window box it should be treated as a hardy annual; if grown down

a wall it can be treated as a hardy perennial although it is very vigorous and may well need controlling. 'Profusion' is the variety most often grown. Sow seed in a cold frame in spring.

Eschscholzia californica
California poppy

Height 15–30cm/4–12in

Spread 15cm/6in

California poppies are one of the easiest of all plants to grow for the seed will take root anywhere, even in a gravel border. The plants self-seed vigorously and need to be controlled. They have single erect flowers on stalks in attractive colors, mainly yellow and orange, but some varieties are red, pink, and white. The most spectacular is the Thai Silk Series that has semidouble flowers in a variety of colors. Sow seed *in situ* in spring.

Fuchsia
Fuchsia

Height (small varieties): 45–60cm/18–24in

Spread 30–60cm/12–24in

Fuchsias are mainly half-hardy shrubs, although there are some hardy varieties that will survive temperatures down to -5°C/23°F. They have pendent flowers, mostly in attractive pastel shades of pink, and many are bicolored. They make excellent shrubs for hanging baskets and containers and can be brought indoors over winter where circumstances permit. Good varieties include: 'Margaret Brown', two-toned pink flowers; 'La Campanella', white and purple; and 'Swingtime', white double flowers with red outer petals.

Gazania

Height 20cm/8in

Spread 25cm/10in

Half-hardy perennials that are grown as half-hardy annuals. They are members of the daisy family and the flowers are daisy-like with rather broader petals. There are a number of series normally grown. The Chansonette Series has flowers in a mixture of colors: yellow, pink, red, and orange. The Mini-star Series is smaller and has a wider range of colors. Sow seed in early spring at 18–20°C/64–68°F.

Heliotropium arborescens
Heliotrope, cherry pie

Height 30–45cm/12–18in

Spread 30–35cm/12–14in

Many varieties of *H. arborescens* make good sized shrubs, but the smaller varieties are usually grown as half-hardy annuals. 'Marine' is the most popular variety and has the characteristic smell of cherries that gives the plant its common name. 'Mini Marine' is a bit smaller and more compact. The flowers are violet blue and they make

Fuchsia 'Tennessee Waltz'

Gazania

Lavatera trimestris 'Silver Cup'

a wide variety of colors: pink, cerise, red, white, some bicolored, held above light green and bronze leaves, some of which can be variegated. They prefer to grow in partial shade and will even provide color in complete shade, making them invaluable for gardeners with shady gardens. Many other series are available. Sow seed in spring at 16°C/60°F. You can take cuttings in summer to overwinter indoors.

Lavatera trimestris
Annual mallow

Height 60–90cm/2–3ft
Spread 30–45cm/12–18in

These are extremely attractive annuals, although some are a bit larger than most. They have that lovely mallow-shaped flower which is like a shallow trumpet. 'Pink Beauty' is white with pink veins on the petals and a darker center; 'Silver Cup' is a deeper pink; 'Mont Blanc' is almost pure white; 'Ruby Regis' has deep reddish-pink flowers. Sow seed out of doors where the plants are to flower from mid-spring onward.

excellent plants for containers in the summer. Seed can be sown in spring at 16°C/60°F but named varieties are best propagated by tip cuttings taken in summer, for they may not come true from seed.

Iberis umbellata
Globe candytuft

Height 15–30cm/6–12in
Spread 20cm/8in

Another extremely popular hardy annual that should be sown out of doors where it is to flower in fall or early spring. The two most popular series are Fairy Series, clusters of pale pink, lavender, and white flowers,

and Flash Series, stronger colors of pink, purple, or red. The flowers are made up of many small petals shaped like a shallow dome and completely cover the plant, giving rise to its common name, which is very descriptive.

Impatiens New Guinea Group
Busy Lizzie, balsam

Height 35cm/14in
Spread 30cm/12in

Almost the most popular summer bedding plant, busy lizzies are half-hardy perennials although they are almost always grown as annuals. The New Guinea Group come in

Impatiens New Guinea Group

Limnanthes douglasii
Poached-egg plant

Height 15cm/6in

Spread 15cm/6in

An aptly named, low-growing annual, that has saucer-shaped flowers, white on the margin with deep yellow centers. It also has lovely bright green leaves. The flowers are attractive to bees and flower throughout the summer. It is easy to grow and seed should be sown *in situ* in spring or fall for earlier flowering the next year. Fall sowings need to be protected from frosts during the winter.

Linum grandiflorum
Flowering flax

Height 45–60cm/18–24in

Spread 15cm/6in

Flax flowers are supposed to be blue, and most perennial flaxes are, but the species plant of the annual flowering flax has rose-pink flowers. Of the named varieties 'Bright Eyes' is white, 'Caeruleum', blue, 'Magic Circles', red and white, and 'Rubrum,' red. They are among the easiest

Lobelia erinus

of all hardy annuals to cultivate. Sow seed *in situ* outdoors in spring. Annual flax is best grown in blocks of color so that it achieves its maximum effect.

Lobelia erinus
Trailing lobelia

Height 10–15cm/4–6in

Spread 15cm/6in

These are low-growing bushy perennials that are grown as annuals. They are the mainstay of hanging baskets throughout the world where the small flowers, generally blue with pale marked centers, hang down the sides. If grown in a rock garden they will fall over rocks and they look their best grown in a blue and white border with silver *Cineraria* (*Senecio*) and the white variety 'White Cascade'. The Cascade Series has pink, red, blue, and white flowers, Palace Series is mainly blue or white. There are border-edging and taller kinds available.

Matthiola incana
Sweet-scented stock

Height 20–45cm/8–18in

Spread 25–30cm/10–12in

Stocks are upright perennials or sub-shrubs but they are usually grown as half-hardy annuals. They are sometimes called "ten-week stocks" for they achieve maturity quite quickly. They have upright spikes of flowers, usually white, red, pink, and purple, and are very sweet-smelling. The Virginia stock, *Malcolmia maritima*, belongs to another genus. There are a number of series available. Brompton Series is grown as a biennial, Ten-Week Mixed has mostly double flowers and Sentinel Series is taller.

Mesembryanthemum criniflorum
Livingstone daisy

Height 8cm/3in

Spread 15cm/6in

Livingstone daisies are a popular half-hardy annual and flourish in dry conditions, but need sun to be at their best. The massed, typical daisy-like flowerheads are pink, white, cerise, and yellow, with paler shades in between. They make good groundcover. Sow indoors in early spring at 16°C/60°F.

Mimulus × hybridus
Monkey flower

Height 12–30cm/5–12in

Spread 30cm/12in

Tender perennials that are usually grown as annuals. There are a number of series: Calypso, Magic, and Mystic are the ones usually grown. They have open trumpet-shaped flowers usually yellow or orange but creamy white, red, and pink flowers are also found. They are often spotted in the center. They prefer slightly damp soil. Sow seed indoors in spring at a temperature of 7°C/45°F or over.

Matthiola incana

Nemesia strumosa
Nemesia
Height 20–30cm/8–12in
Spread 10–15cm/4–6in
Popular half-hardy annuals for the rock and scree garden, nemesias have charming, rather informal flowers that open into two halves and are often bicolored. 'KLM' is blue and white, 'National Ensign' and 'Danish Flag' are both red and white. 'Blue Gem' is sapphire blue with white eyes and plants from the Carnival Series are smaller. Sow seed in spring at 15°C/59°F, or sow in the fall for early flowering the following year. Water the plants well when they come into flower and protect them from frost if they are to be overwintered.

Nicotiana × sanderae
Tobacco plant
Height 30–60cm/12–24in
Spread 20–45cm/8–18in
These are rather smaller than the traditional tobacco plant and the flowers are open during the day, not just in the evening. However they are not so fragrant.

'Lime Green' is a popular variety with green flowers. There are a number of series available, notably Domino and Havana, while Merlin was bred for containers. They should be grown as half-hardy annuals. Sow seed in spring at 18°C/64°F.

Petunia
Height 20–30cm/8–12in
Spread 30–90cm/12–36in.
Undoubtedly the most popular and widely grown of all summer bedding plants, petunias are half-hardy perennials that are almost always grown as annuals. They are divided into two groups: the Grandiflora varieties with large single flowers, and the Multiflora varieties that are bushier and produce a greater quantity of smaller flowers. The range of colors available is immense: single colors, double colors, and many have variegated center markings, either darker or in a second color. The Supercascade Series is extremely popular for planting in hanging baskets, Carpet Series is an excellent bedding plant and the Picotee Series has white ruffled margins.

Sow seed outdoors in spring and deadhead flowering plants regularly through the summer to keep them flowering.

Pelargonium
Geranium
Height 12–60cm/5–24in
Spread 20–30cm/8–12in
A large genus of plants with six divisions. Those most commonly grown in borders are the Zonal geraniums and they have seven further subdivisions, depending on the flower shape. Trailing geraniums are excellent for window boxes on balconies, and also work well in hanging basket schemes. The flowers range from brilliant red, through all the varying shades of pink and purple, to white. Plants from the Horizon Series are compact and bushy—and good for containers—while those from the Orbit Series flower early. There are large numbers of named varieties. Geraniums can be raised from seed sown in spring at 16°C/60°F, but they are best propagated from softwood cuttings. These can be taken throughout the year.

Nicotiana x sanderae

Petunia

Sidalcea malviflora

Phlox drummondii
Annual phlox

Height 10–45cm/4–18in

Spread 20cm/8in

A pretty half-hardy annual that is grown for its attractive clusters of flowers that are slightly reminiscent of a small hydrangea. The flowers are generally white, purple, lavender, pink, and red and the shades are very similar to many petunias. There are several series and they vary in size. Among the most popular are Twinkle Star Mixed with star-shaped petals. Fantasy Series is scented with clear colors and Palona Series is dwarf with bushy plants. Sow seed at 16°C/60°F early in spring, sow outdoors early in summer.

Salvia splendens
Scarlet sage

Height 30–40cm/12–16in

Spread 15–20cm/6–8in

Salvias are a large and varied genus but those grown as annual bedding plants have been developed from *S. splendens* that has such vivid red upright flowers in summer.

Tropaeolum majus

They are among the most popular bedding plants for the summer garden, and work well in a container. Several series have been developed. These include Sizzler, which can be found in eight colours, including salmon, deep pink, pale yellow, lavender, red, and purple, and the dwarf 'Firecracker'. There are also many named varieties. Sow seed at 16°C/60°F in mid-spring.

Schizanthus pinnatus
Butterfly flower, poor man's orchid

Height 20–50cm/8–20in

Spread 20–30cm/8–12in

These are popular house plants when grown in a cool greenhouse but they can also be grown outside as hardy annuals, provided you have a warm sheltered border, and they can also be sown under glass over winter. They have attractive open tubular flowers held in clusters, which are generally white, yellow, pink, red, and purple, and they have prominent yellow, or yellow-red central markings. 'Hit Parade' and 'Star Parade' are the ones most commonly grown. Sow seed at 16°C/60°F in spring or in late summer for plants to flower indoors during the winter.

Sidalcea malviflora
False mallow, prairie mallow

Height 30–90cm/12in–3ft

Spread 10–45cm/4–18in

Sidalceas are perennials that, in the wild, flourish in the grasslands, woodland glades, and by the rivers and streams of the north and west. They grow in almost any soil except when it is waterlogged, and they

prefer full sun. The best small varieties for a container garden are probably the compact 'Loveliness' with pale pink flowers, 'Puck', which has deeper pink flowers in mid-summer, or some of the special bedding mixtures available. As might be imagined from their common name the flowers are open and saucer-shaped, and held upright on stalks above a rosette of basal leaves.

Tropaeolum majus
Nasturtium, Indian cress

Height 30cm/12in

Spread 45cm/18in

Popular climbing plants that are easy to grow in almost any soil and can be sown out of doors from late spring onward. They do prefer a sunny position. There are a large number of varieties and these can be grown as bushy annuals or as semitrailing plants in hanging baskets. They all have yellow and orange flowers in varying shades. The Whirlybird Series is popular as are the Gleam Mixed hybrids that have double flowers

Verbena × hybrida
Verbena

Height 30cm/12in

Spread 25cm/10in

Shrubby perennials that are grown as annual bedding plants. A number of series have been developed in a wide variety of colors from deep violet to blue, red, pink, peach, and white. The flowers appear in clusters and each flowerhead is a bit like a very small primrose. Often they have a strongly marked center. Some series are erect, others are trailing or spreading in habit, which makes them very suitable for hanging baskets and containers. Good series include Sandy and Romance, both erect in habit. The Romance Series, and the varieties 'Peaches and Cream' and 'Imagination' are all spreading.

Viola × *wittrockiana*
Winter-flowering pansies

Height 20–30cm/8–12in

Spread 20–30cm/8–12in

The development of winter-flowering pansy has transformed gardens in the winter. They can be planted out in the fall and will continue in flower for months on end. They are hardy perennials but should be treated as half-hardy annuals and fresh stock planted each year. Grow them in containers to provide individual bright spots in the garden. A huge number of series have been developed over the years, mostly multicolored, or bicolored, but single-colored varieties are available. The colours run from deep violet and yellow, to purple, blue, and white. Most varieties have the typical "pansy" face with its strong

central marking. The Fama, Regal, and Ultima Series are all good winter-flowering plants; many other series flower in the summer.

Spring bulbs

Chionodoxa luciliae
Glory of the snow

Height 15cm/6in

Spread 5cm/2in

Chionodoxa are less well known than many of the early spring bulbs but they are extremely attractive and deserve to be more widely grown. They have small, six-petaled, star-shaped flowers, in varying shades of blue, often with a pronounced white center. Once established they self-seed readily. They prefer full sun. There are a number of varieties but the botanical names have become muddled. You will usually find them sold as *C. gigantea*, blue with white center; *C. g.* 'Alba', white; *C. luciliae*, pale blue with white center, *C. l.* 'Pink Cloud', pink, or *C. sardensis*, blue.

Chionodoxa luciliae syn. gigantea

Fritillaria meleagris

Crocus chrysanthus
Spring-flowering crocus

Height 5cm/2in

Spread 5cm/2in

Crocuses flower both in the fall and early spring, but it is the ones that flower early in the year that attract the most attention. The best known are varieties of *C. chrysanthus* and *C. tommasinius*. The majority are yellow, orange, purple to pale lilac, and white in color. They are easy to grow given a certain amount of sun and well-drained soil. When the flowers open in spring they are a charming sight on a sunny day with the petals spread wide apart to catch the rays of the sun.

Cyclamen coum
Hardy cyclamen

Height 5cm/2in

Spread 10cm/4in

The hardy cyclamen that flower in spring are varieties of *C. coum*. *C. hederifolium* and its varieties look exactly the same but flower in the fall. Both species have attractive small white, pink, purple, and red flowers held aloft on short stalks, a bit like upside-down small butterflies. They prefer soil that does not dry out but they need protection from excessive moisture and grow best in the shelter of trees or spreading shrubs. Mulch in the winter to protect the leaves from frost.

Narcissus
Daffodils, narcissus

Height 30–60cm/1–2ft

There are thousands of different daffodils available and a glance through the catalog

of any reputable bulb supplier gives some
idea of the variety. There are
12 divisions. The best ones for the small
container garden are varieties of *N.
cyclamineus*, Division 6, which, in general
gardening terms, would be called small
narcissi. 'Little Witch' is pure yellow, 'Jack
Snipe', white with yellow center,
'Foundling', white with orange center, and
'Jenny', white with white to pale yellow
center. Other good small varieties are those
from Division 7, Jonquilla.

Erythronium dens-canis
Dog's tooth violet, trout lily

Height 10–15cm/4–6in

Spread 10cm/4in

The dog's tooth violet is another charming
spring bulb that flowers slightly later than
most spring bulbs. It needs moist, shady
conditions and well-drained soil that does
not dry out. It is grown for its attractive
spotted foliage, which gives it the name of
trout lily, as well the flowers that are held
aloft on stalks with widely spaced, swept-
back petals and long anthers. The best

Narcissus

known are 'Pink Perfection'; 'Lilac
Wonder', rich purple; 'Snowflake,' white
with pink markings. There are a number
of other varieties available.

Fritillaria meleagris
Snake's head fritillary

Height 30cm/12in

Spread 5–7.5cm/2–3in

The snake's head fritillary is a popular bulb
that will happily naturalize in grassland.
It is also a good bulb to include in an
alpine garden, for here its charms can be
appreciated at close quarters. The bulbs
need full sun to flourish. *F. meleagris* is

widely available with spotted purple
flowers and there is a white form,
F. m. alba. Other taller and interesting
species that can be grown in the alpine
garden include; *F. acmopetala*, green
bell-shaped flowers flushed pink, and
F. camschatcensis, black-purple flowers
with yellow centers.

Hyacinthus orientalis
Hyacinth

Height 30cm/12in

Spread 7.5cm/3in

Hyacinths make excellent container-grown
bulbs and are equally welcome planted in

Hyacinthus orientalis 'Pink Pearl'

the fall in prepared bulb fiber to flower indoors in the early months of the year, or grown in a container outside. The flowers are held on long spikes and are extremely fragrant. Plant hyacinths in groups of two or three colors: white, lilac-blue, and pink are the most common and the most effective. White hyacinths include, 'Carnegie' and 'Innocence'. 'Lady Derby' and 'Pink Pearl' are pink, and 'Blue Jacket' and 'Delft Blue' are soft blue. Make sure to stake the plants as they are liable to topple over. Bulb suppliers sell special hyacinth stakes for this purpose.

Iris reticulata and *I. unguicularis*
Early-flowering iris

Height 7.5–15cm and 3–6in/30cm/12in
Spread 2.5–5cm/1–2in and
30–45cm/12–18in

The bulbous irises known as reticulata are the ones that flower early in the year along with the rhizomatous *I. unguicularis* and its varieties, which were formerly called *I. stylosa*. They nearly all have lovely blue, violet, and yellow flowers with attractive

Iris reticulata

markings, although 'Natasha' is virtually white. *I. danfordiae* has yellow flowers, 'Cantab', rich blue with a yellow stripe, 'Harmony', deep velvet blue. *I. unguicularis* is pale blue to violet with a yellow band on the fall; good varieties are 'Mary Barnard', violet, and 'Walter Butt', a paler lavender.

Muscari armeniacum
Grape hyacinth

Height 20cm/8in
Spread 5cm/2in

Grape hyacinths are obliging plants for they flower when many of the early spring bulbs are over and they are easy to grow and undemanding in their needs. The flowers are usually differing shades of blue, although violet-pink and white forms are available. The most popular are varieties of *M. armeniacum*, all of which have bright blue flowers. They do colonize freely and may require controlling when they are grown in a restricted space.

Tulipa
Tulip

Height 15–65cm/5–26in
Spread 5–7.5cm/2–3in

There are so many different tulips of varying colors and sizes that any container gardener has to choose carefully according to the color scheme of the garden and the space available. There are 14 divisions that all flower at slightly different times, so if you want a display all flowering together, it is advisable to choose bulbs from the same division. The colors range from yellow, orange, pink and red, to deep purple, almost black, back to white. There are a number of

striped and double colored varieties. Sturdy mid-season tulips (Triumph, Group 3) include 'Don Quichotte', pink; 'Margot Fonteyn', cardinal red, yellow margins; 'Shirley', white, purple margins; and 'Palestrina', salmon pink.

Summer- and
fall-flowering bulbs

Bulbs are not confined to the spring. There are many lovely bulbs that flower in the summer and fall and a number of these are definitely worth considering for the container garden.

Allium
Ornamental onions

Height 60–150cm/2–5ft
Spread 5–15cm/2–6in

Many ornamental onions flower in late spring and early summer but there are some that flower in late summer and into the fall, and the smaller varieties can add much welcome color to an alpine garden in this period of the year. Among the best

Tulipa

is *A. sphaerocephalon* that reaches 60cm/2ft and has deep crimson flowerheads. *A. ostrowskianum* is an excellent rockery plant with heads of pink flowers in midsummer and *A. moly* is another small onion for the rockery with bright yellow flowers.

Alstromeria Ligtu hybrids
Peruvian lily

Height 50cm/20in
Spread 75cm/30in

Peruvian lilies are popular flowers for the summer container garden and should be grown in fairly deep containers, for the tubers should be planted at least 25cm/10in deep. They are best grown in individual containers for they can spread quite freely if they are given enough space. They have wide, flared flowers in varying shades of pastel colors, usually peach, orange, pink, and creamy white. The color varies considerably and they are a most welcome addition to a pale-colored, delicate color scheme in the summer. They prefer full sun.

Alstromeria Ligtu hybrids

Anemone coronaria
Windflower

Height 30–45cm/12–18in
Spread 15cm/6in

Anemones are tuberous perennials that should be left undisturbed when they have been planted. They like light sandy soil and full sun. *A. blanda* and its varieties flower early in spring and are common to many alpine garden planting schemes. Varieties of *A. coronaria* flower in late spring and early summer. These include the De Caen Group, single-flowered varieties, and the St Brigid Group, double-flowered varieties. The usual colors of the blooms are red, blue, violet, and white. The much taller Japanese anemones found in the herbaceous borders of the fall are usually varieties of *A. hupehensis* var. *japonica*.

Colchicum
Autumn crocus

Height 10–18cm/4–7in
Spread 7.5–10cm/3–4in

Colchicums are commonly known as autumn crocuses although in fact they have nothing whatsoever to do with the spring bulbs. They are attractive bulbs with flowering stems that emerge before the leaves, giving them their other common name of naked ladies. The ones most usually grown are varieties of *C. agrippinum*, *C. autumnale* and *C. speciosum*. The most popular individual varieties are *C. s.* 'Album', large white globe-shaped flowers; *C.* 'The Giant', large purple-violet flowers, 'Violet Queen', pinkish-violet flowers, and 'Glory of Heemstede', which has reddish purple blooms.

Camassia
Quamash

Height 75cm/30in
Spread 45cm/18in

Camassias are attractive summer-flowering bulbs with upright spires of flowers and tall mid-green leaves. The flowers are usually blue but vary in color from white to purple and violet. 'Zwamenburg' has deep blue flowers while 'Semiplena' bears racemes of semidouble, creamy-white flowers. They prefer heavy moist soil and sun or partial shade. Divide the clumps when the plants are dormant and propagate by taking offsets from the parent bulb in the fall.

Cardiocrinum giganteum
Giant lily

Height 1.5–2m/5–7ft
Spread 45cm/18in

The giant lily is a spectacular plant, even larger than the regal lily, and if grown in a container it will certainly require staking. It has creamy white funnel-shaped flowers that are fragrant and there are several flowers on each stalk. Plant the bulb just

Colchicum

Galtonia candicans

hang in much the same manner. They prefer to grow in good, fertile moist soil that does not dry out, in full sun. They are not totally hardy and containers of bulbs should be brought indoors in very hard winters. Two species are commonly grown: *G. candicans* and *G. viridiflora*. The flowers of the latter have a greenish tinge and they have a more upright habit.

Lilium
Lily

Height 90–150cm/3–5ft
Spread 25cm/10in

Lilies form a huge genus that has been divided into 9 main divisions and 11 sub-divisions. They make wonderful container plants; a large container filled with one variety can be a most effective focal point. All the large lilies need staking when they are planted. A number of them are exceptionally fragrant. Among the most popular are: *L. regale*, the regal lily, *L. candidum*, Madonna lily, *L.* 'Casa Blanca', white, *L.* 'Citronella', yellow, and *L. martagon*, the turkscap lily, purple.

below the surface in moist rich soil. It prefers partial shade and will not flourish in direct sun. Take offsets from the main bulb after flowering.

Cyclamen hederifolium X *neapolitanum*
Baby cyclamen

Height 15cm/6in
Spread 20cm/8in

This is the autumn-flowering form of the hardy cyclamen. It is a tuberous perennial. The flowers appear from a corm before the leaves and are usually varying shades of pink; there are also white forms. They

flourish in dry shade and grow well beneath trees. The leaves, as the Latin name implies, are marked like ivy. The flowers self-seed freely in good conditions and eventually they form large colonies.

Galtonia candicans
Summer hyacinth

Height 90–120cm/3–4ft
Spread 10cm/4in

This is a large summer bulb that has beautiful spires of white flowers that hang down when the flowers finally emerge in late summer. The individual flowers are shaped rather like large snowdrops and

Lilium 'Sunray'

Nerine bowdenii
Nerine

Height 35cm/15in

Spread 7.5cm/3in

Nerines used to be thought of as very tender and were only grown in greenhouses. However they are perfectly hardy in mild areas, as long as you can give them the shelter of a south- or southwest-facing wall. They have lovely pink trumpet-shaped flowers born in clumps in early fall. The flowers last for quite a long time. The form *alba* has white, flushed pale pink flowers. 'Mark Fenwick' has deep pink flowers on dark stalks. They need to be left undisturbed after planting for they grow best when they are pot-bound.

Sparaxis
Harlequin flower

Height 10–25cm/4–10in

Spread 7.5cm/3in

These are cormous perennials that come from South Africa. There are 6 species but they are most commonly sold under the label Mixed Varieties. They are the most attractive small summer plants, flowering from midsummer onward in varying shades of white through pink to red, each flower having a prominently marked central ring at the base of the petals with a yellow center. A bowl full of them makes a wonderful display. They need full sun and are only suitable for growing in mild districts in temperate climates. They need protection in winter if grown out of doors.

Sprekelia formosissima
Aztec lily, Jacobean lily

Height 15–35cm/6–14in

Spread 15cm/6in

There is only one species of this lily but it is well worth growing as a house plant in temperate climates, although it flourishes out of doors when the temperature does not drop below 7°C/45°F. It has striking scarlet red flowers that give the impression that it is sticking out its tongue. When grown as a pot plant indoors, it needs full light and requires watering and feeding when in growth. It flowers in late spring or early summer. Keep dry when it is dormant.

Tigridia pavonia
Peacock flower, tiger flower

Height 40cm/16in

Spread 10cm/4in

Another unusual summer bulb that comes from Mexico and Guatemala where it grows in dry grassland, sand and occasionally among rocks. In temperate climates they should either be grown as pot plants and brought indoors in the winter, or in mild districts, planted out in a sunny border, lifted in the fall and brought indoors for the winter. They can also be grown permanently as container plants in a cool greenhouse or conservatory. They prefer well-drained, sandy, fertile soil. *T. pavonia* is a bulbous perennial with lance-shaped leaves. They are the most exotic looking plants—the flowers resemble orchids with their three large, white, pink, yellow, and soft red outer petals, tiny inner petals, and contrasting central markings of vivid red and yellow spots. Sow seed at 13–18°C/55–64°F in spring. Separate offsets when dormant, avoiding plants affected by viruses.

Nerine bowdenii

Sparaxis Mixed Varieties

Tigridia pavonia

Anchusa azurea 'Loddon Royalist'

Osteospermum

Phormium 'Pink Panther'

Plant Lists

These lists are a guide to those plants that are suitable for growing in varying parts of a garden or have special requirements. Many of the plants, particularly those where only the genus name is given, e.g. *Rhododendron*, have a number of different species and cultivated varieties (cultivars) available, for instance there are literally thousands of different rhododendrons. Always check in a good encyclopedia or with the garden center how suitable that plant is for growing in containers before you buy a specific plant. You don't want to buy something that grows too big, too quickly.

Plants for sunny places

Most plants flourish in sun or partial shade. The following plants not only need full sun to show their best, but will survive in dry conditions

PERENNIALS
- *Acantholimon glumaceum*
  Prickly thrift
- *Acanthus spinosus*
  Acanthus, Bear's breeches
- *Achillea filipendulina*
  Yarrow
- *Aethionema grandiflorum*
  Stone cress
- *Agapanthus* Headbourne
  Hybrids
  African blue lily
- *Anchusa azurea*
  Alkanet
- *Anthemis tinctoria*
  Ox-eye chamomile
- *Artemesia absinthium*
  Absinth, Wormwood
- *Aster novi-belgii*
  Michaelmas daisy
- *Campanula carpatica*
  Bellflower
- *Carex elata* 'Aurea'
  Bowles' golden sedge
- *Catananche caerulea*
  Cupid's dart
- *Dianthus*
  Pinks

- *Echinops bannaticus*
  Globe thistle
- *Eryngium bourgatii*
  Sea holly
- *Gypsophila paniculata*
  Baby's breath
- × *Halimiocistus wintonensis*
- *Helianthemum*
  Rock rose, Sun rose
- *Helichrysum italicum* ssp.
  serotinum
  Curry plant
- *Hibiscus syriacus*
  Hibiscus
- *Hypericum olympicum*
  St John's wort
- *Iris germanica*
  Iris
- *Liriope muscari*
  Lilyturf
- *Lithodora diffusa*
- *Lychnis chalcedonica*
  Jerusalem Cross,
  Maltese Cross
- *Lysimachia punctata*
  Loosestrife
- *Nepeta racemosa*
  Catmint
- *Oenothera biennis*
  Evening primrose
- *Osteospermum*
  Osteospermum
- *Papaver*
  Poppy
- *Pelargonium*
  Geranium

- *Penstemon*
  Penstemon
- *Perovskia atriplicifolia*
  Russian sage
- *Phlox paniculata*
  Perennial phlox
- *Phormium tenax*
  New Zealand flax
- *Ruta graveolens*
  Common rue
- *Salvia officinalis*
  Common sage
- *Saponaria ocymoides*
  Rock soapwort
- *Senecio (Brachyglottis)*
  Dunedin Hybrids
- *Sisyrinchium striatum*
- *Stachys byzantina*
  Lambs' ears
- *Stipa arundinacea*
  Pheasant's tail grass
- *Thymus vulgaris*
  Common thyme
- *Veronica prostrata*
  Prostrate speedwell
- *Yucca filamentosa*
  Yucca
- *Zauschneria californica*
  California fuchsia

SHRUBS AND TREES
- *Abelia* × *grandiflora*
  Abelia
- *Buxus sempervirens*
  Box
- *Carpenteria californica*
- *Caryopteris* × *clandonensis*

- *Ceratostigma willmottianum*
  Chinese plumbago
- *Cistus* × *cyprius*
  Sun rose, rock rose
- *Convolvulus ceonorum*
  Bindweed, silverbush
- *Cotoneaster horizontalis*
  Cotoneaster
- *Cytisus battandieri*
  Pineapple broom
- *Cytisus kewensis*
  Broom
- *Escallonia*
  Escallonia
- *Eucalyptus gunnii*
  Cider gum
- *Euonymus fortunei*
  Wintercreeper
- *Fremontodendron*
  'California Glory'
  Flannel bush
- *Hebe pinguifolia* 'Pagei'
  Hebe
- *Ilex aquifolium*
  Holly
- *Indigofera heterantha*
- *Lavandula*
  Lavender
- *Myrtus communis*
  Myrtle
- *Olearia* × *haastii*
  Daisy bush
- *Philadelphus* vars.
  Mock orange
- *Phlomis fruticosa*
  Jerusalem sage
- *Potentilla fruticosa*
  Shrubby cinquefoil
- *Rosmarinus officinalis*
  Rosemary
- *Santolina chamaecyparissus*
  Lavender cotton
- *Spiraea japonica*
- *Teucrium fruticans*
  Shrubby germander

CLIMBERS
- *Campsis radicans*
  Trumpet creeper

- *Clematis tangutica*
  Russian virgin's bower
- *Eccremocarpus scaber*
  Chilean glory flower
- *Ipomoea hederacea*
  Morning glory
- *Parthenocissus tricuspidata*
  Boston ivy
- *Passiflora caerulea*
  Blue passionflower
- *Vitis coignetiae*
  Crimson glory vine

Plants for shade

- *Aconitum napellus*
  Aconite, monkshood
- *Adiantum pedatum*
  American maidenhair fern
- *Ajuga reptans*
  Bugle
- *Alchemilla mollis*
  Lady's mantle
- *Begonia rex* hybrids
  King begonia, Painted
  leaf begonia
- *Brunnera macrophylla*
  Siberian bugloss
- *Carex elata* 'Aurea'
  Bowles' golden sedge
- *Dicentra formosa*
  Bleeding heart
- *Digitalis purpurea*
  Foxglove
- *Dodecatheon pulchellum*
  Shooting stars
- *Dryopteris filix-mas*
  Male fern
- *Epimedium grandiflorum*
  Bishop's hat, barrenwort
- *Euphorbia amygdaloides*
  Wood spurge
- *Galium odoratum*
  Sweet woodruff
- *Gentiana asclepiadea*
  Willow gentian
- *Geranium* vars.
  Cranesbill, Hardy
  geranium

- *Helleborus orientalis*
  Christmas rose
- *Hepatica nobilis*
  Hepatica
- *Hosta* vars.
  Plantain lily
- *Houttuynia cordata*
- *Hypericum calycinum*
  Aaron's beard
- *Oxalis acetosella*
  Shamrock, Sorrel
- *Paeonia lactiflora* vars.
  Peony
- *Polypodium vulgare*
  Wall fern
- *Pulmonaria saccharata*
  Bethlehem sage
- *Smilacina racemosa*
  False Solomon's seal
- *Thalictrum aquilegiifolium*
  Meadow rue
- *Tradescantia* vars.
- *Trillium grandiflorum*
  Trinity flower, Wakerobin
- *Trollius europaeus*
  Common European
  Globe flower
- *Viola riviana*
  Purpurea Group
  Dog violet

**SHRUBS AND
TREES FOR SHADE**
- *Acer palmatum*
  Japanese maple
- *Buxus sempervirens*
  Box
- *Camellia*
  Camellia
- *Choisya ternata*
  Mexican orange blossom
- *Clethra delavayi*
  Summersweet
- *Cotoneaster horizontalis*
  Cotoneaster
- *Elaeagnus* × *ebbingei*
  Elaeagnus

Euonymus fortunei 'Harlequin'

Passiflora caerulea

Choisya ternata 'Sundance'

Kerria japonica

Camellia williamsii 'Debbie'

Erica carnea 'Golden Starlet'

- *Fatsia japonica*
  Japanese aralia
- *Fuchsia*
  Fuchsia
- *Gaultheria mucronata*
- *Kalmia latifolia*
  Calico bush
- *Leucothoe fontanesiana*
  Drooping leucothoe
- *Rhododendron*
  Rhododendron
- *Skimmia japonica*
- *Symphoricarpos* × *doorenbosii*
  Snowberry

CLIMBERS FOR SHADE

- *Berberidopsis corallina*
  Coral plant
- *Clematis*
  Clematis
- *Forsythia suspensa*
  Weeping forsythia
- *Hedera helix*
  Ivy
- *Hydrangea petiolaris* syn.
  H. anomala ssp. *petiolaris*
  Climbing hydrangea
- *Kerria japonica*
- *Parthenocissus*
  Virginia creeper
- *Pyracantha*
  Firethorn
- *Rosa* (some varieties
  including)
  Rose
  R. alba
  R. 'Gloire de Dijon'
  R. 'Golden Showers'
  R. 'Maigold'
- *Schizophragma hydrangeoides*
  Japanese hydrangea vine
- *Tropaeolum speciosum*
  Scottish flame flower

Unlike most annuals both
Impatiens (busy lizzies) and
Meconopsis cambrica (Welsh
poppy) will flower in shady
conditions.

Evergreens

Plants marked (s) are
semievergreen and will lose
their leaves in cold winters

TREES AND SHRUBS

- *Abelia* × *grandiflora* (s)
  Abelia
- *Abies* (small varieties)
  Silver fir
- *Andromeda polifolia*
  Bog rosemary
- *Arbutus unedo* 'Elfin King'
  Strawberry tree
- *Arctostaphylos uva-ursi*
  Bearberry
- *Aucuba japonica*
  Japanese laurel
- *Buxus sempervirens*
  Box
- *Calluna vulgaris*
  Heather
- *Camellia*
  Camellia
- *Chamaecyparis*
  (small varieties)
  Cypress
- *Choisya ternata*
  Mexican orange blossom
- *Cistus*
  Rock rose
- *Cotoneaster*
  Cotoneaster
- *Cryptomeria japonica*
  Japanese cedar
- *Cupressus*
  Cypress
- *Daboecia cantabrica*
  Cantabrian heath,
  Irish heath
- *Daphne odora*
  Daphne
- *Elaeagnus* × *ebbingei*
  Elaeagnus
- *Embothrium coccineum*
  Chilean fire bush,
  flame flower

- *Erica carnea*
  Winter-flowering heather
- *Escallonia*
  Escallonia
- *Eucalyptus gunnii*
  Cider gum
- *Euonymus fortunei*
  Wintercreeper
- *Fatsia japonica*
  Japanese aralia
- *Grevillea alpina*
- *Hebe*
  Veronica
- *Hypericum*
  St John's wort
- *Ilex*
  Holly
- *Juniperus communis*
  Common juniper
- *Kalmia latifolia*
  Calico bush,
  Mountain laurel
- *Laurus nobilis*
  Bay tree
- *Lavandula*
  Lavender
- *Ligustrum ovalifolium* (s)
  Privet
- *Myrtus communis*
  Myrtle
- *Olearia haastii*
  Daisy bush
- *Picea* (small varieties)
  Spruce
- *Pinus* (small varieties)
  Pine
- *Pittosporum tenuifolium*
  (small varieties)
  Kohuhu
- *Prunus laurocerasus*
  'Otto Luyken'
  Cherry laurel
- *Rhododendron*
  Rhododendron
- *Rosmarinus officinalis*
  Rosemary
- *Santolina chamaecyparissus*
  Lavender cotton

- *Skimmia japonica*
  Skimmia
- *Taxus baccata*
  Yew
- *Vaccinium*
  Blueberry
- *Viburnum tinus*
- *Laurustinus*
- *Vinca major*
  Periwinkle
  V. minor
- *Yucca filamentosa*
  Yucca

CLIMBERS AND
WALL SHRUBS
- *Carpentaria californica*
- *Ceanothus*
  California lilac
- *Garrya elliptica*
  Silk-tassel bush
- *Hedera*
  Ivy
- *Pyracantha*
  Firethorn

Scented plants

TREES AND SHRUBS
- *Chimonanthus praecox*
  Wintersweet
- *Clethra arborea*
  Lily of the
  valley tree
- *Cytisus battandieri*
  Pineapple broom
- *Daphne odora*
  Daphne
- *Hamamelis mollis*
  Witch hazel
- *Lonicera fragrantissima*
  Winter honeysuckle
- *Magnolia stellata*
  Star magnolia
- *Osmanthus delavayi*
- *Philadelphus*
  Mock orange
- *Pittosporum tenuifolium*
  Kohuhu

- *Robinia pseudoacacia*
  Black locust
- *Rosa* (many varieties)
  Rose
- *Stephanotis floribunda*
  Floradora,
  Madagascar jasmine
- *Trachelospermum jasminoides*
  Confederate jasmine,
  Star jasmine

PERENNIALS
- *Convallaria majalis*
  Lily-of-the-valley
- *Dianthus*
  Pinks
- *Hosta plantaginea*
  Hosta
- *Iris unguicularis*
  Iris
- *Primula veris*
  Cowslip
- *P. vulgaris*
  Primrose

ANNUALS AND BIENNIALS
- *Centaurea moschata*
  Sweet sultan
- *Erysimum cheiri*
  Wallflower
- *Exacum affine*
  Persian violet
- *Lathyrus grandiflorus*
  Everlasting pea
- *Matthiola incana*
  Stock
- *Scabiosa atropurpurea*
  Pincushion flower
- *Viola odorata*
  Sweet violet

CLIMBING PLANTS
- *Clematis*
  Clematis
- *Jasminum officinale*
  Summer jasmine
- *Lonicera*
  Honeysuckle

- *Rosa* (climbing varieties)
  Rose
- *Stephanotis floribunda*
  Floradora,
  Madagascar jasmine

BULBS AND CORMS
- *Crinum bulbispermum*
- *Crocus angustifolius*
  Cloth-of-gold crocus
- *Crocus longiflorus*
- *Cyclamen purpurascens*
  Sowbread
- *Lilium*
  Lily
- *Narcissus*
  Daffodil

Plants that prefer acid soil

All the plants listed prefer neutral or acid soil. For a number an ericaceous soil mix is essential. Check in a detailed plant encyclopedia if you are not certain. Plants that will only grow in an ericaceous soil mix will be marked as lime-haters.

TREES AND SHRUBS
- *Abies* (small varieties)
  Silver fir
- *Acer palmatum*
  Japanese maple
- *Arbutus unedo* 'Elfin King'
  Strawberry tree
- *Arctostaphylos uva-ursi*
  Bearberry
- *Berberis*
  Barberry
- *Calluna vulgaris*
  Heather
- *Camellia*
  Camellia
- *Cassiope*
- *Ceanothus*
  California lilac

Ilex aurea marginata

Viburnum tinus 'Eve Price'

Ceanothus 'Concha'

247

Cotinus obovatus

Mahonia japonica 'Bealei'

Centranthus ruber

- *Choisya ternata*
  Mexican orange blossom
- *Cotinus coggygria*
  Smoke tree
- *Disanthus cercidifolius*
- *Enkianthus campanulatus*
  Redvein enkianthus
- *Erica carnea*
  Winter-flowering heather
- *Eucryphia × nymansensis*
- *Euonymus fortunei*
  Wintercreeper
- *Fothergilla major*
- *Gaultheria mucronata*
- *Indigofera heterantha*
- *Kalmia latifolia*
  Calico bush
- *Lavatera* 'Barnsley'
  Mallow
- *Lithodora diffusa*
- *Mahonia*
  Oregon grapeholly
- *Menziesia ciliicalyx*
- *Osmanthus delavayi*
- *Picea* (small varieties)
  Spruce
- *Pieris*
  Pieris
- *Pinus* (small varieties)
  Pine
- *Rhododendron*
  Rhododendron
- *Sarcococca humilis*
  Christmas box, Sweet box
- *Styrax americanus*
  American snowbell
- *Vaccinium*
  Blueberry

CLIMBERS
- *Berberidopsis corallina*
  Coral plant
- *Forsythia suspensa*
  Weeping forsythia
- *Tropaeolum speciosum*
  Scottish flame flower

PERENNIALS
- *Aconitum napellus*
  Monkshood
- *Alchemilla mollis*
  Lady's mantle
- *Astrantia major*
  Masterwort
- *Campanula*
  Bellflower
- *Centranthus ruber*
  Jupiter's beard, red valerian
- *Ceratostigma willmottianum*
  Chinese plumbago
- *Corydalis cashmeriana*
- *Cypripedium reginae*
  Showy lady's slipper orchid
- *Epimedium grandiflorum*
  Bishop's hat, barrenwort
- *Filipendula palmata*
  Meadowsweet
- *Galium odoratum*
  Sweet woodruff,
  lady's bedstraw
- *Gentiana sino-ornata*
  Gentian
- *Lapageria rosea*
  Chilean bellflower
- *Lupinus luteus*
  Lupin
- *Meconopsis betonicifolia*
  Himalayan poppy
- *Myosotis sylvestris*
  Forget-me-not
- *Ourisia*
- *Phlomis fruticosa*
  Jerusalem sage
- *Santolina chamaecyparissus*
  Lavender cotton
- *Sarracenia purpurea*
  Pitcher plant,
  Huntsman's cup
- *Tradescantia*
- *Trillium grandiflorum*
  Trinity flower, Wakerobin
- *Veronica prostrata*
  Speedwell
- *Vinca minor*
  Periwinkle
- *Viola*
  Viola, pansy

Plants for fall and winter flowers and color

TREES AND SHRUBS
- *Acer palmatum*
  Japanese maple
- *Calluna vulgaris*
  Heather, Ling
- *Ceratostigma willmottianum*
- *Cotinus coggygria*
  Smoke tree
- *Daboecia cantabrica*
  Cantabrian heath,
  Irish heath
- *Disanthus cercidifolius*
- *Enkianthus campanulatus*
  Redvein enkianthus
- *Erica carnea*
  Winter-flowering heather
- *Euonymus fortunei*
  'Emerald 'n' Gold'
  Wintercreeper
- *Fothergilla major*
- *Hamamelis mollis*
  Witch hazel
- *Lagerstroemeria indica*
  Crape myrtle
- *Spiraea japonica* 'Goldflame'
- *Symphoricarpos × doorenbosii*
  Snowberry
- *Thuja occidentalis*
  White cedar
- *Viburnum opulus*
  Guelder rose
- *V. tinus*
  Laurustinus

CLIMBERS AND WALL SHRUBS
- *Celastrus orbicularis*
  Oriental bittersweet,
  Staff vine
- *Dregea sinensis*
- *Humulus lupulus* 'Aureus'
  Golden hop

- *Jasminum nudiflorum*
  Winter jasmine
- *Parthenocissus quinquefolia*
  Virginia creeper
- *Pyracantha*
  Firethorn
- *Vitis coignetiae*
  Crimson glory vine
  V. vinifera
  Purpleleaf grape

PERENNIALS AND BULBS
- *Chiastophyllum*
  oppositifolium
- *Chionodoxa luciliae*
  Glory-of-the-snow
- *Crocus*
  Crocus
- *Epimedium grandiflorum*
  Bishop's hat, barrenwort
- *Eranthis hyemalis*
  Winter aconite
- *Festuca glauca*
  Blue fescue
- *Galanthus*
  Snowdrop
- *Helleborus niger*
  Christmas rose
- *Iris unguicularis*
  Winter iris
- *Narcissus*
  Daffodil
- *Persicaria affinis*
  Himalayan knotweed
- *Primula*
  Winter-flowering primrose
- *Scilla sibirica*
  Siberian squill
- *Viola × wittrockiana*
  Winter-flowering pansy

Plants for an alpine garden

- *Acantholimon glumaceum*
- Aethionema grandiflorum
  Persian stone cress
- *Androsace lanuginosa*
  Rock jasmine

- *Anemone blanda*
  Windflower
- *Antirrhinum molle*
  Snapdragon
- *Aquilegia flabellata*
  Fan columbine
- *Arabis caucasica*
  Rock cress
- *Armeria maritima*
  Sea thrift
- *Aubrieta deltoidea*
  Aubretia
- *Aurinia saxatile* syn.
  Alyssum saxatile
  Basket of gold, Gold dust
- *Campanula cochleariifolia*
  Fairies' thimbles
- *Celmisia coriacea*
  New Zealand daisy
- *Chiastophyllum*
  oppositifolium
- *Corydalis flexuosa*
  C. solida
- *Cyclamen hederifolium*
  Baby cyclamen
- *Dianthus alpinus*
  Alpine pink
  D. deltoides
  Maiden pink
- *Draba aizoides*
  Yellow Whitlow grass
- *Erigeron karvinskianus*
  Fleabane
- *Erinus alpinus*
  Fairy foxglove,
  alpine liverwort
- *Erodium petraeum*
  Heron's bill, Stork's bill
- *Gentiana aucalis*
  Trumpet gentian
- *Geranium dalmaticum*
  Dalamatian cranesbill
- *Gypsophila repens*
  Baby's breath
- *Haberlea rhodopensis*
- *Hacquetia epipactis*
- *Horminum pyrenaicum*
  Dragon's mouth

- *Incarvillea mairei*
  Garden gloxinia
- *Leontopodium alpinum*
  Edelweiss
- *Lewisia* Cotyledon Hybrids
- *Linum arboreum*
  Flax
- *Lychnis alpina*
  Alpine catchfly
- *Meconopsis cambrica*
  Welsh poppy
- *Oenothera biennis*
  Evening primrose
- *Onosma alborosea*
- *Papaver alpinum*
  Alpine poppy
- *Penstemon newberryi*
- *Phlox subulata*
  Moss phlox
- *Platycodon grandiflorus*
  Balloon flower
- *Polemonium pulcherrimum*
  Skunkleaf, Jacob's ladder
- *Polygala calcarea*
  Milkwort
- *Polygonatum hirtum*
  Solomon's seal
- *Primula*
  Primrose
- *Pterocephalus perennis*
- *Pulsatilla vulgaris*
  Pasque flower
- *Ramonda myconi*
- *Saponaria ocymoides*
  Rock soapwort
- *Saxifraga*
  Saxifrage
- *Sedum*
  Stonecrop
- *Sempervivum arachnoideum*
  Cobweb houseleek
- *Silene maritima*
  Sea campion
- *Soldanella montana*
  Snowbell
- *Tropaeolum polyphyllum*
  Nasturtium
- *Veronica prostrata*
  Speedwell

Calluna vulgaris 'Peter Sparkes'

Vibernum opulus

Sedum hispanicum 'Minor Glaucum'

Rhododendron

Diascia

Papaver 'Patty's Plum'

- *Viola*
  Pansy, viola

**ALPINE SHRUBS
AND CONIFERS**
- *Abies balsamea* 'Nana'
  Balsam fir
- *Chamaecyparis lawsoniana*
  'Gnome'
  Cypress
- *Clematis alpina*
  Alpine clematis
- *Cytisus ardoinii*
  Broom
- *Daphne*
  Daphne
- *Dryas octopetala*
  Mountain avens
- *Erinacea anthyllis*
  Hedgehog broom
- *Genista delphinensis*
  Broom
- *Helianthemum nummularium*
  Rock rose
- *Hypericum balearicum*
  St John's wort
- *Iberis sempervirens*
  Candytuft
- *Juniperus communis*
  'Compressa'
  Juniper
- *Lithodora diffusa*
- *Origanum rotundifolium*
  Oregano
- *Picea mariana* 'Nana'
  Spruce
- *Pinus mugo* 'Humpy'
  Pine
- *Rhododendron* 'Dwarf'
  Rhododendron
- *Salix reticulata*
  Willow
- *Taxus baccata* 'Dwarf White'
  Yew
- *Thuja orientalis* 'Aurea
  Nana'
  Red cedar
- *Verbascum dumulosum*
  Mullein

Annuals and bedding plants

Many annuals are listed in seed catalogs under their common name rather than their Latin name. The list here lists the plants in the order that you will find them with the alternative, either the Latin or the common name, given where appropriate. Plants marked (p) are perennials frequently used as bedding plants.

- Agastache (p)
- Ageratum
- Alyssum (annual and perennial)
- Amaranthus
  Love-lies-bleeding
- Antirrhinum
  Snapdragon
- Aubretia (p)
- Balsam
  Busy Lizzie
- *Begonia semperflorens*
  B. tuberosa
  B. rex
- *Bellis perennis* (p)
  English daisy
- Bells of Ireland
  Moluccella laevis
- Bidens
- Brachyscome
  Swan River daisy
- *Calendula officinalis*
  Pot marigold
- *Campanula* (p)
- Candytuft
  Iberis
- Carnation
  Dianthus
- Catananche (p)
  Cupid's dart
- Celosia
  Cockscomb
- Cerinthe

- Chinese lanterns
  Physalis
- Chrysanthemum
  (annual varieties)
- Cineraria
- Cornflower (p)
  Centaurea
- Clarkia
- Clary
  Salvia horminum
- Cleome
  Spider flower
- Coreopsis (p)
  Tickseed
- Cosmea
  Cosmos
- Cynoglossum
  Hound's tongue
- Dahlia (dwarf varieties)
- Diascia
- Dianthus
  Pinks
- Echinacea (p)
  Coneflower
- Echium
- Erigeron
  Fleabane
- Eschscholzia
  California poppy
- Gazania
- Geranium
  Pelargonium
- Godetia
- Helianthemum (p)
  Rock rose
- Helichrysum
  Strawflower
- Heliotrope
- Larkspur
  Consolida
- Lavatera
  Mallow
- Limnanthes
  Poached-egg plant
- Lobelia
- Impatiens
  Busy Lizzie
- Malcolmia
  Virginian stock

- Marigold
  Tagetes
- Mesembryanthemum
  Livingstone daisy
- Ipomoea
  Morning glory
- Nasturtium
  Tropaeolum
- Nemesia
- Nicotiana
  Tobacco plant
- Nigella
  Love-in-a-mist
- Pansy
  Viola
- Petunia
- Phacelia
- Phlox drummondii
- Poppy
  Papaver
- Polyanthus
  Primula
- Rudbeckia
  Coneflower
- Salvia
  Sage
- Saxifrage (p)
  Saxifraga
- Scabiosa
  Scabious
- Silene
  Catchfly
- Stock
  Matthiola
- Sunflower
  Helianthus
- Sweet William
  Dianthus barbatus
- Sweet pea
  Lathyrus odoratus
- Thunbergia alata
  Black-eyed Susan
- Tithonia
  Mexican sunflower
- Verbena
- Veronica (p)
- Viola
  Pansy
- Zinnia

Cerinthe major purpurescens

Suppliers

BULBS
The Daffodil Mart
85 Broad Street
Torrington
CT 06790
800-255-2852

Dutch Gardens
PO Box 2037
Lakewood
NJ 08701-8037
800-818-3861
www.dutchgardens.com

CONTAINERS
Simple Gardens
Box 292 RD2
Richmond
VT 05477
802-434-2624

Seibert & Rice
PO Box 365
Short Hills
NJ 07078
973-467-8266
www.seibert-rice.com

Gardener's Eden
PO Box 7307
San Francisco
CA 94120-7307
800-8229600

Gardener's Supply Company
128 Intervale Road
Burlington
VT 95401
800-863-1700
www.gardeners.com

Home Harvest: Gardening
Supply Online
13624 Jeff Davis Highway
Woodbridge
VA 22191
www.homeharvest.com

HERBS
Johnny's Selected Seeds
Foss Hill Road
Albion
ME 04910-9731
207-437-4301
www.johnnyseeds.com

The Cook's Garden
PO Box 5010
Hodges
SC 29653-5010
800-457-9703
www.cooksgarden.com

Richters Herb Company
357 Highway 47
Goodwood
ON l0C 1A0
Canada
905-640-6677
www.richters.com

Shepherd's Garden Seeds
30 Irene Street
Torrington
CT 06790
860-482-3638
www.shepherdseeds.com

PLANTS
White Flower Farm
PO Box 50
Litchfield
CT 06759
800-503-9624
www.whiteflowerfarm.com

Shady Oaks Nursery (hostas)
112 10th Avenue SE
Waseca
MN 56093-0708
800-504-8006
www.shadyoaks.com

Bluestone Perennials
7237 Middle Ridge Road
Madison
OH 44057
1-800-852-5243
www.bluestoneperennials.com

Rock Spray Nursery (heaths
and heathers)
PO Box 693 Truro
MA 02666-0693
508-349-6769
www.rockspray.com

Wayside Gardens
1 Garden Lane
Hodges
SC 29695-0001
888-222-3580
www.waysidegardens.com

Tomato Growers Supply
Company
PO Box 237
Fort Myers
FL 33902
888-478-7333
www.tomatogrowers.com

ROSES
David Austin Roses
15393 Highway 64
West Tyler
TX 75704
1-800-328-8893
www.davidaustinroses.com

Jackson & Perkins
2518 South Pacific Highway
Medford
OR 97501
1-800-545-3444
www.jacksonperkins.com

Heirloom Roses
24062 NE Riverside Drive
NE OD
St Paul
OR 97137
503-538-1576
www.heirloomroses.com

Weeks Roses
www.weeksroses.com

Pickering Nurseries Inc
670 Kingston Road
Pickering
ON L1V 1AC
Canada
905-839-2111
www.pickeringnurseries.com

The Roseraie at Bayfields
PO Box R(h)
Waldoboro
ME 04572
207-832-6330
www.roseraie.com

SEEDS
W. Atlee Burpee Co
300 Park Avenue
Warminster
PA 18974
800-888-1447
www.burpee.com

Park Seed
1 Parkton Avenue
Greenwood
SC 29647-0001
1-888-222-3545
www.parkseed.com

Johnny's Selected Seeds
Foss Hill Road
Albion
ME 04910-9731
207-437-4301
www.johnnyseeds.com

FRUIT TREES
Raintree Nursery
391 Butts Road
Morton
WA 98356
1-360-496-6400
www.raintreenursery.com

Hartmann's Nursery
PO Box 100
Lacota
MI 49063
616-253-4281

WATERING EQUIPMENT
Gardener's Supply Company
128 Intervale Road
Burlington
VT 05401
1-888-833-1487
www.gardeners.com

Lee Valley Tools Ltd
12 East River Street
Ogdensburg
NY 13669
1-800-871-8158
www.leevalley.com

Dramm Pro Tools ("Rain Wand")
P.O. Box 1960
Manitowoc
WI 54221-1960

Index

The author would like to thank his wife, Anthea, for putting up with him while
he was writing this book.

He would also like to thank Fiona Biggs, Michael Whitehead and Sarah Bragginton
at Bridgewater Books for all their help during the whole process, and Liz Eddison
for taking and sourcing the lovely pictures that appear throughout the book.
Thanks also to Coral Mula and Ann Winterbotham for the charming illustrations.

Finally, he would also like to thank all gardeners who enjoy growing things.

The publishers would like to thank the following for the use of photographs:
Liz Eddison/Designers: Susanna Brown 16; David Brunn 81; Butler Landscapes 83: Chelsea 2000 6–7, 10,
18, 49; Terence Conran: 35, 209; Guy Farthing/Marshalls: 43b; Alan Gardner: 13; Gavin Landscaping:
88bl, 89; Elizabeth Goodwin & Sylvia Whitehouse: 42; Carol Klein: 29; Lindsay Knight: 11, 84; Landart:
82; Wynniett-Husey Clarke: 46–7, 53r; Neil Holmes: 128, 190, 214bl, bc, 219bl, 223bl, tr, 224bl, br, 225bl,
bc, 226br, 227bl, 228bl, 229bl, br, 230bl, 231bl, tr, 233bl, 236br, 238bc, 240bl, 241bl, 242tl, 243bl, 249tr;
Harry Smith Collection: 51, 53l, 94, 95, 122, 123r, 199, 216, 219tr, 220bl, bc, 221bc, br, 222br, 232bl,
234tl, 235br, 243bc, br; David Squire: 104bl, br. With additional thanks to Roger Benjamin, Georgina Steeds
and Smith's Nurseries, New Denham, Middlesex.